THEODOR HERZL

A Portrait for This Age

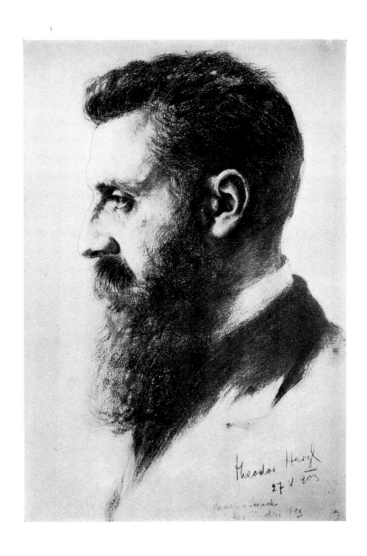

Theodor Herzl
27 V 903

THEODOR HERZL

A PORTRAIT FOR
THIS AGE

EDITED AND WITH AN INTRODUCTION BY

Ludwig Lewisohn

PREFACE BY DAVID BEN-GURION

THE WORLD PUBLISHING COMPANY

CLEVELAND AND NEW YORK

Acknowledgments

"Luz, the Village," "Spring in Elend," "The Dirigible," "In the Dining Car," "Protest Rabbis," "Message to the American Zionist Conference," "Zionism," and "A Blessing on the Journey" were translated by Hella Freud Bernays.

"The Good Things of Life," "Solon in Lydia," "The New Ghetto," "The Dreyfus Affair," "Conditions in France," "The Revision," and "Five Against Two" were translated by Heinz Norden.

David Ben-Gurion's Preface, from an edition in French (Jerusalem, Youth and Hechalutz Department of the World Zionist Organization, 1954) of Herzl's *Judenstaat*, was translated from Hebrew into French by Moché Catane and from French into English by Ben Halpern.

The translation of *The Jewish State* by Sylvie d'Avigdor (London, Zionist Organization, 1936) was revised for this book by Ben Halpern and Moshe Kohn.

The selections from Herzl's Diaries, and Impressions of the First Congress, translated, condensed, and annotated by Maurice Samuel in *Theodor Herzl: A Memorial* (New York, New Palestine, 1929), edited by Meyer W. Weisgal, and revised for this book by Ben Halpern and Moshe Kohn, are reprinted by courtesy of the Zionist Organization of America.

The Addresses to the Zionist Congresses, from *Congress Addresses of Theodor Herzl* (New York, Federation of American Zionists, 1917), translated from the German by Nellie Straus, are reprinted by courtesy of the Zionist Organization of America.

CONTENTS

CONTENTS

PREFACE

AFTER the *Judenstaat* was published, Herzl was advised by one of his friends to read Pinsker's booklet *Auto-Emancipation*. When Herzl had read it, he declared that if he had known this work earlier he might not have written his *Judenstaat*.

History and the Jews should be thankful that it was destined for Herzl to be unaware of the *Auto-Emancipation* and not refrain from writing the *Judenstaat*, even though he himself felt that he had done nothing new. Herzl, in writing the *Judenstaat*, was the discoverer of something far greater than a new idea: *he was the discoverer of himself*, a visionary, architect, and political leader, the greatest to arise in Israel since the fall of Bar Kokhba.

The idea that brought Herzl back to his people, as he himself affirmed, was not a new one. "The idea which I have developed in this pamphlet is an ancient one: it is the restoration of the Jewish State," wrote Herzl in the introduction to his historic work. And indeed, he hardly contributed a single new argument in support of the Zionist idea, neither in respect of the analysis of the Jewish problem—the plight of a people driven to a dead end in the confinement of Exile—nor in respect of the solution through concentration in a national territory. (In the *Judenstaat* Herzl does not yet see in the return to our ancestral country the sole possible road to territorial concentration and the founding of a Jewish State.) In all the theses of Zionist theory, though by no means in the methods of realization he proposed, Herzl had many great predecessors. There was Rabbi Judah Alcalay, the modern heir of two men, Don

Translated from French edition of *The Jewish State*.

9

Joseph Nasi and Rabbi Hayim Abulafia, who were bearers of the Zionist vision among Sefardic Jewry; Rabbi Zvi Hirsch Kalischer and Rabbi Hayim Luria, descendant of the famous Rabbi Isaac Luria who was one of the greatest spirits of Ashkenazic Jewry; two British Jews, Sir Moses Montefiore and Benjamin Disraeli, of whom the former established the first Jewish agricultural venture in the Holy Land in 1856, the Montefiore orchard, and the latter, in 1847, wrote *Tancred*, the first Zionist novel. In America, too, in the beginning of the nineteenth century, arose Mordecai Manuel Noah, an advocate of the Jewish State idea, who wanted to create a Jewish State under the name of Ararat in North America. Moses Hess, the first Zionist-Socialist, a colleague of Marx, conceived the idea of a Jewish State established in the Holy Land under Pentateuchal laws, that is to say, on Socialist principles. In his youth, Lassalle cherished the dream of leading the Jewish people in the conquest of its sacred land. The Hebrew authors Peretz Smolenskin and David Gordon, as well as many other outstanding writers, preached the return to Zion with ardor and persistence. In profundity of thought and power of expression, Leon Pinsker must be given the first place among theorists of Zionism, and his brochure *Auto-Emancipation* has remained to this day the classic and most remarkable work of Zionist literature. In its clear and pitiless grasp of the Jewish problem, its severe and profound analysis of the life of our people and its situation in the Diaspora, in its vigorous, pithy, and precise style, Pinsker's work has no equal in all that has been written on the subject before or since its appearance.

Of course, these authors, too, did not invent the Zionist idea. The Jewish people's hope for the restoration of its national independence in its ancient homeland was never suffered to lapse since our people first went into Exile, and all Jews prayed thrice daily, begging God for their return to Zion.

Yet Herzl was the first—and herein lies his historic greatness—who was able to breathe a new spirit, the will to act, into the faith and nostalgia of the Jewish people, yearning to be revived. He achieved this thanks to the direct, immediate quality of his expression, the true style of rational clairvoyance, and even more to the gift of political draftsmanship which he showed so notably in calling together the Congress, creating the Zionist Organization with its various institutions, and bringing the Jewish people into play as an active national factor in international politics.

Herzl had grasped the secret of historic activity better than any of his precursors. He had discovered within himself and in the Jewish people the mystery of political efficacy. Herzl transformed the Jewish people, for the first time since its Exile, into a political force, a fighting, creative force, a force capable of shaping its historic destiny by its own will and exertions.

Until Herzl the Jewish people had been no more than an object of history, a plaything in the hands of strangers and political forces who used it for good or for ill. Herzl transformed a pulverized people borne on the currents of history by chance winds, favorable or the reverse, into a people who acted out its national will and established itself as an autonomous factor on the international scene. Herzl was the founding father of the revival of Jewish politics. He set the political goal of the people in a simple, clear, and challenging phrase, "The Jewish State," and created the instruments, the means, and the power as well, which were required for attaining the goal. Herzl realized that, despite its dispersion and rootlessness, the Jewish people is a *power*, provided that it can and will organize its capacities and make use of them. The ability and will to do this were the gifts with which Herzl himself endowed the people.

Before Herzl two conceptions, mutually opposed but equally sterile, were current on the question of the Jewish situation among the Gentiles. First, the ghetto conception, according to which, because of the unbridgeable chasm that separated the Jews from other peoples, it was incumbent upon Jews till the advent of Messiah to remain passive and dependent on the good graces of the stranger. The opposite conception was that of assimilation, which had prevailed in the *milieu* of Herzl's rearing and education: for that conception, the Jews are not a people at all, but only a superfluous, transitory aggregation constituted by vestigial doctrines and ancient beliefs which separate them from their neighbors; as Jews learn to adapt to their environment in language, costume, behavior, and customs, the separation will dissolve and the Jewish entity, to the extent that it is unique and distinct, will cease to exist—the Jews will become an organic part of the people among whom they dwell.

Herzl freed himself from this conception thanks to his intense observation of Jewish social reality since his youth, and thanks also to his sense of human dignity, which was offended by the sight of the scandalous treatment inflicted on Jews. Thus he came back to the Jewish people, but not to the ghetto conception that Jews must remain impotent till the Messiah appear.

Seeing the Jewish people as a people, Herzl realized, possibly for the first time in the history of Israel's Exile, that relations of reciprocity could be established between the Jewish people and other peoples, if the Jews organized themselves and acted in the manner proper to a people. Herzl came to the revolutionary conclusion, which today seems to us so natural and obvious, that the Jews are a people like all others, even though it find itself in the worst situation of any people on earth. He said: "A people cannot be saved except by itself," and "The Jewish question can be solved only by the Jews." Precisely because he understood that the Jewish question was an international one and the establishment of the Jewish State an international necessity, Herzl grasped the simple and profound truth that it would never be possible to bring other peoples to aid in the restoration of the Jewish State unless the Jewish people itself concentrated its will, influence, and means upon the achievement of that end.

Upon two things Herzl based his faith in the realization of Zionism: upon the suffering of Israel and the Zionist ideal. Like all great liberators of the past, Herzl knew history's secret: the suffering and distress of masses need not necessarily cause their abasement, surrender, and decay, but are capable of becoming a source of power and strength, grandeur and heroism, if only they are given a *redeeming ideal*, so that the suffering drives those who bear it to revolt against their wretched destiny, and their trials are turned into tools of combat and creation.

When Herzl wrote his brochure on the Jewish State and fashioned the first instrument of political Zionism—the World Zionist Congress—he was ignorant of Jewish life in Eastern Europe, and of the culture, the positive Jewish traditional values with which it was impregnated. He knew nothing of the deep, eternal, inner bond that tied the people to its ancient homeland, and the tremendous creative forces active in the Jewish mass were strange to him. But compensating for his faulty knowledge of Judaism was his intuitive grasp of human nature, for he knew the downtrodden Jews were capable of action, if only they were given a liberating national ideal.

When he appeared in 1902 in London before the Royal Commission on Alien Immigration set up by the British government, Herzl explained in the following terms the failure of the colonization project undertaken in Argentina by Baron de Hirsch: "This failure may be explained in the following way: when a man wishes to colonize, he needs a flag and an idea; one cannot accomplish such things with nothing more than money. Having neither flag nor idea, the project cannot succeed. It is impossible to effect a general movement of great masses with money; they must be imbued with faith in their future, and then alone can one arouse in them a spirit of complete consecration even for the most arduous tasks in the world."

Just as Herzl appreciated the dynamic force of an ideal alive in the hearts of the masses, so did he also grasp the potency of mass distress as a factor in history. He knew that suffering makes men capable of surmounting obstacles insurmountable under normal circumstances, and that distress makes possible the performance of otherwise impossible acts.

Just after the first Zionist Congress in Basle in 1897, Herzl recorded in his diary these immortal phrases: "If I were to sum up the Congress in a few words—words I shall be most careful not to speak in public—I would say: in Basle I founded the Jewish State. If I said that aloud today, I would be met by universal laughter. Perhaps in five years, certainly in fifty, everyone will see it."

Why did Herzl believe he had founded the Jewish State at Basle? In his diary Herzl answers this question: "The essence of a State consists in a people's political volition." Herzl revived and activated the political volition of the people and so opened up a new horizon in Jewish history.

"We have the chance to create a model state," Herzl declared in 1896, prior to the Zionist Congress. "We will use and carry on experiments on every frontier of science in the Jewish land; just as we shall institute the seven-hour day as an experiment for the benefit of humanity, so shall we proceed in everything else in the same humanitarian spirit and build the new land as a land of experiment and a model state."

This brief allusion to a "model state," inserted at the end of the text of the *Judenstaat*, was later developed by Herzl in a book entirely dedicated to this theme, *Altneuland*, subsequently translated into Hebrew by Nahum Sokolow under the title *Tel-Aviv*. In this work, Herzl depicts not only the political independence of the Jews, but a new social system founded upon the co-operative organization of free labor. Herzl was not a Socialist. But he had faith in suffering men and in their ability to liberate themselves by their own awakened will and creative efforts. Herzl had faith in national organization and social planning. He had faith in science and technology. He had faith in the liberating ideal.—On these four pillars, he founded his dream and his conviction that the Jewish State would come into being and that it would become a model state.

His faith was justified—and will continue to prove justified.

The dream of a Jewish State has become reality; it will be the same with the dream of a model state.

When Herzl wrote the *Judenstaat* in 1895, he seemed to hear a beating of wings above his head. He was not deluded: it was the beating of the wings of the Providence that watches over Israel. Over the head of Herzl appeared once more the radiance of our providential destiny, so that it was fated for him to become the cherished object of the people's love, the focus of its secret aspirations, its hopes of deliverance and resurrection. He owed this to the charm of his personality, to his sensitive and loving heart, to his indomitable energy, his capacity for dedicated action, to the magnificence of his spirit and his political genius.

While still alive, from the moment the *Judenstaat* appeared, Herzl appeared to the people as a legendary figure, radiant with grace and splendor, and that is why he continued to be a vitalizing, educating force after his death, for Herzl was the man of thought and of action alike.

David Ben-Gurion

Jerusalem, May 25, 1953

THEODOR HERZL:

A Portrait for This Age

BY LUDWIG LEWISOHN

1. BACKGROUND IN HISTORY

ALL occurrences and characters in Jewish history during the last century and a half must be interpreted under the aspect of that civic emancipation which set in with the French Revolution and was destined to give rise to so much apparent glory and achievement and in the end to so much disaster and to so much shame. It had been prepared for in the minds of men. Abstract and inherent human rights had been proclaimed equally by Judaeophiles like Lessing and Judaeophobes like Voltaire. Frederick of Prussia had announced that in his realm all could seek salvation after their own fashion. The protagonists of the French and the fathers of the American Revolution stood on the ground of the inalienable rights of man as man. The acknowledgment of a Supreme Being in France, the formal Deism of Paine and Jefferson did little or nothing to mitigate the breaking of metaphysical ties and bindings. Abstract man was to live in freedom and equality under the guidance of Reason and of Nature.

According to these formal, logical, and not ignoble principles, all men had, of necessity, to be included in a universal human society. If some groups, like the Jews, were afflicted with "faults," with annoying peculiarities, it was because the light of reason and humanity had but so lately dawned. Let it once shine on them, the "faults" would disappear and the peculiarities fade. It occured to no one, neither to Gentiles nor to the Jews of the West, that these "faults," these peculiarities, were such only upon the application of alien and exterior norms. Dazzled by the prospect of social flexibility and of participation in Western life and having wholly lost the sense of the peoplehood of Israel, a whole generation of Jews forgot that their ways were the ways conformable to their character and that their inherited wisdom might alone be redemptive for them. A self-induced blindness smote them. Three generations of Western Jews, including that of Theodor Herzl, accepted the Gentile estimate. The "faults" of the Jews were due to the oppression they had suffered, a specious defense, since it failed first to examine Jewish character and being according to their own norms. All "faults," differences, or inadequacies were, quite without historical scrutiny, attributed to the Ghetto. Hence, too, when the resurgence of Judaeophobia broke the untenable compacts of the emancipation, this phenomenon was characterized not by Herzl alone as a fragment of medievalism dragged into the Age of the Enlightenment (*"ein verschlepptes Stück Mittelalter"*). Alienation from the sources of one's being was inveterately interpreted as progress. This shameful and disastrous tendency has not yet wholly disappeared.

The Gentile thinkers of the Enlightenment were stricken with an almost equal blindness. Their total repudiation of all the content of the ages of faith, their insistence upon man's goodness and innocence, warped only by wicked institutions, led them into errors almost as shattering as the errors of the Jews. They would have held it to be folly of the darkest and most reactionary sort had someone predicted that, since man is a worshiping creature, driven by irrepressible metaphysical urges, he would, deprived of religious bindings, plunge into orgies of self-idolatry under the symbol of the homogeneous nationalist State. How were they to know it when in mid-twentieth century America thousands of men of apparently normal intelligence still refuse to acknowledge that shattering truth, and when Jewish intellectuals make common cause with those pagan idolatries which are and have been, everywhere and always, the signals of their own destruction.

Excuses, according to an intelligent adage, do not excuse nor do explanations explain. Yet it must be remembered that in recent centuries the Jewish people has been in a twofold sense the victim and object of the historic forces which operate upon the scene of the *Gola*, the dispersion. On the one hand it must submit to the mood, the temper, the policies of the peoples among whom it dwells; it must share their fortunes; it must die in their wars. On the other hand, being even in this dispersion a contemporary people, it inevitably undergoes the intellectual influences of the world. Jews shared the thin fallacies of the Enlightenment; Jews were influenced by the successive waves of Positivism; Jews, in due time, embraced the teachings of Darwin and of Marx; uncritically and wholly unaware of its subjective motivation they accepted the German analytical attempt of the Wellhausen school of Biblical exegesis to destroy the authenticity of their Scriptures. They hastened —a vast majority of them in the Western world—to defile their own sanctities, to strip from their souls vestiture after vestiture, until they stood naked in the storms of the world when the ultimate pagan barbarians reiterated in their vulgar version the statement which Tacitus had made eighteen hundred years ago, that the branch of Christianity could be the more easily destroyed if the tree of Judaism, from which it sprang, could be uprooted from the earth.

II

Now the politicians were Enlighteners too. They were going to emancipate everybody on abstract human grounds. But they were in practice and instinctively concerned with the establishment of a society according to their norms. Therefore Count Mirabeau demanded in 1787 that the Jewish schools be regulated and improved. Whence came his competence to define "improvement"? But this was the slogan here, as it was to be later on in Czarist Russia. "Improvement," he continued, "will raise Jews to the rank of the most useful citizens." He meant adaptation, adjustment to *his* norm and notion. "Freedom," he finally announced, "will heal the evils to which they have been subjected." That would have been true emancipation. Alas, he added: "and the vices which have been forced upon them." What were those "vices"? By what norm were characteristics which he saw only in street or market place "vices"? We have amazed Christian witnesses to the fact that, all during the Middle Ages, when only a rare priest could read his

missal, Jews founded and sustained schools for their boys and
even often taught their daughters to read, and that therefore
Jews had been for many centuries the most literate people in
Europe. Count Mirabeau and the Abbé Lamourette who, two
years later, pleaded for the emancipation of the Jews before
the National Assembly not without sincere fervor—had they
ever seen a Jew except in his public acts of getting his livelihood? Had they ever seen this same Jew at his table, ushering
in the Sabbath, or in his House of Study, communing with the
saints and sages of old?

It is doubtful whether these questions have ever been asked
in this form before. And this circumstance bears witness to the
blindness with which generation after Jewish generation has
been stricken. Yet these questions need to be emphasized not
only to explain Herzl and the men of his time, but the servile
antics of Jews which still cripple and disgrace us. It was, at
all events, no wonder that the well-meaning Abbé Lamourette
was impelled to confess that the existing Jews were "coarse and
slothful"—strangest of epithets!—and to advance in their favor
the simile that those who were excluded from the civil society
about them were "like fish out of water." That he, like all the
emancipators and all later philo-Semites, speculated, whether
quite consciously or not, upon the disappearance of the Jews
is clear from his final statement: "For the Jews are really no
longer a Nation; they are but the remnants and ruins of a folk
destroyed."

The stage was set for that final statement of Clermont-Tonnerre before the Assembly which foreshadowed so early the
nationalistic master state in its pretotalitarian form: "All that
we demand of a religious sect is evidence of its ethical validity.
To the Jews as a nation everything is to be denied; to the Jew
as a human being all is to be granted. There dare not be a nation within the nation." And so Napoleon caused the Jewish
Notables to be convened in the ancient Hôtel de Ville of Paris
seventeen years later and offered them the fruits of the Revolution in the form of twelve questions, on the answers to which
their civic rights were to depend. One year later, with one of
those self-conscious historic gestures of his, he assembled a

Sanhedrin in Paris, of which he demanded a confirmation of the answers which had been given to the twelve questions. "His Majesty, for the exalted protection granted, demands unexceptionable guarantees for an exact adherence to the answers." He demanded, amusingly enough, that these answers be given an authority equal to that of the Talmud. The so-called Sanhedrin assented. What the great historian Simon Dubnow was to call "the sin of 1807" was irrevocably committed.

The questions put and the answers given have never been a favorite subject among Jews. A subtle shame has been at work. It is clear, for instance, that the Sanhedrin was forced to answer affirmatively the third question concerning the legitimacy of intermarriage, that is, to consent theoretically to the destruction of Israel. As Herzl and many after him declared: Biological assimilation is the only kind that really works. From both the dangerous and the harmless questions Jews preferred to avert their vision and to fix it rather upon the formulation of their status and condition as those of a mere sect or abstractly religious community. No experience deterred them from this delusion, not even the edict of the Prussian State of 1812 that Jews were to adopt German surnames, that they were to keep their business records and formulate their contracts and wills in "German or some other living language and in Latin letters." Thus, first here and later in the Austrian empire, the Cerf Bers and the ben Yehudas and the ben Eliezers became those Goldbergs and Veilchenfelds and Perlmutters whose posterity was to blush at these wholly un-Jewish Jewish names. Thus, too, this edict took cognizance of the existence of a living Hebraic civilization which implied peoplehood. Yet Jews, in contradiction of the historic evidence under their very eyes, echoed with joy the well-meant absurdity of the high-minded Wilhelm von Humboldt that "the word Jew need no more be uttered in any relationship except a religious one."

Two voluntarily embraced delusions were now frozen for several generations and beyond. One was that the Jews were mere sectaries in the accepted Western sense of that word. The second delusion, which led in time to the endemic disease of self-hatred, of self-disesteem, was this, that during the centuries

of civic oppression the Jews had become a sordid and slavish
people of usurers, withdrawn and self-withdrawn from the
civility of the Western world and needing to adapt themselves
to the cultures amid which they dwelt. Forgotten were the
sublime creative achievements of the ages of oppression and
self-sustaining Judaism from Maimonides and Yehuda Halevy
through Rashi, through the literature of Responsa and Ethical
Wills; forgotten were the myriads of heroic and saintly lives
which had been led in every generation; the somber glory of
the Ghetto was negated and defiled. Jews agreed that they must
be "improved," that they must be transformed in order to
deserve freedom. Such was the plea of Macaulay for their
emancipation; such was, a generation later, the principle
announced by that pseudoliberal czar, Alexander II, in whom
so many hopes were centered. "The aim must be," Alexander
declared, "the moral transformation of the Jews and their
amalgamation with the ethnically native population." In the
East, then, the *lamdan*, the Jewish scholar, was to try to become a *muzhik*, a peasant; in the West, the Jewish ethical
personality, so often God-dedicated, so often a forgiver of his
enemies, was to turn himself into a pagan warrior and a dueling fool. Is this a reduction to the absurd? Hardly, alas! The
classically minded masses of Eastern Europe stood largely
firm against this degradation. In the West, it almost conquered.
It will be seen that both Herzl and Nordau still accepted the
question of the duel as one which must be seriously faced.

The two delusions penetrated each other. A mere religious
sect, whose members' highest aim was to be their adaptation
to an alien environment, could not well continue those practices which stamped its religion as a national culture; it could
not well continue those daily acts of sanctification by which
the Jew is commanded to differentiate his conduct from that of
the world's peoples and thus to prove himself the member of
a "kingdom of priests and a holy people." The core and essence
of Judaism had to be abandoned. The freedom which Jews
sought, the only freedom which they were permitted to seek,
namely that of another mere sect of Frenchmen or Germans,
forbade both the theory and practice of election and differen-

tiation through *Kedusha,* through sanctification. This theory and these practices began to inspire terror. They were cast aside by thousands with unseemly haste. So brutal and so relentless has been the pressure toward nondifferentiation that today in America, as in those far pre-Herzlian days, there are "Jews by religion only" who are totally ignorant of Judaism, who repudiate it with horror when, unwillingly, they become aware of it; there are theologians who discard the statements of election from the liturgy on the ground that these statements are not conformable to "modern" thought.

Thus Reform Judaism, which may be said to have originated in Hamburg in 1813, was never an organic development from within. It did not—as it has recently begun to do—re-examine the Law, the content of *Halakha,* on its own grounds. It raced to adapt itself. The vernacular sermon instituted by the Hamburg reformers was in historical perspective no great innovation; the use of an organ, though also historically at least debatable, was evidently a showpiece for the world; it was in their formulation that the Hamburg reformers betrayed themselves. New forms were to be found, they declared, using the alien Christian terminology, for all those human acts "which are consecrated by the *Church"*—*"Handlungen die durch die Kirche geheiligt sind."*

It is never to be denied nor to be forgotten that Reform Judaism was and is a bridge over which many thousands of Jews were able to pass from one age to another and were thus preserved to their people. But the historic account of that Western Judaism which shaped Herzl himself and which illuminates the magnitude of his achievement must continue to emphasize that Reform, too, was the issue of the two delusions, embraced under brutal pressure, that the Jews were a mere group of sectaries who had been morally corrupted during the ages of oppression and who must now prove their worthiness of civic freedom by abandoning and repudiating their history and their historic being. A shattering entry in Herzl's diaries may anticipatorily illustrate the tragic state of mind nurtured by the two delusions and by the "winds of doctrine" of a stupid age. The *Judenstaat* had been written, though not yet published. Herzl had returned from London, where, before the Maccabean Club, he had proclaimed his total dream and his regenerative vision. He was at home in Vienna. The date of the entry is December 24, 1895.

> I was lighting the candles on the Christmas tree for my children. Güdemann [the Chief Rabbi of Vienna] dropped in. He seemed irritated by this "Christian" ceremony, No, I won't stand for pressure! But for all I care, let the tree be called the *Hanuka* tree —or of the winter solstice?

The voice of reason and history had never been wholly silent. Many years before this the eminent and learned Rabbi Samson Raphael Hirsch of Frankfurt-am-Main had asked whether it was or could ever have been the purpose of divine truth to be "timely" and conformable to the age, to any and every age; whether, if this truth be true and acceptable, it were not the duty of the age to conform to it? Yet he was no sullen separatist, but declared that no science nor art nor culture need be alien to the Jew if proven worthy by the touchstone of his Judaism. Thus a considerable fragment of Central European Jewry was saved from the depths of assimilatory folly and survived to reorganize its forces in the *Ahdut*, the "Unity" movement as late as 1923. But the apparent leaders of Jewry, the Jews of high visibility in the Gentile world, did not heed the voice of reason or history. Stubbornly they insisted that all traditional beliefs and practices were "antiquated" by nineteenth century intellectual and cultural norms. "New rites conformable to the spirit of the time, the *Zeitgeist*" were demanded. None sought, as many do not still, to regard the *Zeitgeist* critically and question the validity of its demands. Dazzled and duped, every succeeding generation of youth hastened more morbidly and eagerly to repudiate the historic character and faith of Israel. Intermarriage and apostasy flourished. No one chose to observe the circumstance that the birth rate among these Germans and Austrians and Frenchmen of the Jewish or Mosaic persuasion declined rapidly. For to observe that circumstance would have been to see that the extremes of Jewish assimilation lead first to moral and next to physical extinction.

How, it may be asked, did reasonable men sustain themselves under the dominance of two delusions so coarse and obvious as the reduction of the Jewish people to a sect and the negation of its historic dignity and sanctity? The answer is that, roughly, from 1830 to 1875 the more generous errors of the Enlightenment seemed still to prevail and, crassly, to pay off. True, Jews could not become officers in the German army, as they could in the Austrian and, as the example of Captain Dreyfus illustrates, in the French; rare, too, were Jews of full professorial rank in Western universities, so that not even Chaim Weizmann attained that rank at Manchester. But these exclusions and others were interpreted (not by Weizmann, needless to say) as temporary imperfections on the road of an inevitable progress. Again and again Herzl was to argue that Jewish emancipation was irreversible despite the age's bitterly resurgent antisemitism. From 1830 to 1875 even this very affirmation would have been unthinkable. The great Jewish fortunes were founded; Jews were ennobled in Austria, Germany, even a few in Russia, as some had been under the French Empire. The revolutions of 1830 and of 1848, which Heine witnessed with such joy and hopefulness, seemed to confirm the march of the principles of the Enlightenment. If Jews just continued to be mimimum Jews, if only, except for a nominal religious affiliation, they identified themselves wholly with the dominant culture, the golden age of complete equality and equivalence could, except in such barbarous and antiquated polities as those of Russia and Romania, not be far off. Indeed, it might be presumed to be already here.

This view or theory penetrated deeply the consciousness of a majority of Western Jews. A type of character was formed which, tragically and well nigh unbelievably, persists in America, in England, in France, to this day. This Jew is an ardent patriot and an ardent liberal. He is a progressive secularist. Imponderables of any kind are not for him. He looks upon his observant and obedient brethren with the scorn of the enlightened for the obscurantist. He looks upon such remnants of his

immemorial Jewish past as have persisted in his family or in
his early years with a supercilious kindliness. These are antiquated matters which do not touch the modern mind. Sedulously he avoids all contacts with authentic Jews; indeed he
generally feigns unawareness of their existence. With equal
though unobtrusive zeal he seeks the society of Gentiles; he
feels wholly safe only when, with and among them, he can
illustrate to himself his complete likeness to them. Every Gentile acquaintance is a bargain to him; every Gentile friend—
as Wurzlechner to Jacob Samuel in Herzl's play *The New
Ghetto*—is a source of pride, of joy, of security. And he does,
indeed, require these acquaintances, these friends; he needs
the constant reassurance of his likeness to them. For, despite
all protestations, despite the fact that all intellectual currents
seem—and seemed especially from 1830 to 1875—to be on his
side, an element of inner insecurity continues to disturb him.
He compensates for that element by an ever more ardent em-
bracing of every wind of contemporary doctrine, by an ever
more acrid contempt for every vestige of his ethnic and religious past. Thus—and this was and is the "lower depth" of
the assimilatory hell—he co-operated and still co-operates with
all those scientific and antireligious forces which undermined
the validity of the Judaeo-Christian ethic and unleashed that
pagan fury which, first in Germany, next in Russia, was destined to destroy him and his kind.

When it was too late, by far too late, at the turn of the twen-
tieth century, the sagacious and saintly historian Martin Philippson (1846–1916), himself the son of an eminent though
moderate Reformer, wrote sadly enough: "We sought to avoid
everything that might make us seem to appear as Jews in the
face of the world. Our only care was not to obtrude ourselves
and to remind no one of the fact of our independent existence!"
It was far too late. Too late also was the not unpoetic and melancholy delineation of the dealing of that ever old and ever
new wound to the Jew of the Enlightenment in Herzl's dramatic sketch "In the Dining Car" ("*Im Speisewagen*") which
he contributed to the *Neue Freie Presse* in that very year. For
the apparently liberating delusions of the Enlightenment had

already given way to other delusions more monstrous and more devastating. The old religious prejudice against the "faithless Jews," as the Catholic liturgy has it, had perished in dominant European circles with religion itself. Hence conversion was no longer asked and apostasy was no longer profitable. Since everything had to be "scientific," racialism was invented. The Jews were an evil and contaminating race who were undermining and corrupting the cultures and the states of the "Aryans." Such was the doctrine advanced by Eugen Dühring in that book on the Jewish question which so troubled the young Herzl in 1881; it was reiterated by Drumont in *La France juive* five years later. It was to culminate still later in the notorious German summing up:

> What the Jew believes is all the same;
> In the race resides the filth and shame.
>
> (*Was der Jude glaubt ist einerlei;*
> *In der Rasse liegt die Schweinerei.*)

The new doctrine of nonreligious antisemitism, which smote so sorely the precarious equilibrium of the Jews of the liberal decades, expressed itself at first in apparently more civilized forms. Although the Prussian historian Heinrich von Treitschke coined the phrase: "The Jews are our misfortune" (*"Die Juden sind unser Unglück"*) in 1880, he took his stand upon the ground of the old Napoleonic agreements. Civil rights had been granted to the Jews "in expectation of their striving to be like their fellow-citizens." This they had not done. It is easy to imagine how this precise reproach smote upon the minds of the strenuous assimilationists whom Martin Philippson had so accurately described. But they had no opportunity to awaken from their delusions. For their defenders, such as Theodor Mommsen, the illustrious historian of Rome, answered Treitschke with the observation that the German Jews had "honorably fulfilled their sacred duty of a complete merging with the German people," and pointed with satisfaction to the increased number of intermarriages. It was on these terms that the clamor continued. In 1881 a petition was addressed to Bismarck, who was supposed to be not unfavorable

to Jews, reiterating the charge that "the hope of their amalgamation with the German people had proved illusory." And
again, between 1881 and 1885, the philosemites continued to
assert that the Jews had indeed "sought zealously to throw
off their peculiar mode of being," to attempt a "complete
blending" with the autochthonous population and to "substi-
tute German national feeling for their ethnic consciousness."

All forces conspired to lure the Jews of that generation
deeper and deeper into the morass of psychical confusion and
Jewish self-disesteem. The assimilatory race became feverish.
It expressed itself more and more, too, in a contempt for the
Jews of Poland and Russia who, despite oppression and pogroms, continued to defend the ancient citadels of the Jewish
spirit. No gleam of the intellectual life of the East was permitted to penetrate the darkness of the Central Europeans.
Unheard was the voice of Leon Pinsker, whose *Auto-Emancipation* appeared in the German language; unheeded were those
Hebrew essays in which Ahad Ha'am so precisely defined the
miseries of the Western Jews. These warnings reached no one.
Herzl, as will be seen, was wholly unconscious of them. What
he undoubtedly heard were the repeated pleas of that distinguished company of German intellectuals who in 1890 formed
their Society of Defense Against Antisemitism (*Gesellschaft
zur Abwehr des Antisemitismus*) and whose 12,000 members
reiterated publicly their conviction that the Jews had become
sufficiently Germanized. He must have been aware, too, of the
founding in 1893 of the afterwards famous Central Society of
German Citizens of the Jewish Faith (*Central Verein Deutscher
Staatsbürger jüdischen Glaubens*) which, like later defense
organizations, had little traffic with "faith" and was prepared
to act in defense not of Judaism, but of Jews as undifferentiated
human beings.

Not uninfluenced by these controversies, mixed marriages and
baptism once more increased and the birth rate among German
Jews declined to twenty-two births per thousand. Meanwhile
the questions of ethnic nationalism and the dominance of ethnic
culture took on even more grotesque and confused forms within
the various nations united politically under the Austrian crown.

Here Jews, like the families of Herzl and Nordau in Hungary, like the family of Franz Kafka so many years later in Czechoslovakia, were German in their cultural orientation. This was due consciously to the power and breadth of German culture compared to the provincialism of the Magyar and the Czech; it was also due—though the Herzls and the Nordaus would honestly have denied this—to that ancestral late Middle High German speech which had developed into the Yiddish language and literature. Of the latter motivation the schoolboy Theodor Herzl was wholly innocent when, at fifteen, he wrote in his natal city of Budapest:

> Out of the long, long night,
> Through Luther's power and might,
> The German spirit came to light.

> (*Es ist aus langer Nacht,*
> *Durch Luthers gewaltige Kraft,*
> *Der deutsche Geist erwacht.*)

The verses are indeed those of a schoolboy. Yet how significant they are of the tragically false position of a Jew, repudiated by the Germans, acting as *their* defender and representative in the capital of the Magyars. Seven years later, when the Herzls had long since moved to Vienna, Theodor visited Budapest. Half contempuously he wrote home that Hungary had grown more Hungarian in the interval and added with a gesture of defiant pride that he had spoken no syllable of Hungarian during his stay in the city. This was in 1882. Thirty-eight years later Franz Kafka, his vision cleared by what we now know to have been his Zionist convictions, told his young Czechish friend Gustav Janouch the at once exact and symbolic story of the fate of the Jewish writer Oscar Baum. Like all the children of the Jewish middle class in Prague, Baum attended a German primary school. There were frequent street fights between the pupils of this school and those of a Czech school. In such a fight little Oscar Baum was hit over the eyes with a sharp pencil box. The retina became detached and Baum was stricken with lifelong blindness. And so, Kafka summed up: "The Jew Oscar Baum lost his eyesight as a German—as something he never was nor was accepted as being, a melancholy symbol of the so-called Jews of Prague."

IV

Meanwhile, in those far years of Herzl's youth and early manhood, the brawling and tumult of the Antisemites continued. The courts of Vienna rang with the insane accusations of a certain Rohling, who was defeated and exposed in the columns of that *Allgemeine Zeitung*, which was later to give Herzl his first chance as an essayist. All Europe resounded in the early eighties with the ritual blood accusation in the Hungarian village of Tiszaeszlar. By 1890 the German Antisemites, having formed a political party, elected five members to the Reichstag. Thus it is clear that the inner, the spiritual condition of those Jews who had accepted the principles of the false emancipation and who sought an ever more complete identification with their Western cultures, became more and more troubled and precarious. Horace was one of the few poets whom Herzl loved and it is profoundly significant that his favorite quotation was that somber line: *Post equitem sedet atra cura*— "behind the knight sits black care"—*die schwarze Sorge*, as Herzl translated it in his mind. The crumbs of comfort were few and stale. Before the Dreyfus trial and his own turning to Zionism Bernard Lazare in his *Histoire de l'Antisémitisme* preached the old defeatist doctrine that antisemitism would perish if only the Jews would give up their existential separateness; Renan's defense was that the Jews did not constitute a pure and recognizable racial strain, and that of Leroy-Beaulieu, whom Herzl later criticized so tellingly, rehearsed the wilted lie that the virtues of the Jews were native to them while their vices had been historically induced.

So sharp, moreover, was the division between the assimilated Jews of Vienna and those who had either come from the great Jewish centers in the East or were at least aware of their existence, that Herzl actually did not know that in Vienna, perhaps only a few city blocks from his own house, Peretz Smolenskin had as early as 1880 published *Hashahar* ("The Dawn"); that the student Zionist group *Kadima* ("Forward"), which was later to hail him, was founded in 1885; that Nathan Birnbaum ("Mathias Acher") proclaimed on the same streets which they both trod the central principle of Jewish self-emancipation. How much less, then, was it possible for Herzl to have known that in remotest Russia one of the most penetrating minds of the nineteenth century, the mind of Ahad Ha'am ("One of the People," the famous pseudonym of Asher Ginzburg) had with complete finality analyzed the sins, the sorrows, the errors of Western Jewry? The capital essay on the subject appeared in 1891. It was called *Avdut Betokh Herut*—"Slavery in the Midst of Freedom." In brief and sober sentences Ahad Ha'am described the estate of the Western assimilationist. "On the one hand Judaism dare be nothing but a religious community; on the other hand this transcendental bond has been almost wholly dissolved. But in the end—and this is the chief thing—they feel, despite everything, not only that they *are* Jews but that their will is to *remain* Jews." What, then, is this indestructible force within them? Ahad Ha'am asks. Evidently a national bond, a bond which unites the members of a people. But the right to entertain and acknowledge this feeling the Jews of the West had "bartered away" a century ago for those civil "rights" which condemn them to a moral and intellectual slavery of a hundred hypocrisies and attempts at self-annihilation. "In the face of the whole world they renounced their peoplehood and dare no longer recognize its existence and dare no longer admit that they sold something which it was not within their power to alienate." Ahad Ha'am had in mind, of course, the Sanhedrin summoned by Napoleon in 1807, at which the false bargain of the emancipation was struck. It is worth emphasizing once more at this point the very great saying of Simon Dubnow, himself no Zionist but a *Galut* nationalist,* that the first Zionist Congress convoked by Theodor Herzl in Basle in 1897 not only created a caesura, an epoch-making break in Jewish history, "but was a partial atonement for the sin of 1807."

* i. e., a proponent of minority rights in the lands of the dispersion.

2. THE MID-EUROPEAN
AND HIS TIME

I

THE Herzl family came from the borderlands between the East and West of Europe. There was a move in Theodor's great-grandfather's time from Czechoslovakian to Yugoslavian territory where two of his great-uncles apostatized. His grandfather, Simon Loeb Herzl, remained an observant Jew and lived, though at a distance, until Theodor was twenty. From him came vague and unsubstantiated stories of a Sefardic strain and tradition. And it is certain that Herzl had a cast of countenance as well as a *grandezza* of gesture and attitude which do not fit the legend ill. His father, Jacob Herzl, however, displayed no such characteristics. He was a carefully Europeanized middle-class Jew, banker at one time, broker at another, losing one modest fortune only to regain prosperity later, a Jew by habit and nurture but quite without piety or fervor.

Herzl's mother, Jeannette Diamant, came of a family apparently long established in Hungary. Her father was a clothier, a man of some means and standing. Although she survived her illustrious son, we know little that is concrete and specific about her. And this is a great pity, since hers was the commanding influence in Theodor Herzl's life. Tradition has it that she was noted for wit and beauty even in her girlhood. What is certain from internal evidence was that her Jewishness sat lightly upon her, that she was an avid reader of German literature and aware of all the fashionable notions of her day. She was determined from the first that her son should be a very exemplar of German culture and, if possible, a leader within it. She represented thus a type familiar in the history of every Mid-European Jewish family. It was often the woman in that generation who strove most ardently for cultural identification and who constituted the passionate audience of those two Jews who then, and for several generations to come, seemed to illustrate the triumphant participation of Jews in German civilization, Ludwig Börne and Heinrich Heine.

Of these parents Theodor Herzl, dutifully also given the Hebrew names of Binyamin Ze'ev, was born in Pest on May 2, 1860. The house in which he was born on the Tabakgasse stood almost next door to the Liberal Reform Synagogue of Pest. He showed his awareness of a certain irony in that circumstance in an autobiographical sketch written in 1898. He did not permit himself to remember that the proximity of the Temple in that day and place meant that he was born in a densely settled Jewish quarter, in that "Ghetto" which, until the great transformation of his life and even beyond, was to be the object of his fear and his recurrent dismay. But that the place of worship near the house of his birth was called a Temple and was of the Reform wing in 1860 showed the passionate attachment of that part of the Jewish *gass* of Pest to the dominant German culture within which the Reform movement had originated.

The picture is clear to anyone aware of the circumstances and temper of that time and place. All Jewish preoccupations and practices were perfunctory and diminishing. One was ashamed to abandon them and equally ashamed to emphasize them. All hopes and all aspirations were toward a son's penetration into and predominance within the Germanic civilizations, whether of Austria or Germany. One avoided and silently condemned the Orthodox Jews on the next street. One kept one's children from association with them. Since a daughter, destined to die in her girlhood, had been born to the Herzls a year before Theodor, the children needed no other playmates. The family was self-sufficient and lived in a state of hot and brooding intimacy, of intense fixations, dominated by the mother's assimilatory drives. To the end of his life Theodor spoke and wrote of his "good Mama" and his "good Papa." They were his first disciples in the days of the great change; his father was to be the first "senator" in the Jewish State; into the arms of his mother he fell in an interval during the tragic "Uganda" Congress.

Nor was this all. The biographers of Herzl have hitherto taken what might well be called a greeting-card view of the realities of his life and of the psychical patterns formed in his early childhood.* The unrelenting mother dominance kept him far too pure in his magnificient youth and early manhood. As a defense, it rendered him fiercely puritanical. What he yearned for and could not act out must be regarded as evil. But all through his earlier writings, as will be seen, both in the essays and in the plays, there is a hankering after the ribald and a defensive contempt for women and womanhood which jibes but ill with that sincerely enough professed but probably profoundly ambivalent adoration of his mother. The learned and perceptive Leon Kellner read the literary record correctly but dared not quite speak out. Dr. Alex Bein frankly admits that Herzl's mother ruined his marriage. However frivolous and spoiled Julie Naschauer may have been, she had no chance against the entrenched union and unanimity of that mother and her son. Theodor Herzl was from the start a beautiful human being. But his photographs taken at six, at twelve, at sixteen—one can see Frau Herzl proudly taking her adored boy to the photographer's studio—are a singular subject of study. The face is unrelaxed; the expression is petulant and proud; the posture is rigid. It is not only the conventional stiffness of early photography. The poor, beautiful boy had been praised and flattered directly and indirectly. His parents had reached no goal which his mother valued. He was to be fulfillment, compensation, reward. He was to transcend the Jewish Street; he was to be a great man among the men of German speech and deed.

When Theodor was five and a half a private tutor was hired. The *heder*, the traditional Jewish school, so indiscriminately maligned considering the type of mind and character that issued from it generation after generation, was to be sedulously

* From this reproach, based upon the abbreviated English translation, Dr. Alex Bein must be exempted. His original work, kindly communicated by him (*Theodor Herzl: Biographie*, Wien, Fiba-Verlag, 1934), treats all these matters with candor and insight.

avoided. At six, however, the child was sent to the *Pester Israelitische Normalhauptschule*, a German-language normal school, maintained, as the name shows, by the Germanizing section of the Jewish community. Its "Israelite" tepidness and inadequacy can be well imagined. Playing in his childish fancy with grandiose scientific notions, the boy was transferred at ten to a technical high school. There he remained for five years. On May 3, 1873, his parents invited their friends to the "confirmation" of their son. He was, it would appear, called to the Torah as a bar mitzvah, despite the word "confirmation," and must thus have acquired at least a smattering of Biblical and liturgical Hebrew. But the moral atmosphere was unfavorable to any retention of these impressions. At school he slighted all studies except literature and history. He began to scribble both prose and verse. Hence he took a year off to acquire enough Greek and Latin to enable him in 1876 to enter the *Evangelisches Gymnasium*, the Evangelical High School or College, populated, despite its name, largely by Jewish students. The verses on Luther and the awakening of the German spirit mark this period. They complete the picture of his inevitable future as a *jüdischer Literat*, a Jewish writer, *not* creator, according to Jacob Wassermann's penetrating description, within the world of German letters.

In the succeeding years book reviews which he composed were accepted by the *Pester Lloyd*, the famous German newspaper in Budapest. He planned novels; he attempted essays and verse. He yielded, of course—how could he not have—to the prevailing positivism and nihilism which marked the period. Jewish sanctities, which Jews of that period associated with the humiliating separateness which, above all things, they hated and condemned, were not to be thought upon. Hence the mounting pretensions of an immature science, the screaming contempt poured upon any metaphysical speculation, the ardent reduction of human characteristics to an animal level found the readiest acceptance among those Jews who desperately sought an escape from their history and their being. They were "free" once more in the midst of a new slavery and sought to outshout the poignant melancholy, the deep sense of an unrealized loss

which throbbed like a pulse in all their productions. Reflections
of Herzl recorded in those early years complete the picture of
the involuntary wretchedness of these liberations. It was simply
more seemly to laugh than to weep.

II

In 1878 he passed, not too brilliantly, the final examinations
of the *Evangelisches Gymnasium*. His sister died of typhoid
fever and the grief-stricken family moved to Vienna. Here,
according to a custom long prevalent and destined long to continue, Herzl matriculated at the University in the faculty of
Law. Talented young Jews, of whose growing numbers Herzl
was so often to complain, had no prospects in an academic
career. They had none, as he was to discover, in the specific
judiciary service of the state either. But there was always the
chance of a livelihood as a practicing lawyer. Many did, in
fact, choose that practical path. But from long before the days of
Herzl until those of the Hitler madness the ranks of German
journalism were filled with Jewish *doctores utriusque juris*,
doctors of both Roman and German law.

The freedom of a European university student was now his.
His parents, as always, supplied him liberally with funds. He
steeped himself in the peculiar culture, the incomparable aspect,
the massive yet curiously intimate life of Vienna. Here already
Jews, feigning in every outer act and every assumed conviction
to be Austrians and Austrians only, played an influential role.
The two most conspicuous newspapers, especially the *Neue
Freie Presse*, which Herzl was to serve so long, were in Jewish
hands. Antisemitism was grimly on the march. But the notions
of the Enlightenment had not wholly lost their force. Thus
Herzl joined a nondiscriminatory reading club (*Lesehalle*) and
steeped himself in such German literature as he had not yet
read. He joined a fraternity, *Albia*, protested against its growing antisemitic leanings, and was unceremoniously dropped.
He repressed this incident, as he did others. Feverishly during
these university years he wrote plays and essays. The resounding successes of a playwright were to compensate for the inner
conflicts, for his actual or potential rejection as a Jew. The

younger Arthur Schnitzler recalled later how, strolling past the *Burgtheater*, the then imperial and ruling theater, Herzl had said to him: "I'll be in there some day!"

The sense of haste and urgency which was later to characterize his Zionist activities manifested itself in these early years in other forms. He gambled, though not immoderately; he grew the long concealing beard which was to be removed only once more and then for a brief period. He suffered beyond reason or measure under the rejection of his plays and tales and essays. He read Dühring's specific accusations against Jewish character and morality. In the end, of course, his comments echo the babble of the Enlightenment. Even these dark legends concerning Jews would disappear. An enlightened humanity will look back upon all this as one looks back upon the Middle Ages. But the wound burned, although so deeply hidden from himself. And to feverish ambition he added attempts to direct outwardly the aggressive instincts of defense. He was, a few years later, to challenge two men to mortal combat in duels, and was saved from this extreme folly only by the force of outer circumstances. He was later, it will not be forgotten, to insist that manly honor demanded the practice of dueling in the projected Jewish State.

He managed to achieve his doctorate in Law in May, 1884; he worked during some months in the courts of both Vienna and Salzburg. But these incidents remained external and trivial. The shaping of his character both as a man and a writer was deeply rooted in his personal situation and in the repressed Jewish conflicts in his breast. This has not hitherto been observed. His father, after a crash in Budapest in the late seventies, had recovered financially. He and his wife had no aim in life save to guard, to encourage, to amuse, to flatter their son. He in turn accepted their estimate of him; he contrasted it with the low estate of his literary fortunes. He seemed to himself a kind of prince whom the world would not acknowledge. As such he idled about with a mocking and superior air; he went on journeys to the Austrian Alps, to Switzerland, and, after taking his law degree, to Holland, Belgium, and finally to Paris, the culminating point and experience. He frequented the

Comédie-Française; he conceived a just admiration for the great
actor Coquelin, but also, unfortunately, for the French theater of
those years, which was still the theater of superficial intrigue as
practiced by Scribe and Sardou. Only once or twice in the course
of the years was he to mention Antoine's *Théâtre Libre,* which
inaugurated the modern drama, and, among the contributors
to that stage, only the fantastic François de Curel.

He continued sedulously to write both plays and essays, and
finally, in 1885, when he was after all still quite young, won an
honorable mention in a contest sponsored by the *Wiener
Allgemeine Zeitung.* His *feuilleton* was published and a measure of local fame in that tight cultural community was immediately gained. What, it may be asked, is a *feuilleton* and
what was the character of this first one of Herzl's which made
its small noise in the world?

A *feuilleton* is, from the angle of English usage and tradition,
a "familiar essay." It is a personal, apparently undisciplined
and variegated comment on life, manners, literature. From
Addison on it often becomes character sketch and, as in the
famous Sir Roger de Coverley sketches, almost story. English
literature is rich in great *feuilletons,* such as Hazlitt's "On
Going a Journey" or "On the Pleasures of Painting" or "The
Indian Jugglers." Charles Lamb, too, was a great practitioner
of what are known as *feuilletons* on the Continent. The tradition has continued through such writers as the young Aldous
Huxley and the contemporary American E. B. White. Now in
German literature a strange mad thing happened. Since the
older type of familiar essay, imitated from the English practi-
tioners, had fallen into disuse, and since its first and most brilliant resuscitators happened to be the Jews Ludwig Börne and
Heinrich Heine, it began in the eighteen-eighties to be stamped
in German literary circles as the escapist form of the "uncre-
ative" Jew. The German was a *Dichter,* a poet, a creator. The
Jew was a "barren rascal" and his medium the *feuilleton.* This
insane theory was apparently confirmed by the fact that Jews
did excel in this form of writing, from Herzl himself on through
the immensely brilliant and witty Alfred Polgar, and that their
works appeared in the famous German papers—the *Vossische*

Zeitung, the *Berliner Tageblatt*, the *Neue Freie Presse* and *Allgemeine Zeitung* of Vienna—which were known to be owned and edited by Jews. But these Jews pretended to be and to run their papers as undifferentiated German or Austrian liberals. Hence an element of unveracity served further to invoke the hatred and disdain of the German nationalists. It will be recalled that the word "Zionist" was not printed in the *Neue Freie Presse*, in whose often hated and irksome harness Herzl died, until after his own death and, as it were, apotheosis.

In 1885, in the days of his first small successes, Herzl himself would have been the last one to appear as a Jew writing on a Jewish theme. That first sketch of his was called *Das Alltägliche*, which may be rendered as "A Common Incident." A shy and dreamy young man adores a blonde young piano teacher. He has a friend, a blasé chaser of women, a cynic, who laughs to scorn the rose-colored little romance. Hence the young lover introduces his cynical friend to his blonde lily and, of course, it is he, the cynical friend, who marries her at once. The shy young idealist is the dupe. Now this early figure of the cynic continues in the sketches and tales and familiar essays. It is he with whom Herzl identifies himself defensively. His name here is Georg; later it was to be Spangelberg, an impresario, a ruthless scorner of all values, a seducer, ruffian, falsely witty, falsely sentimental, a perpetrator of monstrous practical jokes—a creature of external worldly elegance under which he barely troubles to conceal a profound corruption. Once more it is Leon Kellner who first among the biographers perceived this identification. He does nothing to connect or integrate it with the facts of the young Herzl's situation and character. Yet this tone of harsh and shallow derisiveness is constant in the essays and plays and lasts to the edge of and even beyond the great revelation and change. The pose hardly varies. And it has long been evident that he who assumes a constant pose does so as a defensive measure against the realities of his life. This pure young man, upon whose least expression or impulse his mother veritably hung, wrote: "One has but to amuse women in order to possess them." He wrote in that first travel sketch on St. Jean de Luz with which he made his way into the columns of the *Neue Freie Presse:* "In Tarbes, the principal town of the Pyrenees, I felt compelled to add a codicil to my last will and testament. In the categorical tone proper to the elegance of such documents, I set down explicitly that my remains were not to be interred in this place, in the event I were to die here of boredom." In an otherwise perceptive and ingenious tale he wrote: "Thus matters stood when at a ball one day, Kilchberg met the daughter of a wealthy hardware manufacturer and fell in love with her father's business." The old ache of his early disappointments which were not grave and soon overcome echoes late: "It was at the beginning of my career, but I had already gone far. For I had reached the point at which I still am today." English versions, it may be added, do little justice to the ironic pointedness of these sentences. The cynical phrases were sharp. But their edges and points were, of course, turned inward, not outward.

He dared not admit to himself anything that he was—any of the aching realities within, neither the shattering relation to his mother which kept him "pure," nor the throb of his Jewish woe, his *Judenschmerz.* For the one he overcompensated by the ribald and cynical pose; the other broke out surreptitiously again and again. He cannot keep the compensatory pose out of otherwise rather lyrical writing: "Autumn draws near like a young colonel who is still bent on amatory conquests but who secretly feels the chill of frost steal into his bones." He visited and described a fashionable race track, an epitome of the world of elegance and rank. "A contemptible fool," he comments, "is one who would seek to imitate these. By doing so he betrays the consciousness of his own lack of worth and his desire to penetrate where he is rejected." He plays with the etymology of the German word *Elend,* which now means "wretchedness" but originally meant "exile," being in another land than one's own. "Are there not," he asks, "such islands of the unfortunate in our days too?" Above all, in the adroit dramatic sketch "In the Dining Car" ("*Im Speisewagen*"), the perennial wound throbs for all to see. For the princess in the dining car of the Orient Express is repelled by the raucous vulgarity of the theatrical impresario who forces himself upon her attention; she is charmed by the urbanity and culture of the nameless gentleman who is also drawn into the conversation. Yet she flees in silent but irrevocable dismay when he tells her, against his will and at her importunity, that his name is—Kohn.

The early plays, as again noted by Kellner and Bein, are even harsher in tone than the sketches and tales. Ingenuity is their source, not experience. They are compensatory fantasies in which Philistines are duped, women seduced, duels fought. But indeed, all of his plays except *Das Neue Ghetto*, the immediate prelude to the composition of *The Jewish State*, are belated products of a withered kind. Of the new playwrights of his time he mentions only Max Halbe; late and tentatively he speaks of "the wizard of the Northland, Herr Ibsen"; he seems unconscious of the existence of either Henry Becque or Gerhart Hauptmann. But this is on a level with his general views of the literature of his time. Concerning the short story, of which he himself was no contemptible practitioner in his *Philosophische Erzählungen*, ingenious and telling despite the pretentious title, he observes that the tales of Octave Feuillet are unveracious and pure, those of Guy de Maupassant veracious and impure.

Yet since in a given age tastes overlap and the new does not thrust out the old, Herzl cannot be said to have been wholly unsuccessful as a playwright. A one-act historical play, "Tabarin," more or less inspired by the second-rate French Jewish writer Catulle Mendès, was performed in 1885 by a distinguished Austrian actor as guest on the then excellent German-language stage of New York. When the amazing news arrived Herzl rushed to Berlin, where he was well received in the editorial offices of the *Berliner Tageblatt* and by theatrical managers. But none of his plays was accepted. He returned to Vienna unduly dispirited and was provided with money and sent by his ever-watchful mother to the South, to France, to Italy, the land of the poet's yearning. From there he sent somewhat mellower *feuilletons* to the papers which had accepted him but also wrote the rather revolting compensatory tale "Tumult in Amalfi." Determined, however, to "make" important stages, above all the *Burgtheater* of Vienna, he grimly excogitated a plot which commended itself to a then well-known playwright and journalist. The result was the anonymously presented collaboration *Die Wilddiebe* ("The Poachers"), which was accepted by the *Burgtheater* and enjoyed a fair "run." The "poachers," the thieves of "game," are, of course, professional lady-killers, potential seducers. The silly intrigue, wholly devoid of truth and reality, is skillfully managed, so that every temptation is exhibited and, in the end, no propriety outraged. Local fame resounded, however, and Herzl was appointed to an editorial position on the *Wiener Allgemeine Zeitung*.

These circumstances persuaded the young man of twenty-nine to marry. He had long known the reputedly handsome Julie Naschauer, the daughter of a wealthy Jewish family. The wedding ceremony took place in Reichenau, outside Vienna, and the young couple departed for France on their honeymoon. Except for the birth of three children, two girls and one boy, in the immediately succeeding years, poor Julie hardly appears again on the scene of Herzl's life. His mother remains the predominant figure. The marriage took place in July, 1889. The very next year we find Herzl again voyaging alone in France and in Italy. These trips, according to him and his mother, had become a spiritual necessity. Speculation on the concrete circumstances would be vain. Definitive separations were followed by temporary reconciliations. The more or less official biographers have no good word to say for Julie, who is represented as frivolous, spoiled, and extravagant. She may have been so. But she never had a chance against that mother and her son. Except for his children, for whom he had the tenderest affection and about whom he wrote some of his subtlest and most beautiful sketches, Herzl pursued the same half-lonely path—with his parents in the steady background—that he had always trodden.

Culminations came rapidly in the immediately succeeding years. He had bungled his editorial duties on the *Allgemeine Zeitung* by treating editorial assistants and contributors harshly and dictatorially. He had since written his best pieces for the *Neue Freie Presse*. Once more on one of his voyages, he received at San Sebastian in Spain a telegram from that paper's editor-in-chief, offering him the position of Paris correspondent at the then generous salary of one thousand gold francs a month and all expenses. He proceeded to Paris and established himself there alone. His nonpolitical writings remained in the same old unhappy vein. Life was still delineated from the point of view of a supercilious irony as being a struggle between "the dupers and the duped," an affair at which "the gods must indulge in Homeric laughter." But even in the general essays the tone begins gradually to mellow and to deepen; in the political reports, on the other hand, the objective and analytical faculties begin to be vigorously exercised. Herzl saw the world of power in direct action. He became less afraid, too, of mentioning the word "Jew" in his reports. The book in which these political *feuilletons* were later gathered, *Das Palais Bourbon*, is the maturest and sanest of his pre-Zionist writings. Shrewd observations alternate with sharp sketches of characters. There is also a heightening of interior awareness which culminated in an exquisite letter addressed to Arthur Schnitzler in February, 1893. He had just read Schnitzler's play *Das Märchen* ("Fairy Tale" is the wholly inadequate and misleading English translation) and had been moved by its sincerity and grace. "I feel a nostalgia after the creative process," he wrote. The original is so much more expressive of his mood and so much more adequate: "*ein Heimweh nach der Dichtung*." But, he hastened to add, "I am full of remorse over my former production which was so frivolous, so unrelated to art, so contrived for mere success." He was capable of sitting in judgment of himself and on his past. It is by no means fantastic to fix the beginning of a spiritual and moral awakening in him at this point. Never before had he been anything but petulant or boastful concerning himself and all his works and ways. He had avoided, as has been seen, the plays of the then new playwrights who had introduced depth of tone and veracity into their art and had, above all, sought to avoid the shallow ingenuities of the old theater of the boulevards. Inaccessible to any metaphysical stirrings by reason of the brash and empty positivism of his period, what struck home to him, himself something of an artist, was the music and the method of a work of art.

It took twenty months for the ferment to work. Travel, work,

a hundred personal and professional preoccupations put off the
creative hours. But when opportunity and inner ripening coin-
cided, the process was swift and, as later in the composition of
The Jewish State, almost ecstatic. Between October 21 and
November 8, 1894, he wrote *The New Ghetto* (*Das Neue
Ghetto*), not only his best play but a farewell—though this he
did not yet know—to his assimilatory past.

The play is in four acts; the scene is Vienna in 1893; the
milieu is that of the assimilated Jewish bourgeoisie. There are
the Helmanns, the Samuels, the very successful stockbroker
Rheinberg and his wife. There are the Helmann girl and the
son of the Samuels, Jacob, a Doctor of Laws, of course, a practicing attorney, who get married in the play. There is the mildest
and most conciliatory of rabbis, and the Jewish apostate and
physician, Dr. Bichler; there are the Gentile servants and two
Gentiles who belong to the authentic society of Vienna: Dr.
Franz Wurzlechner, Jacob Samuel's closest friend from boyhood
on, and the cavalry captain, von Schramm. For comic relief
there is a minor stockbroker, a man of constant ups and downs,
named Wasserstein. The first act presents the wedding reception
at the Helmanns. The guests drift in from the Temple, where
the ceremony has been performed. The delineation of type and
milieu here is brilliant. The shabby Wasserstein, among the
earliest guests, complains to Dr. Bichler of the low estate of
his fortunes. "I was afraid you were going to commit suicide,"
Bichler says. "What? Listen, I have other troubles," Wasserstein flings back. And one can hear the Yiddish word *tsoress*
under tone and gesture. They discuss the young Dr. Jacob
Samuel. "I hear he's a lawyer. Has he got much business?"
Wasserstein asks. "So, so," Bichler replies. "Not too much. He's
determined to represent only honorable clients." "Can a man
make a living that way?" The point is that Herzl is careful not
to render Wasserstein contemptible nor Rheinberg, the millionaire stockbroker, ignoble. He still offers for them the old,
wrongheaded excuse of vices historically imposed, as though
there had been in that Viennese world not more Gentile than
Jewish stockbrokers and speculators in invisible properties. But

his mood is no longer that in which, attending services in the great synagogue on the Avenue de la Victoire, he seemed to himself to have seen only the grins of avidity and worldly emptiness.

As the other guests and the young married couple and their parents drift in, the unabashed Wasserstein asks Bichler: "Tell me, why did you have yourself baptized, anyway?" "I rather fancied it the solution of the problem on an individual basis; at least an attempt at a solution. Because, between you and me, it solves nothing." Thus the keynote is admirably struck. The rather too soft scenes between Dr. Jacob Samuel and his parents are, of course, deeply colored by Herzl's relations to his own. Poor Julie Herzl must have submitted to such advice as is here offered by Hermine Samuel's new mother-in-law. Admirably observed are the attitudes of Dr. Wurzlechner. He had known Jacob Samuel since their boyhood and had been permitted to know nothing essential concerning his friend. There had never been moral parity, only subservience on the one hand and patronage on the other. For Wurzlechner, coming from his first attendance upon a Jewish ceremony, remarks in brooding surprises: "How all this has been preserved—those alien customs in our very midst. Strange . . . Jacob himself struck me as an utterly different person today." In brief, Jacob had never shown his true self to his friend but only his mimic and servile self, and so Wurzlechner had been led to believe that the false bargain of the emancipation had been and could be carried out. Did Herzl quite see that yet? He did see the degradation of Rheinberg, who boasts that a Councillor of the Court visits his house, because he lets the astute Wasserstein ask: "Does he appear in public with you?" And he lets Rheinberg awkwardly reply: "What do you mean? *Wie heisst?* If I want him to!"

The inevitable eternal discussion goes on. Rabbi Friedheimer observes that the "walls [of the Ghetto] have come down." "The *visible* walls," Jacob Samuel sharply replies. "I don't belittle it. I only say we must get out of it. . . . These new barriers we must break down after some other fashion . . . the inner barriers we must clear away ourselves. We ourselves! . . ." In brief, the

"new Ghetto" is an inner one, a moral and spiritual one. Here
Herzl is still in the bonds of a strange delusion. For what is
that inner Ghetto except Jewishness, except Judaism, except
the Jew's life and the length of his days? Excellently, as dra-
maturgy, Herzl lets Bichler ask Wurzlechner: "Well, what do
you say to all this, Gentile?" And Wurzlechner replies weightily
and from a troubled mind: "It's another world!"

He comes in the second act to break with Jacob. Not that he
loves him less or values him less. Herzl represents this attitude
as a sincere and not necessarily ignoble one. It is necessary to
remember time, place, and circumstance to understand that.
Through Jacob's wedding and the scenes at the reception Wurzlechner had learned that his friend lives in another environment, another society, into which he can never find his way.
Moreover, he intends to enter politics and dare not be known
as the hanger-on of rich Jews. Jacob is deeply and, to any sane
perception, shamefully stricken and answers shamefully: "I've
learned a good deal from you . . . often without quite knowing
it . . . inflections, gestures . . ." Yet he defends even Wasserstein. "You each stand," he says to his false friend, "where
history placed you." Again and so late there is here once more
the complete implicit negation of all the inherent values of
Jewish faith, wisdom, historic experience. There is the melancholy implication of emptiness on the one hand, fullness only on
the other. And yet Herzl, some years later, sharply criticized
Nordau for a similar negation of Jewish values and traditions
in Nordau's similar play *Dr. Kohn*. His own true awakening
had not yet come. He lets Jacob Samuel horribly lament: "He
was not only my friend—he was the 'Gentile neighbor' who
liked to associate with me. It was quite flattering—there's a bit
of the Ghetto left in all of us." The act ends with the final and
explosive complication of the plot. A leader of the wretched
miners who are in deadly danger from ruined shafts in the
mines owned by Captain von Schramm and financed by Rheinberg pleads with Jacob Samuel to represent them.

He consents to do so. The dreaded disaster takes place. Jacob
turns upon the Jewish speculator, but Herzl gives Rheinberg the

serious and manly defense that Schramm deserves no help. All his actions had been stupid and frivolous, and his was the responsibility for the conditions in the mine. Schramm, of course, throws off all blame and fastens it on the dirty Jews who, speculator and pretended humanitarian, were in the same conspiracy. Jacob strikes him in his just fury. A challenge is issued and it is, of course, the Jew, Jacob Samuel, who sustains a mortal wound. Dying he mutters: "O Jews, my brethren, they won't let you live again until—until you . . . Why do you hold me—so tight? I want to—get—out! Out—of—the—Ghetto. . . ."

It was, on Herzl's part, a cry of the heart. But it was another year before the revelation came to him as to whither Jews were to flee from the Ghetto.Yet in this play, quite the most serious and estimable of his creative works, it seems constantly as though he were trembling on the brink and threshold of perceptions that he could not yet reach—as though, in the fine old Virgilian image, of which he was not ignorant, he were stretching out arms in love toward another shore.

Herzl continued his literary work all during his Zionist period. This, despite his plaints concerning his editorial bondage to the *Neue Freie Presse*, has not been sufficiently emphasized. He wrote no more plays. His essays and tales continued to appear, and though not a few, such as the stories "The Good Things of Life" (1898) and especially "Solon in Lydia" (1900), are deeper in tone and finer in workmanship than his earlier performances, they, too, bear witness to a boundless melancholy and to a bleak negation of even a tragic triumph as possible to the life of man. From that last voyage of his, that voyage to Egypt which concerned the fantastic dream of opening to Jewish colonization the few square kilometers of the desert Sinai Peninsula, he sent a *feuilleton* to his paper, under the somber eloquence of which all the old wounds still burn:

> But properly to celebrate this superb spectacle of the sun, one would really need to have retained in one's soul all the sensibilities of youth. Where has it vanished to, one's youth? It is well that these sensibilities are no longer alive. Yet so exquisite and

ravishing, so rose-drenched and so moving is this dipping down of our beloved sun, that one might truly for a space indulge the foolish wish that youth were back, even at the price of having once more to endure all its perished ills: the burden of studies, the conflicts, the vain efforts, the disappointments—aye, even love itself.

3. THE GREAT AWAKENING

WHAT is "conversion"? Literally a turning *with*, as opposed to "aversion," a turning *from*. And what is *teshuva*, the Hebrew word, consecrated by the centuries as the very aim and fulfillment of the good life? It, too, is a turning, a return—a turning toward and a return to God and good and truth. The thing is known as phenomenon, as fact. It occurs in every age. And it remains an act of grace, for, were it not, it would happen to all and there would be no more the dark, the recalcitrant, those who, from age to age, bitterly hold out against redemption because their minds are frozen and fixed. There were, a Midrash tells us, Jews who did not follow Moses out of Egypt; they had adopted Egyptian names and had painted their walls in the manner of the Egyptians and dwelled beside the fountains of their courtyards. And the rabbis of Berlin and Munich who so acridly opposed Herzl from the depth of their propitiatory and assimilatory Ghetto and whom he dubbed *Protestrabbiner*, were they not sincere and, by the best light they had, honest men? Perhaps, as Matthew Arnold said in a similar context, they had not inquired whether that light of theirs was not darkness.

Thus grace remains for the chosen, the elect. But we do today know the pattern of the process; we can discern the difference between those capable and those incapable of *teshuva*, of the great turning. The human psyche perceives dangers, dangers to its comfort, ease, facile social and civil adjustment. It represses these dangers; it thrusts them below the level or threshold of consciousness. It will not let them rise into the aware mind. It "knows"; it usually "knows" dimly what o'clock it is. But

51

it will not turn its eyes to the dial and ascertain the exact hour. It "knows" and will not let itself *know*. This repressed knowledge is transformed into symptoms—into, for instance, Herzl's mad relentlessness, his aggressive tendencies, his troubled arrogance. "The Jewish question lay in ambush wherever I went," he writes in the early days of his illumination. "I sighed and derided and was wretched. But I would not let it truly lay hold upon me . . ." How clear it is from this that he "knew, but would not let himself know." "At first," he writes in this self-purgating confession, "the Jewish problem hurt me sorely. Perhaps there was a time when I would gladly have escaped into Christianity—anywhere." And it had been, in fact, only two years before, in 1893, that he had thought out a plan by which all the Jews of his generation were to have their children baptized. The fathers were to remain steadfast, whatever he thought he meant by that. They were to carry their children as offerings to the Cathedral of St. Stephen, to the *Stefansdom*, and thereby persuade the Pope to put an end to Antisemitism in Austria. He actually broached the scheme in all apparent seriousness to Moritz Benedikt, the owner of the *Neue Freie Presse*. Even that Austro-German liberal of the supposed Jewish persuasion balked. "You cannot do that; you dare not do that!" Cannily Benedikt added: "Moreover the Pope won't even receive you."

The very extremity of this antic betrayed the nearness of some end in either illumination or horror. The break-through, the beginning of *teshuva*, the cessation of repression, need not be brought about by an external occurrence. It can take place in quietude, in the act of meditation or in the act of prayer. But the great typical story of the classical Jewish tradition is the story of Moses, who saw the Egyptian taskmaker smite one of his brethren and slew the slave driver and escaped into the desert. The *Protestrabbiner* were present in other guise in that original story too. Such was the man who said to Moses: "Who made thee a chief and judge over us—*sar veshofet alenu?*" The Egyptians in Herzl's case were the French. Nothing could have more deeply wounded the liberal Jews in Western Europe. Was not France the home of the Revolution and of the "rights of man"? For the nefarious terms of the Napoleonic enfranchisement, the sin of 1807, had been a subject not of individual but of group repression. Jews acted upon the conditions of that miserable bargain but chose to forget its set and brutal terms.

The brother whom the Egyptians smote in Herzl's case was, of course, that Captain Alfred Dreyfus, falsely accused of treason to the French State, imprisoned on Devil's Island, that foul French penal colony, rehabilitated and restored to his rank only many years later. Herzl, representative of one of the chief newspapers of Central Europe, had to witness the public degradation of Dreyfus, his trial, his condemnation. He had to witness, above all, in the earliest days of 1895, the tumult of the French populace, the cry "*À mort les Juifs*"—down with the Jews, "Death to the Jews"—not "this traitor" but "the Jews." And that concerning one who was in full flight from his Jewishness and had, as symbol of that fact, chosen the military profession and had, probably by reason of the wealth of his family, succeeded in rising to a captaincy and being attached to the French General Staff. Herzl's accounts to his paper of the degradation and trial of Dreyfus were objective, serious, dignified. But the repressions were torn asunder once and for all. An Antisemite was being elected Burgomaster of Vienna at almost the same time. Herzl asked of a French Jewish friend: "Why were *you* overcome by Lueger's election and *I* by Dreyfus' degradation if you are a Frenchman and I an Austrian?" Not only had the illumination come, but a knowledge of its processes. "My Jewishness had been indifferent to me; let us say that it lay below the threshold of my consciousness—*unter der Schwelle meines Bewusstseins.*" In the new light even the old darkness seemed less dark than it had been: "How did I find this thing? I don't know. Perhaps because I went over it in my mind again and again and felt so wretched over antisemitism. Now that everything is clear to me, I am astonished to reflect how often I was on the edge of the solution and passed it by. But that I have found it is a source of great happiness. It will radiate my parents' declining years and be to the lasting honor of my posterity."

The process, the illumination, the *teshuva*, had not at once become articulate. It was not until May, 1895, that he began the confessional diary which he called "The First Book of the Cause of the Jews." The months of June and July were the decisive ones. He may be said to have lived and written in a state of euphoria. He took long solitary walks in the Bois de Boulogne; often he had tears in his eyes. Many of his notations for the Jewish State and its character are still compensatory fancies—compensatory for his sufferings under the scourge of antisemitism, his humiliations, his wants, the falsenesses to which he had been condemned. And now and then there is a harsh and grating relapse, as in the notation of July 5: "What I would like to have been is a member of the old Prussian nobility." Yet on the very next day we find him "harmonizing as never before" with his first disciple, the neurologist and popular writer, Dr. Max Nordau, who had an even falser and more stridently unlovely Jewish past to overcome than Herzl himself. But he had grasped the very root of the matter on June 3 in an early letter to Baron Maurice de Hirsch, the benefactor of the Jewish colonies in the Argentine: "A flag, what is it? A pole and a rag of cloth? It is far more. Under a flag one can lead men whither one desires to lead them—even into the Promised Land." And even somewhat before and more decisively and trenchantly: "During our millennial dispersion we have been without a unitary leadership of our political interests. That is what I consider to be our chief misfortune." When that was said, all had, at least symbolically, been said. This recognition was essence and center of the new era in Jewish life which the far more learned, pure, devoted *Hovevei Tsion*, the lovers of Zion of the East of Europe, had not been able to usher in.

Among his compensatory reveries, which are quite personal —the vision of himself as Doge of a kind of Venetian State, all gold and russet and ceremonious splendor, with a dueling code and a strict hierarchy, secret police, High Priests in ornate vestments, and the Hungarian Jews as hussars and the unpretentious Rabbi Güdemann as the first "bishop" of the capital city of the Jewish State—there are passages of poignant perceptiveness and beauty. And again: "No one dreamed of seeking the Promised Land where actually it is. And yet it is so near us, namely, within ourselves." And finally: "I believe that my personal life is over and world history has set in." There are flashes of practical and, above all, of psychological insight as well. Irresistibly he was swept along, and on June 13 he began that address to the family council of the Rothschilds which was, in effect, the first draft of *The Jewish State*.

It is not to be forgotten that during these weeks and months he was alone. He was alone with a terrifying revolutionary idea. He had not even read George Eliot's *Daniel Deronda*. A friend suggested that he do so. When, some months later, he was given a copy of Pinsker's *Auto-emancipation*, which had appeared in 1882, he remarked with a new humility that it was well he had not seen it, else he might not have written *The Jewish State* at all. He knew neither the *Rome and Jerusalem* of Moses Hess nor the writings of Nathan Birnbaum. He was not aware at this time of the *Hibat Tsion*, the Love of Zion movement in Russia. Alone, unfriended, up to the eyes, as he himself admitted, until but the other day in the most repulsive assimilationism, he announced an implicit negation of the *Galut*, the dispersion of Israel, as a worthy form of human life. No Westerner had ever dared to harbor such a notion. Strolling the beloved streets of Paris, hearing Wagnerian music-dramas at the *Opéra*, he declared that Jews must leave this alien and hostile Continent, that they must take their destiny into their own hands and found a State among the other States of the world.

No wonder that the first friend to whom he spoke was seriously concerned for his sanity, and that the good, mild Rabbi Güdemann blew both hot and cold. Max Nordau was the only soul that was at first kindled. We do not know how soon Herzl communicated in this matter with his parents. And one can not imagine Nordau's agreement to have been a very warming or consoling one. Nordau had noisily popularized the shallowest errors of the period. In *Degeneration*, a document defensive of his own creative sterility, he had declared all the great writers of his time, from Ibsen and Strindberg to Verlaine and Swinburne, as fit only for the madhouse. Nor did he ever relent toward any of the sanctities of Israel. His Zionism always remained, as Weizmann well points out, formal and arid. He performed one immense practical service. He introduced Herzl to Israel Zangwill, novelist, Zionist, authentic Jew, and thus first turned Herzl's vision to England where, in the autumn of that very year, the decisive year of 1895, he was first enabled to declare the substance of his portentous dream.

II

Two months before, in the early autumn of the year, he had resigned his Paris post and returned to Vienna as *feuilleton*, that is, in reality, literary editor of the *Neue Freie Presse*. Paris had become barren. He had set his highest immediate hopes upon the Baron de Hirsch, of whose vast charities he knew. Hirsch, pleading for a delay so characteristically on account of the results of an old wound incurred while hunting, *"une ancienne blessure de chasse,"* wholly declined of course to abandon the condescending charitableness of a European *grand seigneur*. Arriving in Vienna in September, Herzl was at once met by the anxieties of the owner and editor-in-chief of his paper. Rumors had reached both Benedikt and Bacher. They needed and wanted Herzl, whose journalistic reputation was by now one of the first in the German-speaking countries. They did not want him to spoil everything through his new madness. They argued and pleaded. And Herzl needed his salary to maintain himself and his family. This conflict and discomfort lasted until his death. His indomitable pursuit of his ends, while, as he said, he had to tremble for the bread of his children, is not among the least heroic aspects of those last nine years of his too brief life.

Several publishers had meanwhile been too frightened to accept *The Jewish State* for publication. At last a more intrepid Jew, or one at least who counted on a *succès de scandale*, was found. But actual publication did not take place until February, 1896, so that the address before the Maccabean Club in London on November 26, 1895, remains the first public declaration of Herzlian Zionism. The core of his theory is there. What

Jews have lost is their *Staatsmut*, their courage toward political organization. The emancipation, moreover, had "driven
assimilation to the point of saturation." A people remained,
and a people cannot be helped by means of philanthropy but
only politically.

At last *Der Judenstaat* appeared. It was, as Herzl said, to
arouse a mighty "cry of agreement in every place where Jews
suffer." The cry was all the mightier because the Jewish masses
had never expected to hear such a voice from such a quarter—
from a German assimilationist writer and journalist, from one
without a Zionist past, almost without a Jewish one. And this
was a mighty voice. More than a voice. It was a triumphant
bugle call—deep and vibrant because it expressed the liberation
of the man himself, of the man who uttered it. His idea, he
announced, was immemorial. To the depth of his being, he
declared, he was convinced of its rightness, ". . . though I doubt
whether I shall live to see myself proved so. Those who today
inaugurate this movement are unlikely to live to see its glorious
culmination. But the very inauguration is enough to inspire in
them a high pride and the joy of an inner liberation of their existence." The tone was new because the man was new to the idea.
His ignorance became a virtue. He had discovered all for himself. One must, he said, "rethink and relearn," as he had done.
He had shared no long discussions in *Yeshivot* (Talmudic academies) nor among the *maskillim*, the enlighteners of the East,
who had sought to bring the masses Western knowledge in the
medium of a Hebrew tongue renewed. He had not brooded over
exile and home-faring all his life. He had not prayed daily that
a great trumpet be sounded for the *herut*, the freedom of Israel,
which was to consist in gathering the remnants from the four
corners of the earth and bringing them home to Zion. And for
these very reasons, which account also for his blunders and his
blind spots and his occasional relapse into assimilatory vulgari-
ties, his voice was one of unrivaled freshness, power, and poign-
ancy. "The world needs the Jewish State; therefore it will arise."
For himself, he thought, or seemed to think at that moment, that
the publication of *The Jewish State* completed his duty in the

matter. For he was convinced—again at that moment—that
"the Jews who *will* it, shall achieve their state; and they will
deserve it."

So far the preface. The introduction seeks to go deeper. It
asserts the reality of the Jewish problem, which cut the Westerners in their tenderest part, but declared Jewish suffering to
be an anachronism. This, they, too, believed. But Herzl cut off
their shallow hopes. "We are naturally drawn to those places
where we are not persecuted, and our appearance there gives
rise to persecution." The proof he offered was that of France.
Hence, the Jewish problem must be solved by political means.
As for antisemitism, he proceeds, he thinks he understands
it and all its complications and regards it as a Jew without hate
or fear. Here he is weak, but who shall blame him? His old
analysis of antisemitism and even cruder ones than his are
still current. It is still here and there interpreted as *mere* religious intolerance, *mere* social prejudice, eliminable by knowledge, persuasion, or legal devices. Herzl rose above such crudi-
ties, at least. Antisemitism, i. e., the Jewish problem in its hateful
form, is neither a social nor a religious problem. It is a national
problem and must therefore be raised to political world rank.
And then there rises from him, set off in a paragraph by itself,
the great, the liberating cry:

"We are a people—*one* people."

The English version of this cry which created a new Jew in
Western Europe and did lead to a Jewish rebirth, especially
in the lands of German culture, is subtly inadequate. The original: "Wir sind ein Volk, *ein* Volk!" has overtones and re-
sonances which the English word "people," even when we
remember the appellation *populus Romanus*, wholly lacks. In
the first place the word *Volk* is, though differently spelled, also
a Yiddish word. No wonder that the Easterners were thrilled
when a Dr. Herzl of the *Neue Freie Presse* spoke, as it were,
their language and declared his adherence to *dos yiddishe folk*.
And no wonder that Western assimilationists were frightened.
Was not this the concept that had been forbidden since the days
of Clermont-Tonnerre and Napoleon? "There must be no nation
within the nation." And the concepts of nation and *Volk* were

closely allied. Closely and subtly. For what both the foes and the friends of the Jews debated was whether Jews could or could not, would or would not, become part of the German *Volk*. Cultural assimilation in its deepest sense, *Eindeutschung* (German acculturation) *Volkstümlichkeit*—a word that exists in Yiddish, too, with the same deep sense of the spiritually characteristic— this was the problem, this the recurrent question. If the Jews were a *Volk*, then indeed, according to both Antisemites and philosemites in that day and place, there was no room for them.

Nor was that all. Not only did Herzl declare the Jews to be a people; he declared them to be *one* people. And so the proud and servile assimilationists of Germany and Austria, of France and England, who had carefully separated themselves from the "unimproved," "jargon-speaking," even earlock-wearing, authentic Jews of the East, and had done their best, when Russian or Romanian persecution became too barbarous, to huddle them out of the way on immigrant trains and boats to the far corners of the earth—they and these people were to be members of one body and one spirit with a common character and a common destiny? That was too much for Rabbi Maibaum of Berlin and Rabbi Güdemann of Vienna and even Claude Montefiore of England. One wonders whether Herzl was himself wholly aware of the enormity of that cry which, nevertheless, burst from his deepest heart.

For he goes on to say that Jews had done their best in all the Western lands and cultures to become at one with the ethnic populations and had made distinguished contributions to those cultures. And perhaps: "If we were left in peace . . ." "*Wenn-man uns in Ruhe liesse*"? Once more he cries, setting the words off typographically: "But I think we shall not be left in peace." Hence the "strong among us defiantly return to their own (*trotzig zu ihrem Stamme heim*) whenever persecution breaks out." There, of course, is Herzl's weakness, inevitable in his time and place, in the notion that there is nothing positive in Judaism to return to. One returns, as he did, under intolerable pressure, under affronts to one's "honor" and self-respect. Wherever there is any permanence of political security, he continues, we do assimilate. And in this tendency he sees nothing disgraceful. Indeed, a statesman who desired a Jewish amalgamation in the ethnic formation of his "race" would need only see to it that Jews are politically happy and secure. For then mixed marriages, which *alone* (and this a right and great insight of Herzl) can lead to genuine assimilation, as opposed to mere mimicry, would bring about the desired end. One must not ask of Herzl, needless to say, a later and ultimate insight to the effect that precisely security and well-being increase the menace of corroding the spiritual substance of the Jewish people and bringing about its moral destruction.

Side by side with failures in perception he has the keenest insights. After all, he was a man of letters, akin to a poet. From this side of him came the passage concerning the antisemitism of the "fairy tale and the proverb," both inexpressive and inadequate terms for *Märchen* and *Sprichwort*. From this source within him also came the cry: "The Jews have dreamt this princely dream throughout the long night of their history. 'Next year in Jerusalem!' is our age-old motto." And rising to a higher vision still he wrote those truly and actively redeeming words: "Whoever can, will, and must perish, let him perish. But the distinctive nationality of the Jews neither can, will, nor must perish. It cannot, because external enemies consolidate it. It does not wish to; this it has proved through two millennia of appalling suffering. It need not . . . Whole branches of Jewry may wither and fall away. The tree lives on." And in this context he rises to the final declaration which did indeed, once and for all, define the necessary character of all redemptive movements. "No human being is wealthy or powerful enough to transplant a people from one place of its dwelling to another. Only an idea can achieve that. The State Idea surely has that power."

It has not perhaps been sufficiently observed how unsystematic in structure *The Jewish State* is. The reader may think that the question of antisemitism and its pressures has been discussed. It turns up again and yet again before Herzl's actual plan is broached. And these further passages illustrate both his strength and also his weakness, which was, it must be granted, the weakness of his place and personal past. He briefly marks the many shadings of antisemitism in Europe from pogroms in the East to the exclusiveness of clubs in Paris. He echoes the cry of the Berlin vulgarian: "Out with the Jews!" Whither? he asks. And: "May we remain, and if so, how long?" For he knew that no reversal of the current was to be expected.

Thereupon he returns once more to the sources of that old ache in his own heart. Antisemitism (he should have added: in its modern form) is a result of the emancipation. But he misses the evil and unnatural bargain according to which the emancipation was effected, for he is oblivious of the positive forces in Judaism. Hence he must conclude that the emancipation came too late; Jews had become unassimilable in the Ghettos. It is, to say the least, odd enough how he combines the assertion of Jewish peoplehood, of the form, the ethnic personality, with total obliviousness of the internal *content* of that form. But his immense merit lies precisely there—in his failures, his almost total ignorance, despite which he proclaimed with such fire and force the liberating idea. His reasons are all wrong; his conclusions are all triumphantly right. It is melancholy to see him return to that old, vain notion: "Though perhaps we *could* succeed in vanishing without a trace into the surrounding peoples, if they would let us be for just two generations. But they will not let us be." Hence, alas, he seems to himself forced to conclude once more that "*Only* pressure drives us back to our own; only hostility stamps us ever again as strangers"—two deeply wrong and unworthy fallacies. Yet from these fallacies he derives once more a great cry of liberation for the Jews of the West: "Thus we are now, and shall remain, whether we would or not, a group of unmistakable cohesiveness (togetherness: *Zusammengehörigkeit*)." Or as he put it elsewhere: "Of recognizable historic homogeneity." In brief, once more: *Ein Volk*—a people. *It was this preliminary part of* The Jewish State *which exercised two unforgettable historic functions: It united the Jews of the East and of the West under a single banner. It created among a small but immensely influential group of Western Jews a new Jewish consciousness—a new Jew.*

III

Next comes the "plan." And perhaps the most extraordinary aspect of Herzl's "turn" and "turning" is that it made him into a man of action, a man of practical affairs, a diplomat, a statesman. Yet this too is understandable, in view of his past and his psychical structure. He needed to tear himself loose from parental, especially from maternal, dependence. He had, above all, to compensate and overcompensate for what he felt to be the limitations of his literary talents. Had he become a world celebrity, like Schnitzler or Wassermann, his younger contemporaries! But one must not go behind the facts of history. The point to be made, though briefly, is this: that some of Herzl's detailed workings-out of the great "plan" are of an immense and strictly practical astuteness.

The essential nature of the "plan" was foreshadowed on an early page of *The Jewish State* "We shall not leave our old home until the new one is available." Since history upon the whole determined otherwise, though at the cost of so much blood and so much anguish, Herzl's plan has not only almost fallen into forgetfulness, which was natural enough, but the attempt has been made to trivialize it, which is quite unwarranted. He was initially opposed to what he called infiltration into any promised land. For he conceived correctly that thus antisemitism would be dragged into that promised land, too. He wanted the emigration of the Jews of Europe to their promised land to be clean and clear and definite, according to an orderly method, supported by binding legal agreements. Hence his insistence on a "charter"; hence the pertinacity with which through the years he pursued that dream and notion of a "charter," of that assured legal sovereignty over some adequate portion of the earth's surface to which Jews could go and build their State and rebuild their lives, not on sufferance but as of right.

Was that really fantastic? One remembers the enormous relief of old, literally battle-scarred settlers in Petah Tikva, in Rehovot, in Rishon Letsion that at least they were no more at the arbitrary mercy of "the Turk." A "charter," the Balfour Declaration, did finally bring, despite riot and murder, an ultimate relief; the establishment of the Jewish Agency did, in time, give a large measure of at least legal security; the mandatory regime, approved, as Herzl had dreamed, by all the civilized nations of the world, though it ended in so much shame for England and so much Jewish agony, did through the years permit the development of that community in Eretz Yisrael, that *yishuv*, which was strong enough to proclaim itself a State, a *Medinat Yisrael*, and fight its bloody tragic, triumphant war of liberation. Was, then, Herzl's pertinacious pursuit of a "charter," some kind of sovereignty, as fantastic as it has been represented to be or was it far-sighted statesmanship?

He was wrong, to be sure, in desiring no *ad interim* colonization. But this sprang from his new tenderness for his people. Long as the gradual migration from Europe might take, he wanted it to be orderly, dignified, safe. "Who would go with us, let him fall in behind our banner and fight for the cause with word and pen and deed." He meant: fight for the great plan. His final words on the method were sane and reasonable words in the summer of 1895: "Infiltration is bound to end badly. For there comes the inevitable moment when the government in question, under pressure of the native populace—which feels itself threatened—puts a stop to a further influx of Jews. Immigration, therefore, is futile unless it is based on our guaranteed autonomy." What was fantastic was Herzl's forgetfulness of the fact that history does not proceed logically. Discussing the choice of a homeland—whether it was to be the Argentine or Palestine, the discussion being again an illustration of his remoteness from Jewish life and tradition—he decided that, after all, Palestine is our unforgettable homeland. Then he goes on: "If his Majesty, the Sultan of Turkey, were to give us Palestine, we could in return undertake the complete management of the finances of Turkey."

With this formulation he enters upon that part of the "plan" which has often been criticized as fanciful. The finances of Turkey were notoriously on the edge of disaster. Hence the very rich and very powerful Jews of Europe were to persuade the great powers to put pressure on Turkey to grant the Jews

at least a guarantee of autonomy in Palestine. Thereupon the
Jewish people was corporately to rectify the finances of Turkey
and build in Palestine a society as splendid and as unreal as
that delineated, so inadequately, it must be confessed, in
Altneuland ("Old New Land"), the utopian novel published
in 1902. Herzl, in brief, as most of his plays and stories show,
was not strong in the matter of insight into character. This
Sultan was Abdul Hamid II, the slaughterer of the Armenians,
the petrified symbol of a dying age, despised and derided
wherever his name and deeds were known. It is this lack of
realism when dazzled by mere power or the tawdry splendor
of mere thrones which, as will be seen, made Herzl's mission-
ary years so often a kind of phantasmagoria.

But his idea that the security of the Jewish people in its
new home must be guaranteed in public law was wise and
far-sighted. The devices, moreover, which he suggested for the
liquidation of Jewish property in Europe and the transfer of
these values to Palestine, were of a technical acuteness and
reasonableness to which justice has not always been done. With
instinctive foresight he gave English names to the primary
institutions which were to be the instrumentalities of the emigration: The Society of Jews, which actually became the World
Zionist Organization, and the Jewish Company, that bank
which, in fact, he marvelously created out of nothing. The
headquarters of both institutions were to be London.

If the ideological portion of *The Jewish State* was wholly
new to Western, if not to Eastern Jews who knew from Pinsker that the tragedy of the Jewish people was to be without
"cohesion in space" and without "official representation," what
was new to both West and East was form, plan, organization,
a projected policy and controlled action, an aim or goal and
words and acts directed toward the accomplishment of that
aim or goal. Herzl himself, as will be seen, offered in his
own person the immediate and overwhelming example of directed activity. *The Jewish State*, when it appeared, not only
aroused the terror and resistance of the Jewish super-patriots
and servile assimilationists of the West; it not only lit an in-
candescence in the minds of young Westerners who, surfeited

with alien values and impatient of their anomalous situation, were seeking liberation and release. It also had its effect on wiser and more instructed spirits. In Berlin there existed at that time a Judaeo-Russian Scientific Society (*Jüdisch-Russisch Wissenschaftlicher Verein*). The leading spirits of that group were young men whose names were later to attain world fame in Zionist circles and far beyond. Their names were Chaim Weizmann, Shmaryahu Levin, Leo Motzkin, Nachman Syrkin. Wearily they watched the antics of the German assimilationists who repudiated all they were and still feigned at least to believe that "a little enlightenment judiciously applied, and antisemitism would vanish." These words are the words of Weizmann. And so to him and to his comrades, too, *The Jewish State* seemed "an utterance which came like a bolt from the blue." It told them nothing which they had not known all their lives. But they had to bow down, as it were, before it, if not as wisdom, then as *act*.

The most accurate evaluation of the initial Herzlian act, from which so many others arose, may be gathered from the writings of his acutest and profoundest critic, Ahad Ha'am. "I must admit," he wrote a little over a year later, "that Western Zionism is of great use to the Jews of the West, who had almost wholly forgotten their Judaism and whose relation to their people consisted of a blunted feeling, unclear even to themselves. . . . To them the *idea* of the state is an incentive for them to dedicate their powers to the service of their people; it lifts them out of the abyss of assimilation and fortifies their Jewish national feeling." But the Herzlian call, as Ahad Ha'am had difficulty in admitting, struck home in the East too. "In Pinsk (or Minsk or Odessa or Kiev)," as Weizmann admitted, "organized activity simply did not exist." The *Hovevei Tsion* had held their historic conference of Katowice in 1884; the magnificent Hebrew periodicals had been established; modern classical Yiddish literature was being created; nothing, nothing was *done*. A few settlers, a few more, went to Eretz Yisrael and suffered unthinkable hardships; the colonists of the "Baron," the true friend and finally Zionist, Edmond de Rothschild, though relatively safer, were ruled by his squab-

bling bureaucrats. An important system of thought was created
and a body of almost great literature. And hardly a Jew was
saved and hardly a single anomalous aspect of the *Galut* miti-
gated. It was at this dead point that the Herzlian call, inadequate as it was, even, if one liked, fantastic, became a redemptive call of crucially historic impact.

One other passage of Ahad Ha'am, a passage of a hundred
pregnant implications, stamps the character of both his own
and of Herzlian Zionism and points to a future even not yet
realized. "We, however, who, awakening from the brief dream
of the emancipation, have recovered our old knowledge that
we shall never find peace in the lands of the dispersion; we
had meanwhile lost the moral ability of our fathers to be outwardly humiliated and enslaved and to preserve our inner and
spiritual heroism; for our closeness to the other peoples and
their cultures was destined, against our will, to undermine our
faith that all the other peoples wander upon aberrant ways
and that redemptive truth is in our hands alone."

There is a touch of irony in that phrase: "against our will."
The Jewish enlighteners of the East, the *Maskillim*, from whose
ranks Ahad Ha'am arose, had been no less busy, though upon
somewhat other and higher grounds, than the assimilationists
of the West in undermining Jewish faith and Jewish form, in
robbing the Jewish people of that belief in its own uniqueness
and unique rightness, in the positive and eternal values of its
Judaism, which had, in very truth, carried it nobly, if not safely,
across the centuries. All that Ahad Ha'am had to offer was a
secular nationalism without action. It was magnificently expressed, but it was founded upon a mere theory of Jewish
ethical culture, upon an ethic without transcendental validation,
that is to say, without any validation—which men, which Jews,
could take or leave. Herzl, who used more crudely and naively
such terms as "we freethinkers," also offered a merely secular
nationalism. But it was one of immediate urgency, of the immediate act. And it was that secular nationalism that he proclaimed which did, in effect, whatever transformations the
future may bring, establish the *yishuv*, the Jewish community,
in Eretz Yisrael and create a State.

4. THE MISSION YEARS

EIGHT years alone were left him. And during most of the days and nights of those eight years he was both literally and figuratively sick at heart. He organized six congresses. He established the type and exemplar of all future Zionist periodicals, *Die Welt* (The World), in 1897 and impoverished himself by subsidizing it. Once a year he would go briefly and alone to Alt Aussee, the magnificent resort in the Styrian Alps and gaze upon the lake and the Dachstein glacier and inhale the fragrance of the pines. But these rests were brief. How many times was he in France, England, Turkey, waiting there in the outer rooms of the Sultan's palace in morning-coat, silk hat, gloves, however oppressive the heat, doling out from his own purse the ever heavier *bakshish*, the bribes to the Sultan's shabby and pretentious underlings? At home, he would ride a bicycle from "Cottage," the well-known Viennese suburb where he lived, to the inner city to reach the offices of the *Neue Freie Presse*. His adored children were left lonely. Once a day, whatever came or went, he dropped in to see his parents. A "daemon" and a premonition drove him. Rest, unless he was ready to break down, was not for him.

His moods varied immensely, and all contribute to the picture of his mind and character, though he knew himself to be too self-conscious, literary, aware of posterity, to write simply and with simple truth in his diary. But this inevitable circumstance is part of the picture of him. A notation, set down in a Paris spring just after a return from Constantinople, shows him at his highest. It was late; it was in 1901. It was, perhaps, a summing up. "Perhaps a just historian will see it to have been no small thing, that an impecunious Jewish journalist, at a time of the deepest degradation of his people and of the most revolting antisemitism, turned a rag into a banner and a degraded populace into a people gathering in erectness about that flag."

Quoted oftener than this passage is another and even more moving one written at about the same period. "Zionism was the Sabbath of my life. . . . I believe that my effective leadership is to be attributed to the fact that I who, as a man and a writer, have so many faults and have been guilty of so many mistakes and follies have been in this matter of Zionism pure of heart and wholly unselfish."

But he could not sustain those moods. Old aches and disappointments arose to plague him. As late as 1902, returning from Constantinople once more, he wrote on a day of June in Paris: "It seems to me at times that a man of worth, if he is active in two fields, will gain recognition in that field which is not central to his personality. Thus I, for instance, have gained world fame as a Jewish agitator, that is, in a field where I have exercised no high mental powers but only a political skill within the reach of any horse-trader and regarding a matter which only fools could fail to grasp. But as a writer, above all, as a dramatist, I count for nothing, for less than nothing. And yet I feel, I know that I am a writer of high rank or was, at least, but one who did not unfold all his powers because he was revolted and discouraged." It takes no great insight to observe how these lasting frustrations needed to be transformed into ceaseless activity. And it may be added that he could never quite grasp the effectiveness, the evident radiance of that activity and was chilled, rather than warmed, by applause and praise.

But the great drive was immediate. *The Jewish State* had been published in February, 1896. In April he had his first interview with the Grand Duke of Baden in the hope, not abandoned for years, that the German Emperor might lead the Powers to persuade the Sultan to grant the Jewish people a charter of colonization for Palestine. In the weeks just preceding he had tasted a strange immediate glory and also a touch of dismay. Zionists, of whose very existence he had barely known, rose to acclaim him. The Jewish students of Vienna, through their organization *Kadimah* (Forward), gave him a great ovation. "I had to speak," he comments. "I counseled moderation and spoke only moderately well." Nathan Birnbaum and his friends came to declare their solidarity with him. The poet Richard Beer-Hofmann and the Shakespeare scholar Leon Kellner announced their discipleship. Simpler people, too, merchants and brokers came, as it were, running, as men had run once upon a time, as a wit could not but observe, to Sabatai Zwi, the false, romantic messiah of the seventeenth century. The Zionists of Sofia sent resolutions with six hundred signatures; the Viennese Zionists, the rank and file, offered him their allegiance. What moved him more was that individuals sought him out to whom his words had been an immediate revelation. "This," he notes, "is the important difference between my effect on men and that of Baron de Hirsch. Beggars beset and do not love him. They love me. Hence I am the stronger."

Queer and inevitable repercussions came from the Christian world. The Reverend William H. Hechler, chaplain of the British embassy in Vienna, had already reckoned out that, according to certain Mohammedan prophecies, Palestine would be given back to the Jews in 1896 or 1897. He wanted to see this prophecy fulfilled. And this bearded enthusiast, having been a tutor in the family of the Grand Duke of Baden, did indeed open various doors to Herzl and clung to him as the fulfiller of prophecy. On the other hand a notorious Antisemitic journalist and publicist of Pressburg announced his joy over this novel solution of the Jewish problem. The Jews would now get out. And Herzl was not wholly displeased. In the midst of tumult and triumph comes the grievous stoic notation: "Dr. Beck, my parents' old family physician, looked me over and diagnosed an affection of the heart, due to all this excitement. He can't understand why I bother myself with the Jews and the Jews whom he knows don't understand it either." The diagnosis gave him no pause. Perhaps, indeed, the knowledge of his fragile hold on life increased his sense of urgency. Again and again during the years he notes briefly the increasing exhaustion of his heart, always in the stoic temper and never granting himself a prolonged rest. A few days later in that March we find him at the Passover *Seder* of still another organization of Jewish students. Soon thereafter he set out to Karlsruhe for the first of those interviews with princes and statesmen which were to include, in addition to the kindly, avuncular, slightly stupid Grand Duke of Baden, the Grand Vizier of Turkey, Ferdinand of Bulgaria, the Kaiser Wilhelm, the Sultan Abdul Hamid, Joseph Chamberlain and that whole group of British political figures, the Russian ministers Witte and von Plehve, Oscar Straus, the American ambassador to Turkey, the King of Italy, and Pope Pius X.

It all proved futile. No one wanted to give Jews autonomy, self-rule in closed settlement anywhere. Wilhelm II's shallow streak of romanticism was at first aroused but, as Chancellor von Bülow observed, his enthusiasms were brief. The Sultan needed money and wanted to accept it for individual immigrants into Mesopotamia, Turkey, perhaps Syria, anywhere but Palestine. All but the British politicians babbled mere folly. The potentates, even the minor ones, were at most condescending. The Duke of Baden, who liked Herzl as a person, admitted, as if that had been the point, that Jews had many good qualities. He had yet to see a Jew drunk. Wilhelm of Germany insisted on calling Jews Herzl's *"Landsleute,"* his countrymen, although Herzl's very insistence was that Jews had, alas, no country. The argument was also presented that to favor the emigration of Jews was to offend the good and useful Jews in their respective countries. Herzl remained undeterred. He seemed to himself to have observed too often and too cruelly the results of the "infiltration" of Jews as individuals into another country. He wanted them to have an assured home and to go there.

Although, as has been noted, sharp insight into character was not Herzl's strongest quality, he did have the artist's seeing eye for both persons and places. Had he not been occasionally unduly dazzled, as when Wilhelm of Germany seemed to him for an hour the unicorn come out of fabled woods, the portraits would have been still more saliently etched. Nevertheless, they are there within the strange pageant of the agitated years. Herzl makes us see Wilhelm with his withered arm, carefully kept from dangling, the deep bright blue of his eyes, the but half sincere streak of coarse jocularity which feigned equality and was a churlish condescension. We see the stupid, crafty Sultan with his rickety body and his painted beard. We see the rather clever, tired Ferdinand of Bulgaria; the brutally frank and yet stealthy von Plehve, the butcher of Kishinev, who half surlily admitted that, since one couldn't very well drown the Jews where the sea was deepest, there might be something to mass emigration but that his august master was completely guided by religious prejudices. We see, too, kindlier and more civilized men, like the liberal Austrian statesman, Count Badeni, who was as sincere as his situation permitted him to be. He and certain colleagues did play with the idea of placing Herzl at the head of an important newspaper, which they would help found, and thus liberating him from the bondage of his friends and favorite enemies of the *Neue Freie Presse.* In the last years we also see the British proconsuls who were honest and unprejudiced within their strict limitations, who did finally want the Jews to have either El Arish, which was vetoed by Egypt, or Uganda in Africa, but who were not themselves as pure as they fancied, in view of that Royal Commission on Alien Immigration before which Herzl was called in 1902 to testify. For the Commission was instituted—and so deeply and justly confirmed Herzl's prejudice against infiltration—because too many Jews, driven in despair from Russia and Romania, were thronging into London and Manchester. And so even the British had taken fright, even as the Americans were to take fright in 1924 and pass those immigration laws according to national quotas which have never been repealed and were but grudgingly relaxed even during the height of the Hitler fury.

Thus Herzl's conviction that Jewish emigration and immigration and resettlement must take place under a charter according to law was confirmed by every experience, and accounts for his tireless pertinacity, for his half-unwilling involvements with slyly greasy, pretentious though out-at-heels Turkish diplomats and officials. For this he choked down the abominable dinners in Yildiz Kiosk; for this he bought gifts as bribes; for this in the very year of that Royal Commission he offered the Sultan £600,000 for a charter and the following year £100,000 for the legal colonization of the Sanjak of Acca alone. His dashed hopes were from time to time revived by curious circumstances. Among these was the friendship and devotion during certain years of the distinguished Orientalist Hermann Vambery, who had personal access to the Sultan and could speak to him in his own tongue. But Vambery himself had no way, as Herzl had not, of being aware of the sullen resistance to any radical improvement in the situation of Jewry on the part of prince or emperor, Sultan or Pope. For Pius X also found it impossible to make a pro-Zionist statement. All, deep within their consciousness, wanted the Jews to remain as they were, present objects upon whom to wreak *their* impatience of and resistance to that Unity of God and that Law of God which the Jewish people had brought into the world and incarnated within the processes of history. In brief, Herzl and his contemporaries estimated justly the ways and moods and results of antisemitism but had no suspicion of its ultimate cause or character, as, once more, it had been defined for all time by the pagan Tacitus.

If Herzl had the artist's seeing eye for personality and gesture, he had it in an even higher degree for landscape and the aspects of cities. Though he was grieved by the squalor of Palestinian life during those few poor days granted him there in the autumn of 1898, he showed in the later description of a new Jerusalem, of a new Haifa, in the novel *Altneuland*, those scenic visions full of prophetic splendor that he had seen beyond squalor and barrenness and grasped the character of that strange, incomparable land. So, too, the comfortless visits to Turkey never veiled from him the magnificence either of the half-ruined city or of the Bosphorus and all the pageantry of sea and sky. One would have liked his picture of Vilna, the magical, the mystical city of the cobbled streets and the

weird cries and the gilded Russian domes and the old *Shul*
and library and the cemetery with the graves of the Gaon
Elijah and of Count Potocki, the *Ger Tsedek*, the Proselyte.
But it was late. He had barely a year of life left. And for once
his stricken heart was moved beyond control. For the cry
"King of the Jews," which in the West had been one of malice,
burst here with consecrated ardor from the throats of multi-
tudes who hailed him as *Hamelekh Herzl*, King Herzl, and who
truly dreamed, while they hailed him, of the restoration of
the throne of David.

II

The diplomatic journeys, the waiting, as he once said, at
the "gates of kings," though it has been seen how justified
they were in principle, have withdrawn themselves into the
past, into the dimness of a mere historic process. What has
lived and lives still and is still operative in the life of Israel
was that other and crucial notion of his that the Jewish people
must at last face the world as a national and political entity,
as *one* people, and must demand, *as* an integrated people, not
tolerance but justice. Yet the two aspects of his work cannot
be separated. For he saw at once after the composition of *The
Jewish State* that the diplomatic missions in search of a charter needed the support of Jews. He needed to be able to give
the assurance that at least a considerable fragment of a people
stood behind him. Hence an organization needed to be established which, by tireless propagation of the Zionist idea, would
strengthen and increase this fragment and that, finally, this
organization would need to found those institutions which, so
soon as a charter was obtained, would take up the practical
work of emigration and colonization.

His first step was, as has been seen, the establishment out
of his own pocket of the periodical *Die Welt* (The World).
The first issue bore the date of June 3, 1897. The *Magen David*,
the Star of David, was on its masthead. It declared editorially
that the weekly was a *Judenblatt*, a "Jewish sheet," the antisemitic appellation for liberal German papers in Jewish hands.

"We choose this word," the editorial continued, "which has been used as an insult and will turn it into an appellation of honor. . . . For this periodical will be the organ of such men as would lead the Jewish people from this time into better times." The paper was polemical in temper. But its immediate practical aim was to prepare for a kind of constituent assembly, a Congress, which was to formulate the broader policies and the immediate tactics of political Zionism. To this task Herzl applied himself. On March 10, 1897, a preliminary conference was held. An organization committee was appointed. The first choice of a city for the Congress was Zurich, the second Munich. But from Munich issued the voices of the "Protest Rabbis" who declared political Zionism to be contrary to the Messianic doctrines of the Jewish faith. Basle was then agreed upon. Herzl, a seasoned journalist, decided at once that all the principal newspapers of Europe and America were to be invited to reserve places for their correspondents.

There were no offices, no secretaries. He had to attend to every detail! "I must myself forge the tool with which the tree is to be felled." But at last he was on his way to Basle where an unoccupied tailor's shop had been assigned as offices of the Congress, which was to hold its sessions in the dignified Concert Hall of the rather patrician Swiss city. The Congress sessions extended from August 29 through August 31. Two hundred delegates from wherever Jews dwelt and three hundred guests and correspondents were assembled. The *Hovevei Tsion*, the dreamers, philosophers who had from deepest Jewish sources rethought the situation of the Jewish people and who were irritated by this sudden Western meteor, came reluctantly. But they came. Ussishkin came; Ahad Ha'am came; Nathan Birnbaum came and gave the report on cultural activities. Whatever the varying moods, East and West were at last united. To Herzl himself the "appearance of the Russian Jews was the conspicuous event of the Congress . . . for they possess that unity which most European Jews have lost. . . . It used to be argued against me that I would win for my cause only the Russian Jews. Today I would reply: 'That suffices.' " He was

proud too, and justly so, for having united the Orthodox and
the "freethinkers" and himself visited the Basle synagogue on
the Sabbath where, having been told that he would be called
to the Torah, he experienced his most nervous moments, pronouncing the appropriate *brakhot*, the blessings, which had
had to be drilled into him by several friends. No more or little
more would have to be said to illustrate Herzl's immense
achievement. For the first time in history since the fall of that
last State under the hammer blows of the Roman legions which
was recorded by Dio Cassius, a Greek historian, the Jewish
people stood before the world as one, as one people. Before
the grandeur of this fact ideological differences fade. An epoch
was inaugurated.

A veteran leader of the Romanian "Lovers of Zion" opened
the Congress by pronouncing the *brakha* of *Sheheheyanu* in
which the Eternal is thanked for having preserved his servants
in life and permitted them to see this day, literally this time,
this period. Thereupon Herzl gave his opening address. He
had little to add to the arguments set forth in *The Jewish
State*. But his formulations were effective and indeed striking.
Here, he said, "we want to lay the foundations of the edifice
that is one day to house the Jewish people." He declared with
sincere conviction, rising thus beyond himself, as Ahad Ha'am
a little querulously refused to credit, that Zionism meant "a
return to Judaism even prior to a return to a Jewish land."
Formally and according to the best light *he* had, he had done
so. He insisted upon the establishment of a tight organization
and insisted further that this organization, as the active instrumentality of a united Jewish people, must through the
Congress take care of its own perpetuation. His argument
against infiltration that, even at the rate of 10,000 Jews a
year returning to the land of Israel, it would take 900 years
for the Jews of his time to return—this argument which drew
the bitterest criticism of Ahad Ha'am seems today in 1955
to illustrate not without aptness the sentence which, in somber
jest, Herzl proposed for the inscription over his grave: "Here
lies one who had too high an opinion of the Jews." For the

German fury has been succeeded by the Russian fury, and
the gates of the Land of Israel are open, and Jews still remain
in the *Gola*, and many of them practice the same servile assimilatory antics from which Theodor Herzl with just pride
declared himself to have arisen.

He was succeeded by Max Nordau, who shrewdly and even
brilliantly portrayed the estate, above all, the moral anomalies
of Western Jewry. He pointed out the falseness and proven
untenableness of the civic emancipation and described the Jew
who sought to live up to its miserable terms: "In his inner life
he becomes a cripple; his outward life is unauthentic; hence
to a true and delicate perceptiveness he becomes absurd and
revolting, like everything unauthentic and false." Nathan Birnbaum gave the cultural report. His words concerning the Jews
of the West struck even deeper: "They have cast off the stamp
of their own culture without, however, absorbing the nationality or culture of another people. What they acquire are international intellectual values, an abstract hollow Europeanism
which tends to make cosmopolites of them."

But the epoch-making accomplishment of the first Zionist
Congress did not consist in eloquent speeches or cultural anal-
yses. It consisted in those historic and new and permanent
formulations of the needs and rights of the Jewish people—
in brief, in the Program of Basle: "Zionism strives to create
for the Jewish people a secure dwelling place in Palestine,
guaranteed by public law." The language of this and many
succeeding Congresses, it must be remembered, was German.
Hence translations of the Basle Program have never attained
quite the precision of the original formulation. This is equally
true of the wording of the hardly less significant addenda to
that program which represented a compromise between Herzl
and the *Hovevei Tsion* wing: Colonization of Palestine was
to continue; a unifying structure of all Jewry was to be effected
according to appropriate local arrangements (*Veranstaltun-
gen*); Jewish national feeling (*Volksgefühl*) and consciousness
were to be strengthened; preparatory steps were to be taken
toward gaining that consent from governments which would
be necessary to attain the aim of Zionism. The last provision,

Herzl sought to carry out almost alone. The other provisions were put into effect by fairly broad masses of the Jewish people: Colonization, however slowly, was continued; the world-wide Zionist movement was organized and, by virtue of that very fact, Jewish national consciousness was sustained and heightened.

Herzl's first word after returning home from the Congress of Basle was his most prophetic one: "If I were to sum up the Congress in a few words—words I shall be most careful not to speak in public—I would say: In Basle I founded the Jewish State. If I said that aloud today, I would be met by universal laughter. Perhaps in five years, certainly in fifty, everyone will see it." He was sustained in his prophetic moods by what he had of the poet's imagination. During the very hours of the Congress he was planning a play in verse; some weeks later he was outlining—the analogy was inevitable—a drama on Moses and the Exodus. And so poetry and realizable prophecy blended in his mind. "I give free rein to my imagination. But one who has traversed the interval between my dreamy walks in the Tuileries Gardens and the Palais Bourbon of June, 1895, and the Congress of Basle, such an one may yet some day traverse the Mediterranean as a Jew returning to his homeland. Only—I am as tired as an old man." But he uttered not only prophetic and poetic fancies. With exactness and sobriety he set down and defined the epochal character of the Congress of Basle. "All contradictions were set aside; as though by prior agreement it had been decided that in those great moments in which the Nation arises *as* a nation, none was any longer to be Socialist or Liberal or Conservative, neither Freethinker nor Orthodox, only a Jew. All of us who went to Basle to take counsel concerning the solution of the Jewish problem—we were amazed and overwhelmed as though above our heads there came to pass a thing, of the fullness and power of which we had no slightest notion, namely, the unanimity of the Jewish people. And in truth, we were too moved to give ourselves at once an exact accounting of what was happening."

III

Herzl was soon to complain, quite rightly, that, except for practical purposes, the establishment of the Society of Jews, the founding of the Colonial Bank, the assigning of a unitary value to the universal folk contribution, named after the *shekel* of ancient Israel, the setting up of the Jewish National Fund, the *Keren Kayemet LeYisrael*, at the suggestion of the Heidelberg mathematician Hermann Schapira, nothing further remained. What did he mean? That the ideological structure was complete. With feverish and unrivaled energy he applied himself to all these practical tasks. But he had been primarily a man of the word. And, as far as he was concerned, all the words had been uttered and so his most passionate convictions seemed to become commonplaces on his lips. What, for instance, could he say when the second Congress was convoked in Basle precisely one year after the first? "Many people regarded this new Jewish movement of ours as though it were a ghost. The Jewish people was regarded as a dead, a lost people. We, however, had a dark premonition, even before our consciousness became aware, that this was not so. For death is the end of suffering. How then did it happen that we were still suffering? And so we changed the saying of Descartes into: I suffer, therefore I am." And again in London he declared that the solution of the Jewish question presupposed three things: "The existence of a Jewish people; the appropriateness of Palestine for colonization; the securing of legal foundations for that colonization." Before the succeeding Congresses, the third, again in Basle in August, 1899, the fourth in London in 1900, the fifth in Basle late in December, 1901, what could he do except report on the enlargement and growth of the Zionist movement and on those illusory successes in diplomacy which had been driving him from potentate to potentate and from court to court? At times, as during the fourth Congress, he polemicized against the anti-Zionists. What had the "great" Jews and the charitable Jews and the official Jews *done* for either the physical or the moral alleviation of the people's ills? Opening the fifth Congress he was so hard put to it that he began by adducing the adherence to Zionism of the now forgotten but then celebrated Manx novelist Hall Caine. What he was able to announce was the fact that through Zionist clubs, organizations, federations, an unexpected life coursed through the veins of the Jewish people. But he himself did not wholly realize that this—precisely this—not the formulated plan nor the diplomatic goings on—was his achievement, his triumph, and his glory, namely, that he had blown a new breath of life into the Jewish people in Europe and America, in East and West.

At each of the Congresses, too, Nordau performed, as Weizmann ironically puts it, his annual and effective *aria*. But what was supremely important was this continued meeting of a Parliament of Jews which, though later interrupted by two World Wars, survived and has survived as, at least, an ecumenical council in which, since 1948, the Jews of *Medinat Yisrael*, the State, have been represented. It still remains in the face of the world the voice of the authentic Jewish people. Herzl himself derived no very great joy from the succeeding Congresses. He still seemed to himself to be fighting "with a wooden sword"; he was able to observe coolly that Nordau talked too long. At least subscriptions for the bank were coming in. The faithful David Wolfsohn reported £100,000. Yet he was bored during the third Congress, bored and irritated. There were intrigues against him, which he did not suffer gladly. On the same day he was happy to welcome Dr. Richard Gottheil of New York, but took more pleasure in despatching another letter to the Sultan. There were hardly any triumphs of the word left. "The slogans grow dull; the ideas become the subjects of declamations, and declamation is easily blunted." By this time, moreover, he had invested and lost 50,000 crowns of his own money in *Die Welt* and was more dependent on his masters of the *Neue Freie Presse* than ever. A rather poor play of his had failed on the stage at this time. "I will not permit myself to profit by Zionism; I am not permitted by the world to profit by literature. Quite a problem." Yet, in the end, he felt that the third Congress had, at least, "run off smoothly," and that, above all, "a good mood (*Stimmung*) had been created."

The fourth Congress, that of London in August, 1900, impressed him unforgettably with the exquisiteness of certain aspects of English life. He was the house guest of the poet laureate Alfred Austin and seemed to understand the patriotism of at least the British Jews. The Royal Commission of 1902 was to disillusion him on the appropriateness of this sentiment. Yet his hopes from now on were ever more firmly fixed on Britain and its government. The year that preceded the fifth Congress was filled, thronged to overflowing and satiety with plans for the founding of newspapers, which came to nothing, with diplomatic journeys, including an interview with the Sultan himself, which resulted in a Turkish decoration and the gift of a diamond tiepin. It was only a canary diamond, not even one of blue-white. Herzl was not apparently too aware of the irony. His health, too, was failing. He gave his fifth Congress address rather wearily. The Congress again met in Basle but in the depth of winter. Sessions lasted until four in the morning. What almost alone heartened him was the official salutation of the Congress by the municipality of Basle, a precedent set once again for that official recognition of the Jewish people as represented by Zionist Congresses on the part of heads of State. This recognition led to the establishment of the National Fund as a juridical entity under the laws of Basle. Bitter internal dissensions, themselves of no great moment, beat upon Herzl's weary heart. He was glad when the Congress was over. He withdrew himself from acclaim and tumult at the earliest moment. This kind of thing, he noted, gave him ever less pleasure.

IV

A rather conscious race with time set in. In the twenty months that elapsed between the fifth and sixth Congresses, Herzl was twice in Constantinople and once in Cairo and again and again in London, where he met and impressed Joseph Chamberlain and Landsdowne who were at long last to offer that Charter, that possibility of autonomous Jewish settlement for which, not unjustly, as has been seen, nor unreasonably, Herzl had so tirelessly striven. Tragically enough, the Sinai

Peninsula and El Arish projects having failed, the British ministers offered the Jewish people through Herzl a habitable territory in British East Africa, known then and also since as Uganda. Meantime, on April 18, 1903, the notorious pogrom of Kishinev took place. In that idyllic world, still tinged with human feeling and a remnant of Christianity, the slaughter of forty-five Jews and the wounding of two hundred aroused a world-wide storm of compassion and of wrath. And now the very ground seemed to burn under Herzl's feet. The Jewish people needed at least a refuge now. But to stem the tide of horrors in Russia Herzl obtained a passport and went on that pathetically ill-advised journey to St. Petersburg to interview the Russian ministers Witte and von Plehve. These men were courteous with brutal undertones and even promised permission for the establishment of a Russian branch of the Jewish Colonial Trust Company. A feigning, at least, of humanity was still in fashion. Can one imagine a Zionist leader's reception in the Kremlin today?

From Saint Petersburg he went to Vilna where, amid the acclamations of a people stirred to the heart, he received the official confirmation of the Uganda offer. He retired for a pitiful few days to his old resting place of Alt Aussee and hastened with his heart "acting up" to the sixth Congress, the "Uganda Congress" which assembled in Basle on August 23, 1903. The Congresses had grown as the movement had. Five hundred and seventy delegates sat in the Concert Hall of Basle. And to these Herzl announced the British offer. A profound emotional ambivalence arose in the assembled delegates. They were uplifted by the fact that at last, at long last, one of the great powers of the earth, England, the greatest, the humanest, had acknowledged the corporate existence of the Jewish people *as* a people, and was prepared to establish that people autonomously in a land of its own. The Russian pogroms, moreover, seemed to many the beginning of an attempt to destroy the then most populous Jewish centers in the world. Against these terribly and overwhelmingly realistic considerations there was nothing that could prevail except an idea—the immemorial Jewish idea of a return to the Holy Land of Israel, of the restoration there of the people and of the exiled *Shekhina*, the spirit of the Divine Abiding. And as a supreme confirmation of the character and destiny of Israel the idea was victorious over the mere, the sordid facts of life.

But it is no wonder that for the hour and the day men's souls were shaken and divided and many were inclined to accept the clever, artificial formulation of Nordau that Uganda need be but a *"Nachtasyl,"* a lodging for the night in a time of great need, and that the hope of an ultimate return to Zion need not be relinquished. Nor should it be forgotten that a majority of the delegates were secularists, so that even men like Nachman Syrkin and Chaim Weizmann's own kinsmen faltered. The immediate security and dignity of the Jewish people seemed—*seemed*, at least—to be offered as an alternative to what was, in a sense, but a dream, though an immortal dream. Thus the first vote is to be explained. Two hundred and ninety-five delegates (the *Ja-sager*) voted for the Uganda project; one hundred and seventy-five (the *Nein-sager*) voted against; one hundred abstained, including the gifted and distinguished Nahum Sokolow. But the quite ultimate spirit was symbolized, perhaps, by an impassioned nameless girl who raced through the hall to the platform and tore down the map of Uganda which had been substituted for the map of *Eretz Yisrael* above the speaker's table.

It should, of course, not be forgotten that the substance of the vote was simply the accepting of a proposal to send a commission of investigation to Uganda, the costs of which were to be borne neither by the Jewish Colonial Bank nor by the National Fund. Nor should it be forgotten that Herzl declared in his closing speech that no jot or tittle of the program of Basle was to be abandoned, and ended with the ancient asseveration: "If I forget thee, O Jerusalem, may my right hand wither." Yet the conflict, as has been seen, was a real and bitter one. The mainly Russian "Nay-sayers" left the Assembly Hall and wept audibly over what they feared was a second or a third destruction of Zion. To the lasting honor of the Jews it was these men, who had to return to the blood-soaked earth of Russia, who rejected a possibility of immediate security for the sake of their vision. Ussishkin hastened to Europe from Palestine and summoned a Zionist conference in Kharkov which voted to present Herzl with an ultimatum. He was deeply wounded; he refused to receive the Russian delegation from Kharkov. He had, needless to say, staunch defenders, too. But for a time the movement and the organization were shaken to the marrow. Nevertheless, Herzl's immediate subsequent activities restored faith and unity. In the eight active months of life left him he sought again to negotiate with the Sultan and to bring pressure to bear upon that sovereign. He tried even to influence the Russian ministers, writing to von Plehve that what was needed was Russia's favorable intervention at the Ottoman court.

His own reflections immediately after the sixth Congress have their own interest and even beauty: "The hard, great sixth Congress is behind us. When, in a state of exhaustion, I returned from the Assembly Hall with my friends . . . I said to them: If I live to see the seventh Congress, I'll give you the substance of my address on that occasion. By that time I'll either have Palestine or I'll have seen the complete hopelessness of any further efforts. In that case I shall say: It was not possible. Our goal has not been reached. . . . An interim goal is available. . . . I know that this argument will cause a cleavage in our movement and this cleavage will go through my very heart. For though at first I was simply the proponent of a Jewish State— no matter where —I, too, later embraced the flag of Zion and became a lover of Zion. . . . And so, in order to heal the cleavage, I shall re- tire. . . . And all my wishes will accompany those who pursue the dream of Zion restored. Farewell."

He had continued to agitate until, quite literally, he dropped. He slept less and less. He waited wearily in the Pope's ante- chamber; he interviewed and pleaded with the not unfriendly King of Italy; he saw again the ever equivocal Turkish bureau- crats and diplomats; he wrote to Jacob H. Schiff who was visiting Europe; he saw the Austrian minister Gulochowsky and "broke down" (his notation is in English) in the Bohemian spa of Franzensbad; he still wrote to von Plehve, to another Austrian minister and—this was his last letter and his last

entry into the diaries—to Jacob Schiff. This was in the middle
of May. On the third of June he was taken to the resort of
Edlach, near his home in Vienna. A month later pneumonia
set in. On his last day, July 3, he is said to have said to the
students who had constituted themselves a guard of honor that
they were splendid men who would assuredly dwell in the
Homeland. He sustained himself with his last strength to await
the arrival of his mother from Vienna. At five o'clock in the
afternoon he ceased to breathe. He had requested that some day
his remains be brought to their final rest in the Land of Israel.
It is not too much to say that, chiefly through the virtues of
his life and of his acts, it was possible for a grateful posterity
to fulfill his wish. On August 17, 1949, his remains were carried
to the State of Israel to their permanent repose.

5. DEATH AND APOTHEOSIS

No man's death had, for centuries, so filled the living Jewish people with grief, with dismay, with a sense of loss as the death of Theodor Herzl. He, and he first, and he in his time alone, had incarnated for Jews their oneness, their national existence upon the scene of history, and the acknowledgment of that existence by the powers and the principalities of earth. Justly and inevitably that incarnation by him of a new era of unity and of action transmuted his human personality into symbol and myth. Large controversies and small enmities were forgotten. The Uganda project was calmly rejected by the seventh Congress of 1905 and the Territorialists (those willing to accept a territory other than the Land of Israel), though led by so notable a figure as that of Israel Zangwill, faded almost into oblivion. Herzl's history as a person was almost repressed. The panegyrics were nearly all uncritical. Not quite consciously, perhaps, authentic Jews rejoiced in this further evidence of their living peoplehood, that they could in this late and prosaic age create a hero and establish a legend. Thus came into being those hundred images of the great leader and symbol which did for years, and in truth do still, appear in bronze or olive wood or painted fabrics, whether made in the Land of Israel or in many corners of the dispersion, and adorn the interiors of thousands upon thousands of Jewish homes.

The effect of Herzl's life and activities, now sanctified by an early death in the service of his people, had soberer and deeper consequences in the West of Europe. A "new Jew," as the quite representative scholar and essayist Moses Calvary frankly put it, came into being. Who was that new Jew? What was he? The transcendental bindings, as Ahad Ha'am agreed, seemed at that moment of history irrecoverably lost. Hence even Jews who desired to escape the assimilatory yoke and that inner servitude which their Western freedom concealed had neither outer nor inner principle to unite them. Bindings had been needed for long. Herzl had announced such new bindings. In the concept of Jewish nationality a supraindividual form and content were again provided. "In Herzl's writings," Calvary records, "as well as at the Congresses, in public meetings and student conventions, there was sounded a tone which had long been missed—a tone akin to religion in its mood, a tone which, in truth, may well be characterized as religious." Here, of course, a very real danger was involved, the danger that is involved in all secular religions—the danger of idolatry. But that danger was far enough at that time from the earnest, highly ethical "new Jews" of Central Europe who truly felt that "even participation in a common action which is rendered possible by the definiteness of its *form*, gives the feelings of the individual a new intensity." Jews, in brief, who through the loss of their faith in Judaism had been paralyzed and atomized, could once again *belong* to the community of Israel and live and toil and suffer in its service. This elementary fact, this possibility of a new Jewish commitment, seemed so precious and so life-giving to that generation, that the exquisite, learned, deeply poetic spirit Hugo Bergmann, active now for forty years in the land of Israel, spoke early a culminating word when he said: "Zionism is *our Kiddush HaShem*—our sanctification of the ineffable Name in life and death."

It was these new Jews whom Herzl had made—even though he would himself not wholly have understood them—who created a veritable Jewish Renaissance in Central Europe. It was these "new Jews" who founded the incomparable *Jüdischer Verlag* (Jewish Publishing House), who directed such magazines as *Der Jude* (The Jew). For it must not be forgotten that Martin Buber had been present at every Congress from the second on. He, to be sure, had come from Galicia with all that authenticity of Jewish learning and tradition of which Herzl had no notion. Yet it was upon the basis of the national unity in feeling, form, action which Herzl had created that Buber built that new *style* of Jewish living and Jewish thinking and Jewish sensibility, which permits the sober observation that a Jewish renaissance period did set in and is still vitally operative, though in transmuted form and in a transformed spirit wherever Jews live and especially in the contemporary Jewish community of America. At the beginning of all these developments there stood Herzl and Herzl alone. He was *felt* to be source and origin. "It was," wrote Calvary, "an innermost necessity that an artist's spirit like Herzl's should have given the bluntedness of our national life the lift of a living movement conscious of its aims." Here quite obviously something of the mythopoeic spirit is already at work. The hero who is needed is created. Yet it must be observed at once, and will be again, that not every personality lends itself to apotheosis— not even every great personality. He who is apotheosized was destined to be.

The dangers inherent in that earlier phase of Herzlian Zionism—not Herzl's own but as it was supposedly derived from him—should not be emphasized; neither should they be forgotten. A cultural parallel sequence was established between Jewish civilization and the other civilizations: Scholasticism, mysticism, enlightenment, nationalism. This sequence was proposed under the treacherous name of progress. Of such subtleties Herzl himself was incapable. But the glorification of state, of nation, and of nationalism, as practiced not only by the Zionist Revisionists but by many other contemporary elements even in the State of Israel—none of whom shall be spoken of here except with tolerance and tenderness—were implicitly attributed to Herzl. This, too, marks the vastness and decisiveness of his influence, that from him were derived views and doctrines which he never held, which he was not capable of holding, which grew rigid at a certain point, and now, in another age, after other and shattering historic experiences, are a source of dread and danger.

It was a "New Jew" and a Jewish cultural and national renaissance to which the figure and, above all, the actions of Theodor Herzl gave rise in the West. The East needed no "new

Jew." Amid the masses of Eastern Jewry, in Russia, in the
Polish Pale, in Lithuania and Romania, the spiritual city of
Judaism, whether Hassidic or Misnagdic, stood firm on its
divine foundation. Yet, in another sense, a "new Jew" had also
emerged. This was the Jew of the Jewish Enlightenment, the
Maskil, whom the *Haskala* brought forth. This new Jew wanted
for his people the culture of the West. By a strange device of
fate it was he who recreated Hebrew prose in its modern form
and used it as an instrumentality of the Enlightenment, of
bringing Jews into direct contact with Western philosophy,
literature, above all science. Many of the *Hovevei Tsion,* the
Lovers of Zion, were *Maskillim,* enlighteners, and thus their
nationalism, too, quite like Herzl's, was a secular nationalism.
What they lacked was not theory but practice. They wholly
lacked unity and action. It was Herzl, as has been seen, who
created the unity between them and the Jews of the Western
world and inspired this new and single people with the possibility of common action, a common front, a common form.

   The most eminent spirit who finally arose from the *Haskala*
movement was Herzl's severest critic who has already been
spoken of—Ahad Ha'am. What was the essence of his criticism?
That Herzl was, so to speak, hardly a Jew, and that Herzlian
Zionism was without Jewish content. Thence came his famous
jibe after the first Congress. When Herzl said that a return to
Judaism must precede a return to the Land of the Jews, it was,
according to Ahad Ha'am, a meaningless phrase and a rhetorical
flourish. The reproach was not wholly unjust. Undoubtedly
Ahad Ha'am possessed the great tradition, the *Hokhmat Yisrael,*
of whose very existence Herzl was unaware. But he, Ahad
Ha'am, too, had abandoned it; he mourned over the human
forces which had been lost to the world in the *Bet Hamidrash,*
the house of study; he wrote in the preface to the first collected
edition of his essays, *Al Parashat Drakhim* (At the Parting
of the Ways), that "a liberation of the spirit must precede our
national liberation." And what was, according to him, the instrumentality of that "liberation of the spirit"? An attempt to
blend the world-view (*Weltanschauung*) of Judaism (was
this not, too, a mere phrase?) with, of all things, Darwinian

evolutionism as elaborated in the philosophy of Herbert Spencer. Is it not clear from this that Ahad Ha'am's famous formulation that Zion was to be primarily the citadel of Judaism rather than of Jews, a cultural center rather than a dwelling place for people, had a most dubious content? Ahad Ha'am remains a fragmentary thinker of permanent interest and value; he remains one of the great stylists in modern Hebrew. But that "new ideal" which he demanded in the preface of the second edition of the essays was one of the bleakest and most barren in the world. Was it by means of this ideal that "the idea of the nation" was to be made to live again and to arouse the "people from its long slumber"? The last word on the matter was spoken long ago, in 1902, by the then young Martin Buber: "The creative spirits are not the 'intellectuals'; the pure 'intellectuals' have too much logic and too little mystery (*Geheimnis*). They take their stand upon 'truth' not upon 'reality.'" The *Haskala*, the Enlightenment, he added soon thereafter, "used the slogans of knowledge, civilization, Europe. It sought to 'enlighten' and, like all enlightening, it was shallow. . . . He who has lost his God is profoundly orphaned. Upon his new way to God the love of his people may be a first stage." This truly prophetic utterance transcends both Herzl and Ahad Ha'am. Its prophecy has, alas, not yet been fulfilled. But Herzl's pre-eminence over Ahad Ha'am, over other classical critics and opponents, is once more defined by Buber: "The creative spirits are the hidden kings of the people. They direct its subterranean destiny, of which the outer manifestation is but the visible reflection." Herzlian Zionism did create a people and a State, and it is both fact and symbol that Ahad Ha'am passed his declining years in a white cottage on Ahad Ha'am Street in the city of Tel Aviv.

II

An attempt has been made to define and describe the psychical pattern of Theodor Herzl. It may be restated as follows: The concentration upon the only son by his parents, their boundless indulgence of him, their boundless admiration for him and exorbitant hopes for him—especially his mother's—hampered his maturing and crippled his judgment both of the world and of himself. He seemed to himself a prince in exile, unknown, unloved, unvalued. Only immediate and brilliant success, only wealth and glory could rescue him. Since these did not appear, he devaluated the world and mankind which would not grant him these rewards and assumed for many years a pose of harsh cynicism. And in the measure in which he needed compensatory wealth and glory, they never came. He remained, despite inner protestations, merely a not quite top-ranking journalist and a mediocre playwright.

Then came the great awakening. His repressed hurts and sorrows as a Jew leaped into consciousness. He transmuted himself into a man of action. He became, as the Vilna Jews cried out to him, a *melekh*, a king. The old wounds were, as the diaries show, never wholly healed; a complete compensation was never achieved. But for those last eight years he burned with a continuous flame and was himself consumed by that flame. He was priest, altar, and sacrifice upon the altar he himself had built. When his ashes had crumbled upon that altar the glory he had striven after was achieved.

This analysis of Herzl's psychical pattern is probably correct. It is borne out by all the incidents of his life and by the more powerful evidence of all his rather voluminous writings. And this sort of analysis has been taught us by Herzl's near contemporary and fellow-Viennese, Sigmund Freud. But the Freudian psychology, unrivaled in the fruitful insights it has brought us, is, after all, only a science. And what is the mark of a science? That it deals exclusively with proximate causes and never with ultimate ones. It can tell us *that* such and such phenomena are likely to occur in such and such sequences of time, never *why*, as a rule not even *how*. The situation of Herzl and his parents, the Oedipus complex, his mother's consuming ambition for him: the brooding, intense, forever reiterated cry, expressed or silent—If not *I*, then *you*, you, you must raise us out of obscurity and discomfort into the light of the world!—in how many families, in how many thousands of Jewish families, especially in that period of the false emancipation, did not this thing happen, was not this pattern formed? My son *must* be a doctor—a doctor of some kind or, especially in Central Europe, a writer, an artist, a luminary of some sort in the world of the Gentiles. And so societies of that kind, as Herzl himself complained again and again, are filled with Jewish intellectual and artistic mediocrities for whom their world had little use and who therefore often enough became radicals and foes of that order which, according to them, had used them ill. None of them was able to transmute frustrations into action; none of them was able to give form to the formlessness of a whole people—his people; not another became a torch, leader, redeemer. Not another—not one rose to consecration and greatness. The explanations of science, like the mathematics of insurance actuaries, can tell us about averages. They can tell us nothing about greatness or consecration. These are and will forever be the fruits of election and of grace. Therefore, despite his obvious weaknesses and his cultivation of the grandiose gesture, Herzl radiated in those years of his burning and self-consuming an indescribable influence upon all who knew, saw, heard him; therefore he transcended his own lack of specifically Jewish content; therefore the myth and the legend into which he and his life were transmuted inhered in his very character and destiny and are, for that reason, permanently justified.

SELECTIONS FROM

THEODOR HERZL'S WRITINGS

LUZ, THE VILLAGE

In Tarbes, the principal town of the Pyrenees, I felt compelled to add a codicil to my last will and testament. In the categorical tone proper to the elegance of such documents, I set down explicitly that my remains were not to be interred in this place, in the event I were to die here of boredom. For I would almost rather be consigned to live in Tarvis [a small town on the border between Austria and Italy], than to be buried in Tarbes. To my great surprise, however, I did awake on the following morning and was able to continue my journey to Pierrefitte.

. . . So these are the Pyrenees? I had pictured them as more awe-inspiring. My thoughts returned longingly to our Tyrol. How much higher those mountains are, and yet the inhabitants are no less simple! . . . At Pierrefitte you leave the train. The station itself offers so little in the way of interest or entertainment that the porters take hours to unload the baggage of a traveler or two, a task that ought to take only a few minutes. Beyond Pierrefitte, the mountains really begin in earnest.

We traveled in the stagecoach of a worthy *paterfamilias,* as they say in the Roman law books. He proved to be a very sleepy *paterfamilias,* with but little regard for his own welfare, and just when the road began to be both steep and dangerous, the good man dozed off. The deep gorge through which the Gave river rushes down to the valley apparently no longer has any attraction for him, not even the fascination of danger.

"Luz, das Dorf," in *Feuilletons,* Vol. 2 (Berlin, J. Singer & Co. Verlag, 1911), pages 111–118.

I was sitting next to him and attempted in vain to keep him awake by my conversational arts. Not even when, as if by chance, I began to poke him in the ribs did he wake up, merely kept babbling some woman's name, which gave me a certain insight into his family life. A small carriage with which we collided as it came tearing down into the valley finally aroused him. From this encounter, ours was the victory! For we rendered the opposition vehicle absolutely useless for further combat and compelled the enemy to proceed to Pierrefitte on foot. Yet we ourselves bore some minor wounds from the fray, although they were honorable scars of battle. Our left front wheel was damaged, several windows in the coach were broken, and an umbrella belonging to one of the passengers fell into the chasm. The umbrella gave our coachman little concern, but he did not cease to bewail, until the very end of the trip, the condition of his conveyance, and the fact that he would have to make good to his employer the damage that had been done. Since anguish prevents a man from sleeping, we kept it a secret from him, as long as we were still under way, that we, the passengers, would assume the cost of the repairs. Only after we had arrived at Saint-Sauveur did we take up a collection. In addition, at his request, I gave him a written testimonial to the effect that he had not been the one to blame for the collision. Perhaps he even succeeded in shifting the entire expense of it on to his employer. To show his appreciation, when he made change, he gave me a five-franc piece which I shall have to treasure forever as a memento of this simple-minded man of the mountains, for there is not a soul in Navarre or in all of France who would be willing to accept it from me.

Saint-Sauveur-les-Bains lies almost half way up the side of a mountain, stretched out like a snail that has just crept out of its shell. As the name indicates, it is a watering place; its name, however, does not reveal the fact that the baths are exclusively for women. That is why there are to be seen here mostly rather old, rather damaged specimens of the weaker sex. The men who do come here, evidently not aware of the special nature of the resort, arouse the ridicule (not always of a kindly nature) of the women who are accustomed to sit outside in front of their little houses. How greatly the women benefit by their stay in Saint-Sauveur can best be observed at the Hotel de France. In this excellent hostelry, the master of the house supervises the kitchen, while Madame, with energy and efficiency, looks after external affairs. What a truly happy solution of the Woman Question! Woman's lust for power is given its due, without thereby wholly dispensing with the usefulness of Man. Every now and again the door of the kitchen opens up, and the fiery red, shaggy-bearded face of the stately host peers out, like a Cyclops, as he announces that the cutlet or the rice pudding is ready. But, observing truly masculine decorum, he does not leave his hearth. Noiselessly and discreetly, he reigns inside the house, admonishing the girls and instructing the boys. Thrice happy may that wife be called, who, one day, leads to the altar a youth trained by such a man as he. . . .

The very sight of the guests at Saint-Sauveur inspires you to go on excursions. But there is no way of avoiding the others, for there is only a single walk, that over the Napoleon Bridge into the gorge which leads to Gavarnie. This bridge, which spans the chasm of the Gave magnificently in a single arch of noble proportions, was built at the behest of Napoleon III, in 1860. The Emperor himself deigned to designate precisely the spot where the daring construction was to be erected. So we are told on a stone, by now as worn as the gratitude-underorders that erected it, in an inscription with gold letters faded like the Byzantinism of those bygone days. On the other side of the bridge, to the right, the road leads to Gavarnie, to the source, high up and far away, of one branch of the Gave. On the left, the road winds gently down to Luz.

Luz! What a delightful spot! What a fine abode for convalescents of all sorts! The foolish hurry on, to Barèges, and to the Pic du Midi, and to Gavarnie, and to the Pic du Marboré, and to the Pic de Gabiétou, and to all the other Pics, whatever their names may be; and then back again, and then on once more. Luz, village of villages! It lies on the banks of the stream of tourists which helps to turn its wheels; yet in and of itself, it is a quiet place, this village of Luz. Through it rushes the stream of the Gave de Bastan, hurling its foaming waves, ever new yet ever the same, against the selfsame rocks. And yet this heady current produces only a single, soothing, sleep-inducing melody of only a few notes.

Whoever does not wish to make use of this heavenly quiet for work will find many a way to be entertained. For example, there is the blacksmith, whom you can watch while he is shoeing the horses. It is all very interesting. You see how the worn-out horseshoe is removed and the new one heated in the fire as the young apprentice stands at the bellows, illumined in a Rembrandt-like glow, all red and black. Then the iron horseshoe sputters on the hoof, singes it, and presses in, then is cooled in the trough, and finally fastened to the horse's foot with strong nails. Whereupon, prouder than ever, the old steed takes his departure.

. . . Nor should you neglect the shoemaker. He sits on the sill of his window and works at the old boots outside the window, leaning forward like a demagogue making an impassioned speech. But the true inhabitant of the Pyrenees takes his footgear for repair to the carpenter or even to the blacksmith, for it is made of wood reinforced with nails, to last not for the insignificant span of but a few short years, but for eternity.

However the pearl of Luz is the barber. When I say the barber, I mean also the postman who sometimes doubles as the grocer as well. Every now and then you see men roaming about in the market place of Luz. They are not ordinary idlers; if they were, their expressions would not be so somber. No, these are men who cannot make up their minds to enter the barbershop because they know what manner of man the barber is. However, he waits for them smiling coldly; he knows that they cannot escape him. In the Pyrenees, custom demands that the men be clean-shaven; only the women, some of them, allow their mustaches to grow. Finally, some stouthearted fellow tears himself away from the others, stops to exchange final handshakes with his friends, casts a mournful glance at the mountains of his youth, and steps boldly inside the barbershop. The door seals him in, for there are no windows in this establishment. It is a tiny room, whitewashed like a ship's cabin, on whose bare walls there is nothing to delight the eye. Neither gaily colored perfume bottles nor evil-smelling concoctions for encouraging hair growth mitigate the terrors of getting shaved. A chair into which the victim is strapped stands in the middle of the room. That is all there is. What takes place goes on in total darkness. When the barber wants to get around to the other side of the chair, he has to open the door, because the room is so small and so narrow. Then, for those few seconds, the men on the outside see in and silently nod their heads. In their eyes you see the look of understanding of those who are familiar with suffering. The man's throat is rattling, but he is still alive. And even so, getting shaved is not by any means the worst; often it takes only an hour. But to have your hair cut! Since I have no desire to describe atrocities, may I be permitted to maintain silence on this score? . . . Furthermore, there are baths in Luz, too, but the inhabitants make no use of them. They bathe solely in the pure mountain air.

Luz, village of strange customs! I am quite aware that it is the capital of a province, the home of some 1,514 souls (and in that number I do not include the people of rank). For me, it remains Luz, the village. How else could I be expected to accept the funerals of cows? I myself once saw one. The village crier came storming through the narrow streets, luring us out in front of the house. With great dignity, he strutted at the head of the procession, his drum hanging from his shoulder by a broad leather strap, behind him a pathetic-looking calf, and, bringing up the rear, the object of all this ceremony—a woebegone cow, hung with garlands, her flanks draped in colored fabrics. She had come to the end of her days, and an inexorable fate had summoned her to the slaughtering block. While we humans can no longer hear the fine words that the chairman of our party speaks in tribute to us at our funeral, this cow prior to her demise is given the opportunity of en-visaging the void that she is going to leave behind her. Does this make her departure any the easier? That is the question. At any rate, at our next regular meeting, I should like to make a motion in respect to this. To be sure, I can already hear the objection being raised: But what would happen if the individual in question were not to die subsequently? Compose yourselves, gentlemen, everybody dies eventually.

And all the other things there are to be seen in Luz! Half-starved Savoyards with their monkeys. A bear trainer, trudging along leading two of Atta Troll's successors by their chains. Troll, of course, was at home in these parts, as our worthy Mr. Heinrich Heine tells us. The dancing bears are getting rarer all the time who can still cavort in all this melancholy. You will see, beasts of prey, too, will yet vanish completely from the face of the earth, and finally, man himself will have to take their places. For the time being, men regale themselves by watching trained fleas and performing poodles. In Luz there are six poodles and innumerable fleas. At present they are still young—I am referring to the dogs—and their private trainer suffers loyally on a par with them. But we shall doubtless come upon them in better circumstances at some later date, in the capitals of Europe, being feted by our very best society. . . . On the other hand, the faded songstress who to the accompaniment of her guitar sings the delightful old ballad of the rose and the butterfly, as well as her companion, the comic, have nothing ahead of them except the dust of the high road. She used to perform in the garden, in the evenings, for those guests of the Hotel de l'Univers who, on the morrow, would be trudging along on their donkeys to Gavarnie and to the many variously named Pics. To help them digest their dinners, she used to intone tender love songs and sly Béarnais ditties. . . . In Luz there is quite an assortment of other mournful wags who make others laugh and dream, although they themselves no longer laugh nor dream.

Gavarnie. You hear that name repeated so often that at last one fine day, in spite of yourself, you start out for there. It is only a matter of two and a half hours, two and a half hours of bells ringing and whips snapping, and ride. Here, too, you see coachmen on the box. They even have red vests and blue coats bound in silver, but they do not, as in the Tyrol and in Styria, pour out their whole heart and soul, and their thirst, in blowing their horns. The ride proceeds in silence, as somber as the landscape. . . . Beyond the Napoleon Bridge, the narrow roads shuts us in fast. How austere is the landscape of the Pyrenees! The steep road is carved out of the side of the rock. Every now and again, the walls widen out, and then it becomes just a green valley without any inhabitants. Nature is generous, lavishing on us, all mixed up together, the forbiddingly steep and the gently sloping. The keynote is always sad. And far below, the river Gave goes rushing by. In the dim past this was the stream that hollowed out this ravine for itself in its attempt to make its way to the Lake of Luz. Or did this formation, perhaps, appear all of a sudden, as the result of a single natural upheaval?

We proceed on our way along the Gave. Now it no longer swirls and eddies in a chasm but murmurs gently on a level with the road. Soon again, it becomes fierce and awe-inspiring far below us, then once more familiarly close by our side—and at last we are in Gavarnie. Before the tourists' hostelry, an army of donkeys, mules, and horses stands inside an enclosure. Here, too, the donkeys play the largest role. It is still a good hour's ride before we reach the hollow of Gavarnie. On the way, we can see, high up there on the ridge, the huge gap that the great Roland smote out of the rock with his trusty sword, Durandal. What a mighty blow that must have been! And yet, the legendary hero went down to defeat in the Valley of Roncevaux.

Now once again the Gave whispers more gently to the pebbles. There are cows at their ease up on the pastures, chewing their cud, and gazing gently, with mild irony, at the travelers who lumber past with so much effort. For these cows have already been in the arena of Gavarnie. And there it is, the bowl or, as it is more properly called, the arena. Yes, a colosseum. A round structure with tremendously high walls, arranged in tiers that get ever wider, the farther up they go. There is snow on the upper gallery already. A few small waterfalls break into spray on their way down to the heaps of boulders. Here is where the Gave rises! The whole landscape is so desolate, so shut in. It is like the great sadness at the end of all questing.

But how differently we human beings are able to view the selfsame thing. Perhaps the woman behind me was right:

"Isn't it pretty?" she asked in English.

And in the same language, another agreed: "Really, very nice!"

As for me, I sing the praises of Luz, the village. It is "really" not even "nice." And yet it is the home of my friends: the blacksmith, the shoemaker, the barber, and many another, who are dear to me because they wear the picturesque dark blue beret. Now as always, they stand silent in the public square. When they speak, it is a dialect that sounds "Spanish" to me, and indeed it practically is. The one thing I can always understand, wherever I come upon it, is the Gave—the Gave de Pau or Gave de Bastan—the blissful murmuring of the brook. When I follow along its bank, it leads to many a lovely valley. If only we could continue to wander along the Gave, on and on . . .

(1891)

SPRING IN ELEND

In Vienna there used to be a street called Im Elend (In Misery). I rather think it is where young Grillparzer used to live. There are those alive today who walked through the Zeughausgasse when it was still called Im Elend. In Viennese dialect, *Elend* is pronounced *Oelland*. It is a good old word that has come down to us from a time when men's hearts were closed against each other even more tightly than they are today. The word is made up of *el, al* (ἄλλος, *alius*), meaning different or strange, and *land*. Thus it signifies a different or strange land, the dwelling place of someone who has been ostracized or banished. In the Middle Ages, that section of a city where the lodgings for strangers were located was frequently known as *Elend*. Thus, natives and foreigners were kept apart by a permanent wall of ignorance and distrust. The *Elend* came to be an island, the island of the unfortunate. Nothing is harder for human beings in any case than to understand each other in simple human relations, so that a vast amount of suffering and misery must have developed in those islands.

In the *Elend* or strangers' quarters of old, besides all the other misunderstandings that can come between even close relatives and kinsfolk, there was added the fear of anything different or strange. The Middle Ages were a conglomeration of fears. The inhabitants of foreign areas in those benighted times had little freedom of movement. To travel was a hazardous adventure which only the foolhardy dared to under-

"Frühling in Elend," in *Feuilletons,* Vol. 1 (Berlin, J. Singer & Co. Verlag, 1911), pages 144–151.

take. So the suspicion of being the cause of catastrophes rested on anyone who settled in a new country. Such a hapless creature who might have lost his way or been banished would then have moved about somewhat timidly, keeping to himself, in this neighborhood which was strange to him. This timidity of his in turn made him still more an object of suspicion, and the unforgivable separateness and difference became greater with everything that he did or refrained from doing. The longer he was seen in the same place, the customs of which remained a semimystery to him because he was shut off from contact with the majority—the longer he was seen, the uglier he became in the sight of others. The *Elend* or foreign quarter was made up of distrust on the one side and timidity on the other, and from this all the rest of the evils inevitably followed. Those evils must have been very great. They included contempt for the poor, unwillingness to help the sick, and hostile prejudice in the face of any accusation. Anyone who had ever been in *Elend* was so weakened, as a result, that he was never able to get away from it. Thus in the course of time, this fine old word *Elend* acquired its present meaning of misery or wretchedness.

But let me ask, has that condition of misery and wretchedness every really disappeared? I am not referring here to the out-land or *Elend* to which, even in our own society, people manage to consign, time and time again, certain groups through organized agitation. Are there not such islands of the unfortunate in our days too? When we come upon them, we can expect them to waft up to us something of the spirit of a time long past. It is even possible that the misery of *Elend* has a special bliss of its own, and that by recognizing its existence we might feel our way a little closer into the heart of humanity.

Elend in the old sense of the place of the banned or outcast exists to this very day, and every city has one of its own. In Vienna it is located on a gloomy street. Two imposing buildings stand guard over the entrance. On the right are the barracks, and on the left the courthouse. On the one side, the state safeguards its order; on the other, it administers its laws. Passers-by timidly look up at both of them with curiosity, and hurry past. Funeral processions drive by day after day. Further up, on the left, is the Foundling Hospital. If you stand at the entrance and look down the Alserstrasse, you will notice that where the street divides it always looks as if it had been dipped in a faint, doleful mist. This is the most important street in the whole city because more of the life of the people takes place here than anywhere else. To the right, behind the barracks, lies the *Elend* or island of misery.

It is called the General Hospital, and its very name inspires fear and trembling. If you have to go this way, you find yourself hurrying quickly past its huge entrance gates. The very air reeks of strong disinfectants. Anyone who has to pass by here often unwittingly takes the other side of the street. Age-old fantasies hover in ghostly fashion round about the hospital, even now, in broad daylight, and it is not hard to imagine what it must have been like in the dark period of history when the Great Death bestrode the world. The powerful odor of cleanliness which pervades the very walls ought, surely, to set everyone's mind at rest. And yet, uneasily, one tries to give it a wide berth; and that is the first characteristic sign of the old *Elend*. A strange thought must occur to anyone who ever happened to notice this, namely, that in the midst of all this commotion, where thousands live and still other thousands come to visit, there must be something that is entirely strange and unfamiliar. What is commonplace is the hardest thing to discover. No one seems able to see what is ordinary and usual, and yet there is nothing more remarkable, nothing so stirring. Who that is not forced to do so by dire necessity ever goes to a hospital? Those who are carried in on stretchers, or who, exerting their last ounce of will power, drag themselves there, are benumbed by the catastrophe that has befallen them. A visitor does not have the self-possessed calm, either, with which to gaze upon this strange region. Everyone does his best to escape as quickly as possible so that he may breathe freely once more. The young medical students would appear to be the ones best fitted to discover this world for us, but, at the beginning, they themselves have a serious crisis to go through to get used to the horror, and once the crisis is passed they are accustomed to the strangeness. Then when they gaze around, their look has the cold dispassionateness that is required, and they no longer can see the pain for the sufferers. They get lost, as indeed they should, in the "fascinating details" of the individual "cases," and thus this world of sickness as an entity, of which, by the way, they themselves are also a part, escapes them.

What a remarkable world, what a wonderful locale for the most human of stories, novels, fiction! It provides slices of life, pieces of raw flesh cut from the very heart of society, still quivering, still raw, still bleeding. But you must not think of this place as filled with continuous and unending affliction, no matter how much horror is to be found there. The gaiety is muted, yet it does exist, and this in itself is miraculous; its gentlest note, by its very contrast, is as impressive as though it were the most resounding paean of joy. If ever you wish to behold the blissful awakening of Nature in its true form, then you have to go to the *Elend*.

A day in very early spring. The air gentle and mild as if it were May. If you enter by the huge gate from the Alserstrasse, you find that just a few steps further on all the noise has died down. Here there is a quiet court, spacious and airy, planted with trees that now stretch their delicate young arms up toward the pale sky. The tips of the dark brown branches are lighter in color, swollen by the force which deep down under the earth is pushing up with so much power that it must needs come thrusting out above.

Strange figures stroll along the paths—the inhabitants of this city of the sick. They are dressed in odd garments. It looks like some paupers' masquerade. The men in their blue-and-white-striped trousers, wrappers, and caps, many of them with a coarse blanket on top of that. The women wear white skirts and bed jackets, some of them even make some small attempt at adornment by wrapping themselves in their woolen blankets. These are the ambulatory patients who are lucky enough to be allowed to walk about in the court. Of course they are not permitted out into the world, but here they can go about almost as if they were outside. In the huge inner court there is always a great deal of coming and going of doctors, employees, and visitors. The patients seem to feel their prisonlike garb as a mild form of shame; as they pass, they lower their eyes, and that is another characteristic mark of the *Elend*.

And yet these are quite cheerful walks for them. Particularly right now, when our dear young mistress, Spring, comes dancing along over the sunny courtyard, everything is so cheerful and life appears so easy. In fact, and this is amazing, one even comes upon contented, happy faces. And yet a person has to be really sick to pass the test in that foreboding admissions room over there. How to explain it? The hospital must have its own particular brand of happiness. It is not the frightful place that our fear of it makes it appear to be from the outside. At least in spring, the sun manages to shine here, too. Life has such powers of seduction that it can work its magic even in the midst of *Elend*. Most human beings are like those hardy plants that manage to get along quite well even on arid rocks.

For many people the very act of entering the hospital is a comfort. You had to be very sick indeed to get there, that is true, but now, it actually feels good. You suffer pain, of course, but also, what a sense of relief! For many a weary soul, being sick has something good about it. A man can lie in bed so nice and peacefully; he is looked after and cared for. His heavy burden has been laid down. When a worker gets sick, he has mixed feelings of shame and well-being. For a short time, he is socially extinct, like a bankrupt, and yet he breathes the more freely. Gradually there steals over him the joy of nonactivity, which is still not laziness; and from his sickbed, he begins to learn to love life. Then slowly his strength returns. He gets up. He is permitted to go outdoors. This poor hospital courtyard becomes a veritable paradise. Spring outside, spring inwardly. For recovery from sickness is in itself a springtime, and nowhere is it lovelier than in *Elend*. For those who are rich, inactivity is something they are accustomed to, but for the inmates of the hospital, it is a rare, fine addition to the joy of getting well. Many an individual may give himself up to this delight with his spirits aflutter, for fear that they might stop putting up with him any longer if he seemed to be getting along too well.

When the patient is getting better, he goes visiting other courts, perhaps leaning on the arm of some comrade from his own ward who already has gotten some of his strength back. What pleasant walks those are! You get to know other people and their troubles. Really, people aren't so bad; only as a rule, they don't understand each other. In *Elend* they get closer to each other. There is a gentleness in their attitude towards each other. The soul of the convalescent, as though it were a field that has been freshly ploughed, is ready to take in new impressions. What a lot of strange sicknesses there are: unrecognized consumption, frightful nervous afflictions, disturbing occupational diseases, not to mention the leprosy of old, of which the poet Hartmann von Aue tells so delightful a tale. Everyone shrinks away from the lepers. You can recognize them by the distinctive stripes on their clothing. Thus there is an *Elend* within *Elend*. But these very lepers are the ones who seem to show the most eagerness for life; the guard has a hard time chasing away these half-gay, half-impudent patients from the main court, which they are not supposed to enter.

There are more somber courts into which even the spring is unable to bring a smile. If you don't enjoy the thrill of horror, I warn you not to go through that section. The medical students whom you meet there have a solemn look in their young faces, because they have just come from the eternal mystery.

And here is the most friendly court—actually not a place of sickness at all—the maternity court. These women are awaiting their hour, dreaming gently in the sunshine, perhaps of some past disappointment or the future smiles of their little ones. They are quite ordinary simple creatures, who live out their days in complete unawareness, and who none the less are performing their part of the great work of Mother Nature.

All these poor people together make up an entity that must

command our respect: the people! The people from which life springs eternally, the people whose sorrows we must feel and understand, if we ourselves are ever to attain a new morality. The road to the future must go by way of the *Elend*. There everything seems to come together. How much there is for us to learn from this place which is not horrible at all, once we have gotten over our first dread of it. The number of those who die there is greater than anywhere else in the city, but then so is the number of those who are born. In this place the heart of life seems to beat with a stronger heartbeat. Everything human is intensified in a strange sort of way, for suffering elevates and transfigures human beings.

Many a lovely sight is to be seen as we wander thoughtfully through this garden of sorrows. How was it that Hartmann had his poor Heinrich healed? Through the power of love. Really, there is no other place where you can see so much of true love but in a hospital. On that March day of which I speak, a thin, pretty, young girl in patient's garb walked across the great courtyard. She was taking the young man who had come to visit her as far as the gate. Beyond that point she was not permitted to go. He looked poor but neat, his little black jacket was too short and too tight, and the band of his little round hat was of velvet. But to her he was the personification of manly elegance. They said good-bye. He left. He had already disappeared on the other side of the entrance gate. But she still remained watching the place where he had been, with a look of dreamy tenderness, and as she stood in her shabby attire under the trees with their sparse foliage, it was a picture of old-fashioned devotion. Her love exemplifies the same force which drives the tender pale green shoots up out of the dull brown wood. A breath of green hovers over the dark earth. There is a delicate twitter of birds in the twigs. Once again, it is the time to be young.

(1896)

THE DIRIGIBLE

A GOODLY company of men and women were sitting in the twilight under the trees. From the tone of the conversation, in which however only the men participated, you could tell that the women were of the finer sort. They were discussing all sorts of things with the utmost freedom, yet there was no vulgar joking. No one thought of wasting time gossiping or discussing the ordinary news of the day. It is always the women who set the tone in any society since the men take their cue from them, whether it be high or low. In this particular gathering, every now and then, they dared to allow their imaginations free play and to indulge in modern fairy stories which might have sounded foolish in other surroundings.

One of the men, just returned from Paris, told of his trip. He reported on the new styles, but not in the way a couturier might have done; rather he took pains to go into the origin and significance of what he had seen. Then he started on the subject of bicycles, and how they were changing the entire aspect of the city. Who would have dreamed, just a few years ago, of the upheavals for which this mere toy would be responsible? Now horseless carriages were beginning to make their appearance. What sort of changes would they bring about? Every innovation in transportation can effect the most unexpected changes, with repercussions on the welfare and morals of the great mass of the people. New diseases may make their appearance, or else people may grow healthier.

"Das lenkbare Luftschiff," in *Philosophische Erzählungen* (Berlin-Wien, B. Harz Verlag, 1919), pages 27–39.

Right now the conditions under which we live are undergoing more rapid changes than at any other time in history.

For a while they discussed this. Then the doctor remarked: "You know, I'm surprised that no one has yet made any mention of the dirigible airship."

"We have all been thinking of it, though," Robert, the painter, remarked in his quiet way.

"You're right," the Parisian declared, "for it is absolutely sure that it will be invented sooner or later. Perhaps the man is even now alive who is going to provide this greatest of all surprises for the human race. I should like to know how the world will look once that has happened."

"For my part," one of the woman added, "I should like to know what the man who discovers it will look like. I am sure that he will be a great hero, a demigod, at the very least."

"I rather believe, on the contrary," the doctor contradicted her, smiling, "that he will cut a pretty poor figure. Some crotchety, impractical devil. Chances are that he will permit his secret to be stolen from him. Others will get rich on it, and he himself will come off with nothing but a monument— after he is dead. But his life, most likely, will be embittered. Serves him right, too! It's going to be a simple invention, something really quite obvious. We will all wonder how in the world we ever managed to miss it. What an insult to our intelligence! I think that if I were to hear that one of my friends had actually invented the dirigible I would give him a beating. Why should he have done it, and not I?"

At this, Robert, the painter, said in his deep, sonorous voice: "The truth of the matter is that the dirigible has already been invented, and I know the man who invented it."

By now it had grown so dark in the garden that the speaker's features could no longer be distinguished. He was a man who delighted in a twilight sort of tale, midway between fact and fiction. The women all knew this, and so they begged him: "Oh, do tell us all about it, please do!"

And this is the story Robert told:

"His name was Joseph Müller. That is not a particularly

outstanding name, but it's the name his father gave him. Older residents of Laudongasse in the Eighth District [in Vienna] would no doubt remember his father, the cobbler, who used to sit at work in his little shop, looking cheerily out at the world like some ancient Greek philosopher. You will note that I am taking pains to give you these details precisely, so that you won't think that I made this story up out of whole cloth. Doctor, just you go and inquire in the Laudongasse whether a cobbler named Müller didn't formerly live there.

"Joseph was apprenticed to a master toolmaker, and in time he got to be a journeyman. One fine day he invented the dirigible. It seems that he came upon the underlying principle as the result of very considerable and concentrated thinking. I don't know much about physics myself, so that I am afraid that my explanation will leave something to be desired.

"I know only this much, that Joseph Müller started out from the apple. He had observed that an apple in space behaves quite differently from the way the globe does, for example. An apple has to be laid on a table or supported in some other way if it is not to fall to the ground. The globe, on the other hand, floats freely in space. Müller came to the conclusion that motion can be substituted for the support, and that a body can be kept up in the air as long as you please, provided there is a definite correlation between its weight and its velocity, forward and rotational. He worked out precisely what this correlation must be, and he also found in certain explosive gases, whose names escape me at the moment, the necessary force to insure the continuity of the motion. You see, in his spare time he had also studied chemistry, because he had long suspected that motion in the air could be accomplished only by an uninterrupted succession of tiny, controlled explosions. Just how he transmitted the force of the explosions, and just how he controlled the flow of the gases before they were permitted to escape, so that they would propel and steer the craft, I shall not bother to explain in detail. It would only bore the ladies. After all, I am not trying to give you an exact description of the airship but only an account of the strange fate of its inventor.

"For fourteen years, Joseph Müller had cogitated, studied, calculated, and experimented. But he did not neglect his work on that account. He was a conscientious industrious workman and employee. Only for his own pleasure and for possible affairs of the heart did he not have time. Only after he was thirty, in the very year that he made his discovery, did he become acquainted with a sharp-tongued spinster, for whom he suffered the pangs of love. In other respects, he was a very sensible man. That can best be seen in the way he later talked about his invention. According to him, he had made the discovery by the purest chance; no credit was due him at all; he had just happened to stumble upon it while he was experimenting around. Naturally, it proved to be a great emotional shock when he came to the realization that he had solved the problem of flight. In the loneliness of his wretched little room, he burst into tears and sobbed long and loud. For the moment it was only the simple principle that he had hit upon, comparable to the melody; but immediately he knew the full orchestration that he was going to give it; he had a notion of the splendor of the performance, and he already heard the wild acclaim of the audience.

"Then he pulled himself together and started to work out his project in the minutest detail. Once again it required an incredible amount of work. When he had completed his drawings, calculations, and cost estimates, he took them to his employer. He wanted the master toolmaker to join with other toolmakers, and then have this group, augmented by a number of technically trained scientists, issue an appeal to the public to raise the necessary funds. For a vast sum was required—no less than two million gulden. A special factory would have to be built to turn out the parts. In addition, they would have to have special laboratories to produce the gases for the explosions. In short, two million gulden—that was the only way it could be done.

"His employer just laughed at him. He must get rid of such

foolish notions, it was a crazy idea, and no one in his right mind would ever take it seriously. Müller was mortified and slunk away. But his invention had by no means been driven out of his head. He just told himself that he must not count on the good will or co-operation of others. And with his iron determination, he began to look for a practical way out.

"Meanwhile, it had been noised about in the shop that Joseph Müller had gone crazy. The other workmen began to tease him about his dirigible, and at first when they tossed their coarse jokes at him he laughed good-naturedly with them. There was, however, among the other journeymen a certain wag, the sort of clown that you will always find in any group. He behaved particularly badly. For a while Müller did not pay much attention, but one day the buffoon made fun of him in front of the prankish maiden of his dreams, and she laughed so loud and so long that it really cut the poor fellow to the quick. She even added some malicious remarks of her own; but Müller held the fellow responsible for these, too, because he was still in love with her and could not bear to admit how heartless she was. When the man started anew with his tomfoolery the next morning, Müller gave him a good, sound thrashing. They carried the windbag out into the courtyard for dead, but he quickly recovered. Whereupon Joseph Müller went quietly about his work once more, now the object of a certain respect among his comrades.

"A few hours later, his boss called him away from his work; there were two strange gentlemen here who had heard about the dirigible, and they wanted to speak to him. Eagerly, and with great enthusiasm, Joseph Müller explained it all to them. You could see that they were favorably impressed, and they invited him to come with them. He got into their carriage, and they drove him to the insane asylum.

"There were several other inventors of the dirigible there. In his quiet, superior way, Müller made friends with them. He listened patiently to their mad talk. He very quickly recognized his mistake. An inventor such as he is not permitted to let himself go in passionate outbursts in a world where everyone takes offense at anything a man who plans great things may do. No other journeyman would have been taken off to the madhouse for a brawl of that kind. But he bore his fate with equanimity. He enjoyed feeding the birds in the beautiful institution garden; in the spring he listened to their cheery songs; and he noted with the utmost care the manner in which they flew. In this way he came upon a number of improvements for his invention. He was able to instill into the minds of his doctors the idea that he was on the way to recovery. And so, after several months, he was discharged as cured.

"Joseph Müller was by no means stupid, although he was a genius. He had a keen sense of reality. He saw very clearly just what men need in their established routine. He told himself that he would merely have to screw his powers of imagination down to a lower level in order to be regarded as a 'useful' member of society.

"He went to work for a manufacturer of electrical products. Within a short time he had improved several of these so that the man immediately took him into partnership in order not to lose him. There was no longer the slightest mention of a dirigible. However, he did invent a new type of corkscrew, a pants presser, a laundry mangle, a fuel-saving flatiron for tailors—in a word the sort of inventions by which a man wins general acclaim. Beyond that, it must be admitted, he did not get much else out of his inventions because he did not have them patented all over the world. But he got rid of even this last remnant of idealism when he constructed his automatic railway brake. He sold his brake idea for fifty thousand gulden to some promoter who got rich on it. When that frolicsome young lady heard of this, she sidled up to him with a great show of admiration and affection. He handed her some money and told her to stop bothering him. He grew more and more practical, and became more and more honored. Next he invented an indestructible rubber bicycle tube, and made his first million out of that. A new incandescent gas lamp brought him his second million, as well as world fame. Finally he set up a huge factory, turning out powerful locomotives.

"At this point, Joseph Müller turned over all his enterprises to his business executives and left. He had a splendid yacht built which he called *Aegaeon*. He commissioned the wall décor for the dining saloon and lounge of his yacht from me; that is how I got to know him. He was a man of cheerful disposition, self-sufficient and with a hearty contempt for his fellow men. Often, in his fine yacht, he would sail from Trieste to one of the southern Cyclades. No one had the slightest idea what he was doing. Even to his intimates, he would say only that he was building a new factory on some island. If I had been familiar with his earlier history, I might perhaps have guessed what he was secretly up to. I did not find out about it until he invited me and two others for a trip on his *Aegaeon* one spring. While we were aboard, he told us his story. He had wanted nothing more than to be a successful inventor, not one of those martyrs to progress who are made to suffer all their lives. That is why he had followed the practical course, from corkscrew to locomotive.

"By the time night fell we had reached the island. At the top of the rock we could see the outlines of tall buildings, from many of which myriads of electric lights gleamed. Müller said good night to us; he himself boarded a small boat to go ashore. The three of us stayed up on deck chatting for perhaps an hour. Suddenly, at almost the same moment, the three of us cried out. For the dark front wall of one of the buildings high up there had dropped or been lowered, and a great flood of light poured out over the ocean. Through a wide opening there rushed, rumbled, and roared out something enormous, with gleaming eyes. The thing had disappeared into the night before we could regain our composure, and deeply moved the three of us cried out, 'The airship!'

"The hours that followed were exciting. We waited in vain for the return of the strange bird. At last, worn out by lack of sleep, we all dozed off in our deck chairs. At the first gleam of the sun's rays, Müller woke us with a laugh:

" 'I fancy you have already seen my *Halcyon*, haven't you? Last night, I flew over Constantinople and Cyprus in her. Now, in daylight, I should like to show her to you.'

"He led the way up the hill. In the building which was lo-

cated close to the steep side of the cliff, and which looked somewhat like a boathouse, the *Halcyon* was resting on iron tracks.
It rather resembled a dragonfly in shape. Its solid parts were
made of aluminum; its soft ones of white silk carefully pieced
together out of hundreds of tiny scraps. Müller stepped into
the wondrous craft and with a gesture beckoned us to follow
him. We did. My heart beat fast. Two Greek youths who were
versed in the intricacies of air travel fastened us into our seats
with safety belts and then jumped quickly on board. Müller
gave the signal, and we glided outward and upward. At first
I was overwhelmed with fright, but soon I experienced a
great sense of freedom and exhilaration. We were sitting behind a wedge-shaped crystal windshield and felt no discomfort whatsoever, no matter how fast we rushed along. But
every now and again we hovered in the air motionless or
streaked downwards in a wide spiral, with the *Halcyon*'s
shimmering wings extended like an eagle's. When we got too
close to the water, all that was necessary was to press a certain
button, and that would drive us up at an angle once more.
One of the Greeks had a golden stringed instrument and in
a jubilant voice kept singing ancient verses to it. I took the
harp and began to sing the 'Spring Song' from *Die Walküre*.
All of us sang—ordinary speech was wholly inadequate. Only
the captain of the *Halcyon* sat silent and deep in thought,
while he steered us through the air.

"In this way we passed two whole days skimming over the
various coasts of the Mediterranean. Joseph Müller had arranged for way stations on the tops of several mountains where
our craft could be refueled. It was a wonderful opportunity to
see the world from above.

"On the third day, we had to embark once more on the
Aegaeon. We were surprised to see that there was a metal
towline connecting the *Halcyon* with our yacht, and that we
kept trailing her along behind us like a corpse. No one of us
had the courage to ask the captain what it meant. He appeared strangely distant and unapproachable. Once we were
far out at sea, he gave the command for the chain to be
loosened. The floating airship had been connected with the

Aegaeon by a thin wire which kept unwinding from some sort of huge reel. We had already left the delicate air-traveler far behind. What we could see dancing out there on the waves resembled nothing so much as a dead seagull. Now Müller came to us and said:

" 'This is where I shall take leave of the *Halcyon*. I have kept my promise to myself, and that is the main thing. A few of my good friends know what I have done. I do not have the slightest wish to do anything for mankind in general. When I was poor and helpless, they tormented me. When I grew stronger, they sickened me by the miserable way they behaved. Corkscrews and fuel-saving flatirons and incandescent-gas lamps are good enough for them. The race of man is not worthy to fly. Crawling on their bellies is good enough for them.'

"He smiled, and pressed a button. We heard the dull roar of an explosion. Where the *Halcyon* had been skimming along on the surface of the Mediterranean, the water churned and foamed in an enormous rush of spray. From way back there, bits of the white silk of the wings were wafted up front to where we were. Our hearts were heavy as we sailed farther and farther over the wine-colored waters . . . "

Robert had come to a halt. For a long time it seemed as though his story were still trembling on the quiet air.

Finally the doctor cried out: "Your Joseph Müller was really not so stupid at all. His *Halcyon* would surely have come to no good end. First of all, it would have been misused for warfare, and then it would have been made to serve the well-being of only a few power- and money-greedy men even while it spread new forms of misery among the poor."

"You are too socialistic for my taste, my good friend," the Parisian replied. "Müller was all wrong. In the first place, he did not fully understand the significance of his discovery. He should not have thought only of the people of his own time, and least of all the miserable creatures in his immediate environment. A man who wants to pave the way for the future must be able to look beyond the present. In days to come there will be better human beings than we have today."

One of the women, however, turned to the storyteller, and her gentle voice seemed to sparkle through the still evening air: "For true greatness your hero lacked one thing—and that was the power of forgiveness."

(1896)

[*Concerning this feuilleton, we find the following entries in Herzl's diaries.*]

May 12, 1896

Great things do not need to have a firm foundation. An apple must be put on the table so that it should not fall. The earth swims in space.

In the same way I may perhaps found and secure the Jewish State without a firm hold on anything.

The secret lies in movement. I believe that on this principle the dirigible airship will ultimately be invented. Weight is to be overcome by motion. And not the ship, but the movement, is to be steered.

June 1, 1896

My yesterday's feuilleton, "Das lenkbare Luftschiff," was quite generally understood as an allegory of *The Jewish State*.

THE GOOD THINGS OF LIFE

Four young men, fresh from the university, sat together one evening twenty years ago to say farewell. They knew their paths would separate, now that they had won their diplomas. They had seen some merry times together at school, and a sense of gravity came over them at the thought of taking leave of one another.

"Life is upon us," one of them said.

"It's true," sighed the second. "I wonder how it will be for us."

"The real question is, what will become of us?" the third one remarked.

But the fourth declared: "I think that will depend in large measure on ourselves. If there is any meaning to these long studies that have taken up our youth, it can only be to send us out into life as men of character. No longer does chance toss us this way or that. We ourselves are at the helm of the ship. I know what I'm after, though I don't know whether I'll reach it. Even so, I've already been raised above the vulgar throng, because I have this consciousness of self."

"And what do you mean to gain by your conscious self?" he was asked.

"I don't think you'll like my answer, but I'll give it to you truthfully. I want wealth."

"That's a vulgar enough dream," said Wilhelm, who had been the first to speak.

"Nonsense! You're the one who's mooning, while I keep my feet on the ground. I want wealth because in our society it

"Die Güter des Lebens," in *Philosophische Erzählungen* (Berlin-Wien, B. Harz Verlag, 1919), pages 149–162.

means everything. Turn up your nose all you want, Milord. What is it you want of life?"

The young man they had dubbed Milord compressed his lips a little and said dryly, "Honors!"

"You're a pack of fools," said the one who had heaved a sigh before. "You want to become a millionaire and you a titled gentleman. What about happiness? Unless you take happiness into account, you're no better than a herd of cattle, with all due respect! A man should seek only what will serve to make him happy—a decent living to make a home for his sweetheart."

"Go sing us a song about your Amy!" mocked the incipient millionaire.

"Alas, Romeo he is and will die of love!" remarked Milord.

"I should like to see you twenty years from now," cried the butt of these gibes, without losing his composure. "Then we should see which of us was the real damfool. Let's make it a date—but something a little better than the usual graduate pledge. Twenty years hence—let only those of us meet here who have really reached their goal. Will it be all four of us? Or only three, perhaps two, a single one—none?"

"Not a bad idea!" said the Millionaire. "Let only him come who has won the success he sought. We've mentioned wealth, honors, domestic happiness, and—say there, Wilhelm, you haven't formulated your demands on life!"

"Well," replied Wilhelm, "you seem to have no doubts about the matter. I have. As I was listening to you, Schopenhauer's three categories were passing through my mind: what a man is, what he does, what he represents. The Great Pessimist lists only these three basic categories for the good things that life aims at. But aren't there others? I can't tell you at this point, for I haven't quite come to terms with myself, as you have. It's in my mind, but I can't put it into words. Perhaps I can come closest to it by saying: that which fulfills a man."

"You aren't saying anything very definite," declared Milord.

"Never mind," said the Millionaire. "He's a good fellow despite his dim aspirations."

But they firmly agreed to hold the reunion. They would meet again twenty years from now, in this very taproom by the ancient campus—if success had attended each on his own terms—and they pledged to give an account of the good things in life they had attained, an account as forthright as they had given this day. . . .

The twenty years passed by, as years will. At first they dragged on, at a wretched snail's pace. Day upon day had to be mastered at the cost of struggle, care, deprivation, and anxiety. Then the pace of time began to quicken, for as one grows older the years grow wings. In the beginning the friends saw one another often, but later on meetings became rarer. As for the reunion of success, they reminded one another of the agreement from time to time, both in jest and in earnest, so that the memory of it stayed fresh. When only half the span of years had elapsed it was already clear that the two who were after wealth and honors would indeed attend. There was ample evidence that they were well on their way. The other two were lost in the mass of mediocrities.

When the appointed day came, Wilhelm was the first to appear at the old meeting place, at the same hour as before. Next came the one whom they had nicknamed Romeo. The two of them shook hands but then had to stand in the street and wait, for the student tavern had long since shut down, when the university moved far away to its new, palatial quarters. Wilhelm looked a little shabby in his threadbare suit. Romeo had acquired a paunch and when he doffed his hat the lamplight was reflected from his bald pate.

"Strange that we should be the first," he said in astonishment. "Are we to be the only ones?"

"I suppose you didn't even expect me at all," Wilhelm smiled.

Just then a splendid carriage drove up behind a fine team of horses. The lean figure that descended, nervously flinging a few words to the coachman, was the Millionaire of yore. He offered Wilhelm his right hand and at the same time Romeo his left.

"Well, to be sure, it's out on the street for us," he said. "We thought our own hopes might go bankrupt, but we never thought the inn could, too."

"We're doing better," Romeo chuckled. "Three of us on hand, a fair percentage at that. Could it be that we live in the best of all possible worlds? I can't understand why His Excellency isn't here. Surely he has reason enough."

"Rather too much," said the Millionaire. "Perhaps he's afraid he'll have to tell us how he managed it all, how he weaseled himself into high places, how he managed to marry that homely woman with the family connections that served to pave his way."

At that moment a smartly dressed gentleman turned the corner, glancing behind him as though concerned lest someone trail him into this unkempt little side-street. It was His Excellency.

"All present and accounted for!" cried Romeo. "I wouldn't have believed it. Well, we can't very well stay here. Does anyone know where the Green Wreath Tavern is?"

"We do look like a gang of conspirators," whispered His Excellency. "I would prefer a quiet, congenial spot for our get-together."

"Some place where we're not likely to be observed," the Millionaire remarked meaningfully.

"I have a suggestion," said Wilhelm. "I have a place quite near by where we won't be disturbed. It isn't much of a place, I should tell you."

"So much the better," exclaimed the rich man. "It will take us back to the old times. I'll send the carriage away."

He did so, and they walked a few blocks, with Wilhelm in the lead. He halted in front of a dilapidated house.

"Here we are."

His companions were no little taken aback.

"Where's the Green Wreath?" moaned Romeo.

"You won't die of thirst," Wilhelm countered. "Come along."

They crossed a dark courtyard. Beneath a lamp and beside a door hung a sign: "Employment Exchange." They entered an anteroom onto which gave several rooms. Cards on the doors said: "Dining Room"; "Reading Room"; "Office." A bell had tinkled at their entry and a young man came to meet them from the dining room. For a moment the door stood open and they caught a glimpse of a long table around which ill-clad men sat humbly enjoying a meal.

"What an inspiration!" said the Millionaire. "He's taken us to a soup kitchen! Will we at least have a private room?"

"Of course," Wilhelm laughed. "You're not going to the soup kitchen, by the way, but to my quarters."

His Excellency stifled a remark and inwardly regretted that he had not been more discriminating in his youthful associations. A table for four had been neatly but unpretentiously set in the office. Some maps and charts hung on the walls. There was a glass case with models of the kind used in craft instruction. One could see into a second cubicle, furnished only with an iron bedstead, a washstand, and a wardrobe.

"That's where I live," said Wilhelm. "I anticipated that you would follow me and arranged for a supper. It may strike you as a bit modest, but it's quite a treat for this house. I'd rather my protégés out there didn't know about it. Beer isn't permitted on the premises. Wine is reserved for the ailing and undernourished."

"Apparently you are exempting us from the rules and regulations," exclaimed the Millionaire. "You seem to be the lord and master here!" His eyes twinkled merrily at His Excellency, as though to say: The man must be stark raving mad!

Wilhelm nodded soberly. Then he had his young assistant serve the meal. By and by chilly spirits began to thaw. Romeo pronounced the beer quite acceptable. The Millionaire went so far as to discover a peculiar fascination in savoring the Sunday fare of the poor—a real change. Soon old memories came to the fore and the diners grew visibly younger over their talk. Even His Excellency lost his initial stiffness, and by the time the table was cleared the companions had almost regained the informal tone of old. Wilhelm dismissed the steward with a gesture.

"We have kept our word," he began, "to ourselves and to one another. This is our celebration of success and now we must fulfill our pledge. Each of us is to report on the good things of life he has gained. I must point out to you that our confessions will have little value unless they are sincere. You will remember the homely way our good Romeo put it twenty years ago—we were to find out which of us has been the real damfool. What we had in mind when we made our philosophical wager was the inward meaning of success, for what we represent to the outside world is something we have already made known to each other, even though we have drifted far apart in life. And I suspect that once this meeting is over we shall again pursue our separate ways. For that very reason we should now display the love of truth that marks the true philosopher. I think we shall sense whether any of us speaks from the heart or not. Who'll be the first?"

"I will," said the Millionaire. "I'll show you I'm not afraid to confess the truth. I must say, Wilhelm, at first this background made you appear a little—peculiar. . . ."

"Come right out and say mad!" Wilhelm interjected.

"But there's something in what you said that touches me on the raw. Well, what I planned was simply to tell you that I have indeed reached my goal. A million, I said at the time. If it's possible to reach a goal ten times over, I've done it."

"Ten millions?" Romeo gasped.

"I'll be damned!" murmured His Excellency.

"Something like that—I couldn't give you the exact figures until my next balance sheet is drawn up. But I want to balance my books right here. That's what you have in mind, Wilhelm, isn't it? Assets and liabilities. I slaved during those early years. No one will ever know just how I slaved. My sheepskin I tossed by the boards almost as soon as I had it. The law was too trifling and barren a career for me."

"Thank you, indeed," said Romeo.

"Forgive me. I forgot that you're an attorney. What I meant is that one can't get rich at the bar. I went into railroading, which seemed most promising to me. I started at the very bottom, as a local agent. Friends, you have no idea what a life that is, banished to a godforsaken depot, working fourteen and sixteen hours at a stretch. It's both stultifying and nerve-wracking, at one and the same time. One is responsible for every last train that roars down the tracks. One has one foot in jail, the other in the grave. As it happened, I was assigned to a timber region and had to do with deliveries of ties. I got to know the suppliers and the lumber business, in which there are ways to work up to something big. I decided to change over and took a job with a lumber firm. Again the work was hard. Within a year or so I opened up my own business, on a pitifully small scale. Have you ever watched an ant climbing over a pebble with a morsel in its jaws? How it slips, loses its prize, regains it, tries once more? I was ruined several times, but always came back. It took energy beyond imagination, and I'll never know where I found it. I do know I wouldn't like to go through it again for anything. I had neither time nor inclination to marry, at first because I was so badly off, later on because I was too well off. I poured all my profits into new enterprises—but the details would only bore you. In any event, I'm on top."

"And how are things on top?" Wilhelm inquired.

"Not quite as they are pictured in the popular success stories. It's true, if I suddenly stopped working, I'd probably die of boredom. But I don't stop, I keep up the mad chase. Will I come a cropper in the end? Will I have to come to you, Wilhelm, and beg for a bowl of soup like those men out there? Actually that uncertainty is about the only thing that still fascinates me in life. I'm not gregarious, because I know people too well. Everyone wants something of me. As for you, my friends, if I hadn't pledged myself to this reunion when I was still a penniless lad, I would have shunned you like the plague. . . . Forgive me!"

His Excellency cleared his throat: "I will say, you're calling a spade a spade, but I suppose the utmost frankness is indicated at this unusual meeting. Well, I won't let you outstrip me in truthfulness. I too have found my goal—indeed, more than I asked for. I can put it even more briefly than you. Once I sought patrons. Now I'm a patron myself. True, I must still bow and scrape and probably always will. I envied you as you related your adventures in pursuit of wealth, even though the balance sheet was not all to the good. At least you could lay about you. The likes of me are fettered in their honors. It is as though one were confined to a room with mirrored walls all about and nowhere a restful place to get away from oneself. If you were to make a single uncontrolled movement, the chances are you would smash a mirror. And the constant humiliation! People salute my title and position rather than myself. It doesn't seem to matter who is cloaked in the robes of office, I or another. I used to feel hurt when a superior failed to take notice of me. Now I know it was of no importance. The worst thing is the servile obeisance of a subordinate. How well I remember why I paid homage to everyone above me! Now they do it to me, and for the same reason. The whole thing isn't worth a pinch of snuff. What matters is to have children, a few strapping children, and to live in obscurity. Our worthy Romeo was right."

"I was right, I was right," Romeo mused, rubbing his bald pate. "I wonder if I really was! Listening to you, I think I am; but I wasn't so sure before. My sights weren't raised as high as yours, hence I had an easier time reaching my goal. I worked to win my wife like Jacob in the Bible. For I served seven years in the law office of my prospective father-in-law, as his clerk and finally his partner. He died and now the practice is mine, a fair living. I can afford to have spring frocks made for my good wife and to see that my children get a good education. We're all in good health. I often tell myself that I have every reason to thank God that all my ambitions have been fulfilled and that I am content in heart."

There was a brief pause. Somehow the sentence sounded unfinished. When the attorney still hesitated, one of his friends asked:

"Still, something seems to trouble you?"

"Yes, there is something. At times I have a strange feeling—not so often by day, when I am busy with many things. Usually it comes over me at night. I wake up to the nocturnal stillness. I don't know what to call it. Fear? A sense of emptiness? Perhaps it is dread of death—unless it be the fear of living. I know my wife and children are close by; I can hear them breathe, snore. Yet I have a feeling of utter loneliness and I despair of ever knowing why I am here. I suppose it will last another twenty or thirty years. I shall continue to win some of my cases and lose others. I shall pay my taxes and butcher bills. I shall collect my accounts. But why? Can anyone tell me to what end?"

"I'm afraid there's no answer to that," said the rich man softly.

Wilhelm took the floor. "Well, we have heard about the deprivations of wealth, the humiliations that come with honors, the frustrations that haunt family life. Now listen to my life and the reasons why I was bold enough to attend the reunion, though I am nothing, have nothing, and represent nothing. After graduation I tried my hand at writing for a time. Then a small inheritance enabled me to give up that occupation, which only fills you up to here with disgust because of the envy, intrigue, and nepotism you find everywhere in it. I traveled. In England and France I learned about modern movements of social welfare, and here you witness my modest efforts to follow in their path. I live among poor and ignorant people whom misery brings to my doorstep. Once I have cheered and fed them a little, they go on their way. A staff of high-minded young men soon rallied to my side. We bring useful training to the poor, and not political catchwords. It seems to me that all the new discoveries and inventions should not profit those alone who already have enough. I teach my good people how grand and vast and fair is God's world, that they must not strike the flag at the first setback. I teach them to hope by showing them our great cultural achievements. For we live in a time that reminds one of the glorious age of the Renaissance and the Reformation."

"Tell me," interjected the Millionaire with a cynical smile, "don't you often find your watch missing after such a lecture? Do you keep books on ingratitude?"

"I have none because I expect no thanks. Whenever there is a new arrival I say to myself: Welcome, ingrate."

"The man's an altruist," His Excellency remarked bitingly.

But Wilhelm concluded unshaken: "The good things of my life, you see, are my sense of fulfillment. It's the thought of the future. Truly, the future is a season of springtime. This takes the sting even from the thought of my own passing. I am a citizen of the future even now, because I serve on behalf of the future. Did not the Great Pessimist himself always address his Congregation to Come? He too, above and beyond his negation, believed in the future. This is the only thing in which one is never disappointed."

"Because it is never attained," the lawyer added.

(1898)

SOLON IN LYDIA

SOLON was in the prime of his years and powers when he resolved to leave the City of Athens. His laws were inscribed on the tablets, but to the citizens they were still all too new. Day after day men came from all the districts to regard the code of Solon with astonishment or misgivings. His friend Hipponicus addressed him thus:

"You see that your laws displease all classes of taxpayers."

"Because they are new, Hipponicus. My laws are not yet good, but neither are they bad. Young laws in some respects resemble wine. They must mellow."

"Dear Solon, you have satisfied none. I do not wonder that the Pentakosiomedimnes, the Knights, and even the Zeugites are against you, for you are a friend of the fourth class, to which you yourself do not belong. Even the Thetes are muttering under their breath, and if they did not worship you so blindly because you have eased their burden of debt they would probably rise against you."

"Laws, dear Hipponicus, cannot please all. Only a fool, a dreamer, or perhaps a scoundrel would seek to satisfy anyone with legislation. Law can rest only on the dissatisfaction of all."

"A tyrant would agree with you."

"But he would not say it, my dear Hipponicus. The secret purpose of my laws was to create a state of tolerable dissatisfaction on the part of all. This state has now been reached. My only concern is to maintain it. That I alone can do."

"Then you desire to become king, Solon?"

"Solon in Lydien," in *Philosophische Erzählungen* (Berlin-Wien, B. Harz Verlag, 1919), pages 3–23.

130

"Of course not! How little you understand me—you who are my friend! True, I am quite capable of making that sacrifice, too, of taking the seat of my exalted ancestor Codrus in the Acropolis. Who of the Eupatrids would prevent me? But why should I repeat the adventure of Cylon? For I should soon be made to look like Cylon and my code would appear to have been contrived for my own advantage. Demagogues would exploit the unrest that is the secret virtue of my laws. Even now I am worried over my own power, because it poses a danger to my laws. Every day men come to me from the coast and the hills, asking whether there is no way of softening my ordinances. As the First Archon, they say, I, the all-powerful, should be able to do as I please. But shall I, like Penelope, unravel by night what I have woven by day? Then again there are others, mainly among the small craftsmen, who want to know why some of the laws have been enacted. It would be a waste of time—indeed, it would be harmful—to try to explain to the individual what becomes comprehensible only from the viewpoint of the state. There are severities in my laws, and sometimes I am filled with pity for those whom I must hurt. I would feel better if I could lay down my office as archon. But in an emergency they would always recall me, for in all Attica I am the only one whom all trust. Then the day would come when I would breach my own laws, from compassion or to retain popular favor. I am a man, Hipponicus, and I distrust my own weakness."

"It is indeed a difficult situation," said Hipponicus thoughtfully. "And what do you propose to do? I read some resolve in your eyes."

"I had thought of dying. It would be noble to drain the hemlock cup. No one would be left with sufficient authority to alter my tablets. But Athens still needs me. Lycurgus and Miltiades son of Cypselus and Megacles and my kinsman Pisistratus would probably tear the land to shreds upon my death. Pisistratus, who will probably recruit the disaffected Diacrians, I regard as most dangerous, because of his great charm. Hence I propose to arrange matters so that I shall not be altogether lost to the people even though I withdraw from them. I shall undertake a long journey. I shall ask the citizens to give me leave. By the time I return my laws will have become flesh of their flesh. In my absence none will dare alter my work, for fear of my avenging return. Solon afar is more terrible than Solon seen day after day. In this way shall I guard my tablets against parties and tyrants, and against myself."

Solon did as he had proposed. It was his notion to stay away from his homeland for ten years. He explained to the citizens that, having fulfilled his duties as archon, he must now attend to his own affairs. For he sought no advantage from the state. He was a merchant and desired to be nothing else.

Solon's departure distressed the Athenians greatly, and the general dissatisfaction turned to gratitude and affection as the legislator took his leave. A fair wind blew him across the wine-hued sea. Lovingly he looked back over the coast of Attica, paling and vanishing in a sunny haze. His breast heaved with sighs and his eyes were brimming with tears. The Muse became his solace, and as the ship slipped past the rosy-tinted Cyclades—past Andros, Tenos, Naxos, and later Rhodes—into the Carpathian Sea, Solon banished sorrow from his soul in felicitous hexameters. As in the days of his youth, he was now all poet and merchant.

In Egypt, where he tarried a while, Psenophis of Heliopolis and Sonchis of Sais were the companions of his meditations. To these shrewd and learned priests he owed his first knowledge of the Island of Atlantis, which on fine days had gleamed beyond the Pillars of Hercules, only to vanish beneath the surface of the sea because of its magnificence. Having drunk in the wisdom of Egypt, Solon went on. On Cyprus he was the welcome guest of a ruler whose royal hospitality he repaid in Solonic fashion. The capital, Aepeia, was situated on an unsuitable knoll. Solon counseled and aided the king in moving the whole city down to a splendid plain. For Solon's eye was ever directed toward grandeur and the welfare of mankind. In honor of the high-minded Athenian, the king named the new city Soli.

Thence Solon traveled to Sardis and Croesus, the fabulously

rich king of the Lydians. Croesus, in the manner of vulgar people, at first sought to impress Solon by displaying his treasures. The Greek regarded this ostentation with courteous indifference, failing to express the admiration Croesus had expected, which pained the vain overlord of Lydia. Yet Croesus remained well-disposed toward his guest, patiently putting up even with Solon's constant philosophic observations on the true nature of happiness. What if Solon, in his voluntary exile, did profess that none could be called happy until the day of his death?—why, Croesus knew better. He was happy. Wealthy Lydia was his and did his bidding. There was nothing to fear, neither from Greeks nor from Persians. At home there was a tranquillity that made ruling the purest pleasure. Added to this were the joys of family life. Croesus had a blossoming daughter, named Omphale after the legendary queen of Lydia and lovely to behold in her maidenhood. And Croesus was ingenious too in filling his life with exquisite enjoyments. He created pleasures of the spirit, without which wealth and power can please only coarse minds. He entertained artists and philosophers with grace, and the greatest figures of Hellas were his friends. At this time, for example, Aesop, the teller of fables, was his guest at Sardis. To this enlightened poet Croesus revealed in confidence his surprise at Solon's coldness.

"Do not wonder, O King," cried Aesop. "Such is the way of sages. They are not taken with the passing scene. They toy forever with the thought of eternity, like kittens with a skein of wool."

Solon tarried long at Sardis, and in time Croesus conceived great respect for the Athenian, so inflexible yet mild in spirit. One day they were gathered at a love feast, the king, the Attic statesman, and the poet of the fables, their heads wreathed with roses. Croesus had drained his cup with fewer words than usual. Neither dancers nor flute players managed to dispel the frown from his brow, the while his two companions were sunk in halcyon dreams. In the end Aesop took note of the king's mood.

"I shall tell you the reason, my friends," spoke the king, waving to the slaves to go. "Today," he continued, "the gravest challenge of my reign has come to me, as suddenly as fate. Never before have I implored the gods so fervently to point the way."

"What is it, Croesus?" said Solon calmly.

"A youth of Ionic descent, from Bolissus on Chios, appeared before me to ask the hand of my daughter Omphale."

"Is he of royal blood?" inquired Aesop.

"He may be more than any king," Croesus replied, "though his father labors only as a poor artisan at Bolissus."

"I do not understand," Solon remarked.

And Croesus said: "The youth maintains he has found something that will forever banish human want from the world. He offers it to me, or rather to the Lydians—indeed, to all mankind. He asks, as his only reward, my Omphale, whom he professes to love dearly."

"The lad has good taste," Aesop chuckled.

But Solon probed further: "What is this means he says he has found?"

"Let him explain it to you in person," cried Croesus and ordered the youth to be summoned.

Eucosmos of Bolissus entered. He was a fine figure of a man, wearing the Ionic chiton with a flair. His countenance was as of milk and blood and his cheeks gleamed from under a youthful beard of light brown. His blue eyes, proud and smiling, commanded the scene.

"Eucosmos," said the king gently, "these are my friends. You may speak freely before them, as you spoke to me. Tell us about your panacea."

"Here it is," Eucosmos said in a vibrant voice that went straight to the heart of his listeners. And he flourished a small bag.

"What have you there? Gold?" inquired Aesop.

"More than that!" Eucosmos smiled. "Much more than gold! . . . Flour!"

The amused teller of fables turned to Solon. "Our royal host must be playing a joke."

"No," cried Croesus impatiently. "It is quite in earnest. At least, so he insists. Speak, Eucosmos!"

"It is flour!" reiterated the youth from Bolissus. "Flour I myself have made."

Aesop held his sides with laughter: "Indeed! You tilled the soil, harvested the grain, and ground it to meal betwixt stones. I seem to have heard of that before."

The eyes of Eucosmos were fixed calmly beyond Aesop's head. "I plowed no acre, reaped no crop, hence could not mill it. I made this flour in different fashion."

"In different fashion?" Solon muttered.

"Yet it is the equal of the finest wheat flour," Croesus added. "The bread on which we dined was baked of it."

"Its taste was exquisite." Aesop marveled.

"Do not play tricks on us, lad," Solon now upbraided the youth. "The king may fall in with your jest, but respect for our years should keep you from repeating such nonsense."

Eucosmos replied calmly: "I know you are Solon, and I honor you. I swear by the eternal Zeus that it is as I say. I have found a way of making flour without the fruit of the fields. I make it from a substance that occurs in nature in inexhaustible amount. I can make as much of it as I please, with trifling effort. One man, in a single day, can, by my method, do what would take hundreds of peasants a year."

"Describe your method," Solon said, "or I shall despise you as a liar."

"I own nothing but my secret," Eucosmos replied. "The king knows my price. It is that or nothing else in the world. I should sooner be torn to pieces. True, I might slowly turn it to gold, if I craved base profit. But whom the gods have vouchsafed such a treasure must surrender his gift only for something equally precious. On the day my wish is fulfilled I shall give mankind bread for ever, bread without sweat or blight, bread to surfeit to the end of time . . ."

"We have heard you," said Croesus, shaken. "Go hence and await my verdict."

"If this is true," Aesop remarked, "what is to keep him from beginning by making flour for the poor? Why should they starve a single hour without reason? Keep your secret to yourself for the nonce, my dear Eucosmos. If you have a heart and wish to please others likewise endowed, then begin by being magnanimous."

"Gladly!" said Eucosmos. "All I ask is the king's promise that no attempt be made to watch me surreptitiously or extract my secret by stealth."

"Eucosmos, you have my royal word!"

The youth bowed and departed.

"Well, what do my friends say?" said Croesus when they were alone.

"Give him your daughter, king of Lydia," Aesop cried fervently.

"And what is your counsel, Solon?"

"Put him to death!"

Croesus and Aesop turned to the Athenian in consternation. A strange fire burned in Solon's look.

The king was the first to regain his composure. "You mean, Solon, if he had deceived me?"

"No, king of the Lydians! Put him to death if he has spoken the truth!"

"Solon, I do not understand you!" moaned Aesop. "You would have mankind's greatest benefactor executed?"

"I should not hesitate a moment," Solon declared.

"But I shall!" cried Croesus. "True, I am angry at the lad for daring to reach out his hand for my daughter. But to kill him?—I would not dream of such a thing."

"Then you are unworthy to be a king," Solon replied with cold fury.

Aesop grew anxious and sought to intercede, but Croesus smiled:

"I am king enough to suffer the harsh words of any man. Finish your thought, dear Solon!"

"My thoughts, Croesus, are simple as always—as simple as yours. The only difference lies in my sense of time. It is for that reason, I believe, that the Athenians did well to entrust me with making their laws. You measure an advantage in terms of hours, weeks, or at best years—while eons sift through my fingers. . . . That young man represents one of the greatest dangers the world has ever faced. Let me not speak to you in the language of children or pious folk, else would I indict the blasphemer who dares meddle in the destiny of the immortal gods, preventing Persephone from descending into the underworld. We are men who have peered behind the veil. We know what is behind the hierophantism of Eleusis. The earth brings forth fruit not because Demeter so wills it, but because it is steeped in the sweat of the tiller. And this lad would change all that! He would rid mankind of care, the knave! He would rob it of the best thing it has: hunger! What then? Shall we return to the rude age of the Pelasgians? Shall settled life and morality vanish in the wake of agriculture? . . . King of the Lydians, put him to death—if you are indeed a king!"

"Solon, you are crushing me!" Croesus groaned.

"A king must know when to kill," Solon went on relentlessly. "Not merely the wicked, the malefactors—that is easy and agreeable. He must exterminate the good as well, if the people's welfare so demands. This, too, you must achieve—that is why there is no earthly power above you. Indeed, such is the secret justification for your power. The teller of fables may find me heartless. Let him! Picture me in your verses as a raging beast, Aesop! You deserve to be popular. But I say to you, there is no greater deed to be done in this our age than to destroy that luminous youth to whom my heart went out at first sight. I shall weep for him when he dies; but I should weep more bitterly were he to live. When we murder him, we shall have struck a blow for Hellas and the world, and that shall be our reward. It will be a quiet deed of grandeur, one of these lofty achievements beyond the ken of common man, unheralded by history, unsung by Homer."

"Hold!" said the King, deeply moved. "It has not yet been settled."

"Thanks be to the gods!" Aesop exclaimed in relief. "I shall offer a special sacrifice to Musagetes, in gratitude for having saved me from a public career. . . . Listen to me, dear Solon! Suppose all is as you say. How can you know whether another will not tomorrow find what Eucosmos found today? Chance brought him here, of all places, made him love Omphale, caused us to be the witnesses. Another we might not know, yet he too would abolish hunger, an end I, for one, would not mourn. For I, Solon, have known the taste of hunger. Perhaps that is why I am a poet of the people."

"I honor your reasoning, Aesop," Solon replied. "It is indeed possible that Eucosmos will have a successor. But the question is: When? It may be a matter of thousands of years. These will have been won for mankind, rather than lost, as you believe in your poetic benevolence. Consider the heights to which Greek culture has risen compared to older ages. This we owe to hunger, which taught us the value of work. At its highest, work is ennobled into art, just as pondering one's own advantage may be enhanced to the loftiest peaks of philosophy. Who knows what Island of Atlantis may yet await the discoverer on unknown shores? I can conceive that in times to come men will travel from Athens to Corinth in swifter chariots than we. I can even imagine ships more seaworthy than our mightiest triremes. Do not hobble my vision! Perhaps, on some far-off cloudless day in history, man will no longer need the goad of hunger. I cannot see that far. . . . Croesus, put that lad Eucosmos to death! . . . You still hesitate? Very well, I have a proposal to make to you. There is one man who is wisest of all the Greeks. Let him settle our dispute."

"Thales of Miletus?" Aesop said.

"Thales!" Solon confirmed. "Make the whole matter known to him. Our friend Aesop will write it down with his customary clarity. Say nothing to me. Let Thales judge without prejudice. I shall accept his verdict."

"Excellent!" cried Croesus, glad of the chance to escape an immediate decision. "Let Thales tell us where lies our duty in this unprecedented case."

The next morning a royal courier hastened to Miletus. A reply from the sage was soon received. "King!" it read. "You must grant me time for contemplation. In so grave a question of conscience I cannot at once give you my final word."

Months passed by. No further news was received from

Thales. Croesus dispatched another messenger to Miletus. He returned with a curious intelligence. Thales was away on a journey and none knew where he had gone. Croesus shook his head in perplexity, but Solon said:

"Never mind! Thales always knows what he is about. You will yet hear his judgment and savor it like a ripe fruit."

In Sardis things did not stand still. Eucosmos had become a welcome companion of the king and his friends. The grace of his spirit, his keen and virile serenity, were a source of unending delight to them. Solon loved him most of all. Often he would say to the youth: "When I return from exile to see my son again, I only hope he will resemble you!"

On such occasions Croesus would take him aside and ask him: "Do you still cling to your opinion?"

"Indeed I do!" was Solon's unvarying reply.

No one barred Eucosmos' way to the lovely Omphale. He confessed his love to her, and it was spring.

It was spring when Omphale replied to him: "Eucosmos, I too love you and I will become your wife when your ordeal is over."

For all she knew was that her father had imposed upon her suitor an indefinite time of trial.

It was a strange springtime in Lydia, bringing joy and lassitude to the people. An inexplicable flood of wealth had poured out upon the land. At least there were no more beggars or folk in want. It had begun some months before, with the distribution of free flour, made in the name of the king, in Sardis and throughout the towns and communities in the land. In the beginning only the poorest of the poor accepted the gift. But by and by, since the supply seemed as inexhaustible as the benevolence of their good ruler, and since anyone might take away as much flour as he needed for his household, others came. Flour was as plentiful as water from the public wells. A few sought an explanation for this wondrous event and managed to ferret out that Croesus, by dint of a skillful foreign policy, had succeeded in importing vast supplies of bread grain. But most people accepted the situation without question, happy at the boon from above, until in the end they took it for granted.

True, there were some who were irked—peasants, land-owners, merchants. The price of grain fell and even acres already planted were abandoned. The rich wheat fields of Lydia went to seed. None troubled to cultivate them or guard them against blight. Let the birds and the vermin devastate the acreage!—what did it matter? As long as the king's flour bins were never empty—and they never were—everyone was protected from extreme want. The greater the need, the greater was the supply. The peasants, though not without some muttering, surrendered themselves to the harsh fate of plenty.

The new situation had a curiously enervating effect, like a sultry wind, on those Lydians who derived their living from pursuits other than agriculture. All activity slackened. Men grew lazy and at once restless. They had fewer worries than was good for them, hence gave themselves over to all manner of idle and dangerous pastimes. They grew slovenly and contentious, their energy seeking outlets work no longer provided. They turned to politics, among other things, in an unruly and rebellious way. They began to mutter against Croesus, and a radical opposition party formed with ringleaders from among the impoverished small landowners.

"There are your Diacrians, Croesus," Solon said when these events were reported at court. "I know them from Mount Pentelicus. People are the same everywhere."

"What our Lydians need," remarked a brawny general of the king, "is a small war. Only a triumph or a defeat will calm them down. We might, for example, start something with Cyrus of Persia."

There was indeed a war party as well at the court of Sardis, and these words were spoken from its heart. Croesus, however, persisted in opposing such plans.

About this time a visitor arrived from Miletus and mentioned casually that he had seen Thales.

"What is this?" Croesus said. "He has come home and still sends me no message? Can you offer an explanation, Solon? Here we are awaiting his verdict and he keeps his silence!"

"Do you still need it, king of the Lydians?" Solon countered, pointing outstretched arms down toward the city.

"Now more than ever," Croesus cried hastily. "Disquiet has invaded my soul. Once I knew to which side I inclined. It was to you, Aesop! Now I no longer know. It is your fault, Solon!"

"Send a messenger to Miletus," Solon said calmly. "The wisest of the Hellenes will free you of your doubts. Meanwhile let us spice a cup of fragrant wine with a swift-acting poison."

"Let us also prepare the ritual quince consumed by young couples," Aesop urged.

"So be it," Croesus declared. "Both shall be in readiness, quince and poison cup. Let us hear what Thales has to say."

Another messenger hastened off to Miletus. Returning, he had difficulty making his way through the streets of Sardis, which were filled with riotous crowds. The soldiers of Croesus were battling the disorderly mob. The clash of arms could be heard in the king's private chambers, where Solon and Aesop were in the company of Croesus and the young couple. A golden goblet and a choice quince stood before Croesus.

"Omphale," whispered Eucosmos, "never fear. I shall defend you with my life if the mob gets to us."

"I am not afraid, Eucosmos, if I only have you. Let them drive us out. I shall follow you to Bolissus and wherever you go. I want to be your bride—yours, yours, yours! For better or for worse, yours alone! I love you."

Croesus had read Thales' reply. With a deep sigh he passed it to his friends. Aesop read in a low and trembling voice: "King! I journeyed away to do your bidding. For within myself I found not the wisdom you demanded of me. There is but one man among the Greeks who has studied statecraft profoundly enough to solve such a problem. I went to Athens to seek him out. But he had left his native city. I followed his trail and traveled to the land of the Egyptians. He had already departed. Not until I reached Cyprus did I learn where he is, with you. That is why I kept silent. Should I bring you wisdom in a bucket, when you can drink from the well? . . . Do, King, as Solon bids you."

Tremblingly Croesus reached for the golden goblet, tremblingly he gave it to Solon, then covered his weeping eyes with his hands.

Solon approached the lovers: "Omphale, I must have serious talk with your betrothed. Your father desires that we men be alone. You may give him a bridal kiss . . . And now, go!"

Blissfully the bride fell into Eucosmos' arms. There could be no more exalted moment in life, this she knew. With a parting smile from tender eyes she freed herself and took her leave submissively, because the men wished to be alone for their serious affairs.

"And now, Eucosmos," Solon said, "do you still hold to your view that men can be made happy? You hear the tumult down below. That is what your divine gift has brought about. Do you still wish to proffer them everlasting bread, without care, without labor? Would you not rather keep your secret to yourself? Destroy it, forget it! Omphale is yours, because you are worthy of her. Croesus will bestow her on you even if you never reveal your magic gift. Do as I say. Let the people sweat in the fields as of yore. Let them toil and drudge. It does them good. They lift themselves up."

Eucosmos stood erect. "I can assume only that you are putting me to some test, Solon. You would discover whether I am so base in spirit as to break my word. Omphale is my bride and tomorrow I shall make my secret known. The method is not mine—it belongs to all mankind and I merely hold it in trust. The mob down there may rage, but that does not abrogate its rights. They rage because they do not know. I shall open their eyes."

"You have guessed it," Solon said in a gentle voice. "It was a test. I love you, Eucosmos, as you are. Never have I loved a man as I love you. Dear dreamer, benefactor of the people! You have deserved your own dream, the dream of Omphale. Surely your soul is now pervaded with her lovely fragrance. You were never happier, Eucosmos, and should you live to an old age you will never be happier! . . . Verily, Croesus, once we spoke of true happiness. Here it is before your eyes: Eucosmos! He loves mankind and Omphale. All who know him love him. . . .

Eucosmos! Drink this wine. It comes to you from Croesus by my hand. Drink to the welfare of mankind and think of your beloved!"

And Eucosmos drank.

(1900)

IN THE DINING CAR

A MELANCHOLY FARCE

SCENE: The dining car of the Vienna-Prague-Berlin Express

Characters

THE PRINCESS
THE THEATRICAL PRODUCER
A GENTLEMAN
A WAITER

The Princess, aged thirty; pretty rather than beautiful; a certain delicate charm; finely chiseled features, with deep lines around the mouth, as if she laughed a good deal. She is dressed with the utmost simplicity, with a subtle, seductive elegance that a connoisseur would appreciate.

The theatrical producer, aged forty; red mustache, the proud sweep of which bespeaks the use of a mustache bandage; in his buttonhole a gaudy rosette proclaiming him the possessor of high Asiatic and African decorations. He is reading the Paris Figaro, *with its masthead ostentatiously turned to the outside. Nobody can help noticing that this particular gentleman is reading the* Figaro, *and on the line between Vienna and Prague that cannot but make an impression. He is wearing a black silk traveling cap. A monocle dangles by a black silk cord.*

The gentleman, in the late thirties; a globe-trotter with no regular occupation; black mustache, aquiline nose, dark eyes, hair graying at the temples; impeccable behavior; apparently

"Im Speisewagen—Ein elegischer Schwank," in *Feuilletons*, Vol. 1 (Berlin, J. Singer & Co. Verlag, 1911), pages 114–122.

absorbed in reading a yellow, paper-bound book, the pages of which he has just finished cutting.
The waiter, a sleepy boy.

PRODUCER (*who had previously made frantic efforts to attract the attention of the Princess, now becoming audible*). *Garçong*, have you a good brand of *fine champagne?* (*with emphasis*) *Fine champagne!* But genuine . . .

WAITER. If you please, sir, we have only genuine bottles.

PRODUCER (*joking*). I can well believe that the bottles are genuine, my good fellow. Well, anyway, go ahead, bring me one. (*Looks around triumphantly as if to say: "What a fine fellow I am!"* PRINCESS *gazes out of the window, smiling slightly.* PRODUCER *now considers the time ripe for approaching her.*) *Aimez-vous aussi la fine champagne, Madame?* (PRINCESS *shakes her head in denial and looks intently out of the window.* GENTLEMAN *who knows them both by sight—the princess from the races at Ascot and Deauville; the manager from a first night in Berlin—bites his lips and continues to read with great interest.* PRODUCER *puts his monocle in his eye, examines the bottle of cognac with the serious mien of a discoverer*). Hm, yes, the bottle is all right! . . . (*takes a sip*) But the contents! *C'est incrédible!* (PRINCESS *laughs a little at the error.* PRODUCER *interprets her laugh as encouragement.*) *On est très mauvaisement—*(*stops to think*) *soigné dans les wagons-lits. Vous ne trouvez pas, madame?*

PRINCESS (*offhand and in a low tone*). *Non, monsieur.* (GENTLEMAN *finds something extremely funny in his book, laughs out loud, but blushes slightly as the* PRINCESS *lets her glance, for the first time, rest on him.* PRODUCER *looks suspiciously at the gentleman.* PRINCESS *gazes earnestly out at the landscape, but the corners of her mouth are trembling.*)

PRODUCER. *Madame est française? Je voudrais jurer dessus.*

PRINCESS. *Non, monsieur.*

PRODUCER (*now really eager to show that gentleman over in the corner how things stand*). *Pourtant vous parlez très bien français—je m'en connais dedans.* (PRINCESS *is silent. Pause.*

GENTLEMAN *laughs gently as he continues to read.* PRODUCER *gets purple with rage). Garçong . . . (Taps noisily on his glass with his knife; the boy appears.)* Check!

WAITER. If you please, sir—Do you wish to pay in crowns or in marks?

PRODUCER (*grandly*). No matter—I have both.

WAITER. It comes to eighteen crowns sixty—if you please, sir.

PRODUCER (*gives him a ten gulden note*). Never mind the change. *Pour-boire.* . . . By the way, tell me, haven't I seen you before?

WAITER. Yes, if you please, sir, you have—right here in the dining car.

PRODUCER. Ah, yes—didn't you wait on me last month, too— when I (*looks around triumphantly, and with great emphasis*) was traveling with the Duke of Franken?

WAITER (*laughs*). Yes, that's it. You were the only one in the dining car with the Duke.

PRODUCER (*under his breath*). See! (*aloud to the boy*) Yes, we were together, just the Duke and I.

WAITER. And afterwards he was very angry.

PRODUCER (*unsuspicious, rocks back and forth in his seat*). Really? I didn't know anything about that.

WAITER. Yes. His staff officer told me when he paid the check. The Duke had come in after the regular dinner hour because he wanted to be alone—and then you came and sat down next to him and started to talk. (PRINCESS *and* GENTLEMAN *strain to look out of the window at the passing landscape to keep from bursting out laughing.*)

PRODUCER (*obviously annoyed*). You must be mistaken.

WAITER. No sir, if you please, sir. The Duke even asked me himself, himself in person.

PRODUCER. Well, what did he ask you?

WAITER. I don't know whether I ought to tell you.

PRODUCER. Go ahead—tell me!

WAITER. The Duke asked me about you.

PRODUCER. Yes, of course. . . . Just what did his royal highness ask?

WAITER (*hesitating*). What he asked me was: "Do you by any chance know who that impudent fellow was?"

PRODUCER. You're a fool!

WAITER. If you please, sir, if you please! (PRODUCER *gets up abruptly and rushes out of the dining car.*) That's what he is, himself! (*Clears the table, and goes out into the kitchen.* PRINCESS *laughs till the tears run down her cheeks.*)

GENTLEMAN. I must say that I enjoyed that thoroughly. (PRINCESS *continues to laugh more quietly.*) Especially since I know both of you, Madam, you and him.

PRINCESS (*looks at him in great surprise; is silent for a little while considering whether she should take the stranger to task or not; but he does not make a bad impression, so her curiosity gets the better of her and she finally asks hesitantly*). Who is this—gentleman?

GENTLEMAN. He is a Berlin theatrical producer. A comical fellow. By the way, I really don't think that he is as stupid as he appeared to be.

PRINCESS. That would be frightful.

GENTLEMAN. As a matter of fact, his misfortune might have happened to a much cleverer man.

PRINCESS. What misfortune?

GENTLEMAN. To be laughed at by a woman on whom he was trying to make a good impression. (PRINCESS *smiles deprecatingly, and once more looks out of the window.*) I can't tell you how pleased I was when I saw him trying to strike up a conversation with you. (PRINCESS *laughs.*) I noticed him from the very first moment when he sat down in that corner and ordered a dinner that was supposed to have its effect on you. You see, he did not have the slightest idea who you are, or else he would not have tried to impress you with truffled goose livers.

PRINCESS. I wonder what he ordered when he was traveling with the Duke of Franken.

GENTLEMAN. I am sure that it was something equally conspicuous. . . . By the way, the man is typical. I have met fellows just like him all over the world. The instant they catch sight of a lady in their railway compartment or on a ship, their first thought is to start a flirtation with her. As if there were anything of that sort any longer.

PRINCESS. And you mean . . . there isn't?

GENTLEMAN. You can take my word for it, there isn't. I manage to get about all over. I would know. Never on my travels have I struck up an acquaintance *en route*.

PRINCESS. You don't say so!

GENTLEMAN. I never try to enter into conversation with any lady who happens to be traveling in the same compartment with me.

PRINCESS. I noticed that. . . . And you say you travel a good deal?

GENTLEMAN. At least six months out of the year. That is the only thing I take pleasure in. If, once in a great while, I do stay quietly in one place for a few months, this is only to whip up to the highest pitch my desire for travel. I know all the big cities and every country in the world, and everywhere I am a stranger. When I get tired of the Ringstrasse, I go strolling on the Rue de la Paix, or on Regent Street. When I am bored with Granada, I try the Nevsky Prospect, or the fine Grachts of Holland. . . . Everywhere I know people who do not know me, and that, of course, is very entertaining.

PRINCESS. I can well imagine. . . . Where did you meet me?

GENTLEMAN. At the races. I think the first time I saw you was at Goodwood. You were there with the Duchess of Devonshire.

PRINCESS. Quite possible. . . . You know the Duchess?

GENTLEMAN. No, I only know her by sight. I told you that I have no connections of any sort, anywhere.

PRINCESS. How strange!

GENTLEMAN. You are beginning to want to know who I am. *Je voudrais jurer dessus*, as that buffoon just remarked. It would be better if you continued to let me be rude and keep my name a secret.

PRINCESS (*raises her eyebrows, measures him fleetingly and smiles*). That's very amusing, really.

GENTLEMAN. You must know so many embassy secretaries, so many officers of the guard, and so many others of the mixed multitude of the drawing rooms. All of them have names, important names, brilliant names, old and honorable names—it must be quite a unique experience for you to become acquainted with a man without a name. Although, I, too, have the pleasure of being the bearer of a very ancient one.

PRINCESS (*almost graciously*). Ah, you see, that's what I thought right away. It's not difficult to recognize where a person comes from. . . . But you are quite right: It is a very original idea of yours to engage in conversation in the role of a man without a name. It has never happened to me before.

GENTLEMAN. Then I am sure that you will not forget me, even if you never see me again.

PRINCESS. I must say that you flatter yourself.

GENTLEMAN. No, that's not it. Actually I am overwhelmed at the fact that we are talking to one another.

PRINCESS. So am I.

GENTLEMAN. Just now, when that clown was annoying you, I thought to myself: How can anyone be so stupid and so wanting in tact as to enter into a conversation with someone like you? And then, all of a sudden, I myself was stupid enough and . . .

PRINCESS. So wanting in tact?

GENTLEMAN. I see that you understand. It is *mauvais genre*. But it must have happened in fairy tales, in delightful fairy tales. There the princesses do not know, either, who the stranger is. And that, of course, is the best part of the fairy tale.

PRINCESS. Do you think so?

GENTLEMAN. It makes it so much easier to talk. In society, people always talk with full awareness of the social position which they occupy. But in a case like this, other words come to one's lips, unexpected words, words that one never used before—words for which one is really not responsible.

PRINCESS. That's true.

GENTLEMAN. When I stop to consider, I see that I have been traveling all over the world for the last fifteen years just so that I might meet you, Madame.

PRINCESS. Me? Wouldn't it have been simpler at Goodwood?

GENTLEMAN. No. I don't mean actually you. Naturally, I never dared even to think of you, although the lowliest serf may dream of the Queen. . . . You see, I am really very shy.

PRINCESS. No one would ever notice that.

GENTLEMAN. I never care to have anything to do with people whom I meet on the road.

PRINCESS. You are absolutely right. When one travels, there are always the most impossible people whom one is barely able to avoid: business men, common people, Jews . . .

GENTLEMAN. How do you mean?

PRINCESS. You know, all mixed up together. You saw just now, even the Duke of Franken had to put up with that creature.

GENTLEMAN. Yes, that's the way it is. The railroads have to cater to ordinary passengers, too; as a matter of fact, I rather think that they are the ones who keep the roads going. But we, we others, who know how to appreciate what is rare and unusual, we get the short end of it.

PRINCESS. You speak after my own heart.

GENTLEMAN. And at that, traveling could be so delightful. Outside, the landscape rushes past. How wonderful that we, too, can rush along with it. That gives you such a warm glow of pleasure. All sorts of unconnected thoughts, grave or gay, course through your mind, like that flock of birds over there, high up against the pale sky. Then the only thing that is missing is some woman with whom you can share your thoughts. But she has to be someone exceptionally proud, exceptionally sensitive in her perceptions, absolutely unapproachable, and she must be attuned to the melody that you are able to awaken in her.

PRINCESS. Tell me, who are you?

GENTLEMAN. A dreamer who passes by.

PRINCESS. Your talk is very different from the way our mixed multitude talks. I would really like to know, who are you?

GENTLEMAN. Perhaps the Rogue of Bergen.*

*"The Rogue of Bergen," a ballad of Heinrich Heine, in which a low-born fellow is raised to the nobility by his love for a lady of high degree: a romantic-satirical tale.

PRINCESS. And who may that be?

GENTLEMAN. Don't compel me to tell you my name, Princess! What I should like is to go on talking to you until we get to the next station. Then I shall get off the train, and vanish. If you have any notion what fairy tales really are, you must prefer it that way. Then for a short while, you will continue to think of the mysterious stranger. As for me, it will be the most beautiful experience that I have ever had in my whole life. It began in the midst of jokes and laughter and got lost in a beautiful dream. I was not just any man who had a name, and you were not an actual lady with a long genealogy —you were a faraway Princess. I was the zephyr that breathed gently over the strings of an Aeolian harp.

PRINCESS. Now I must really know who you are!

GENTLEMAN. You will be very angry with me if I tell you, after all this.

PRINCESS. On the contrary, I will not forgive you unless you do tell me. Hurry!

GENTLEMAN (*resolutely*). Well, then, Your Royal Highness, my name is Kohn.

PRINCESS (*in consternation*). Indeed? . . . That is . . . (*Looks out of the window.*) I wonder just where we are now? . . . (*Rings the bell on the wall to summon the waiter.*)

WAITER (*appears*). Madame rang?

PRINCESS. My lady-in-waiting will be coming in to pay the check. (*Gets up, nods slightly, and leaves the dining car.*)

GENTLEMAN (*under his breath*). It was only to be expected. . . . (*The train continues to rush on.*)

(1900)

THE NEW GHETTO

A PLAY IN FOUR ACTS (ABRIDGED)

Dedicated in warm friendship to Dr. Max Nordau

D r a m a t i s   P e r s o n a e

HERR HELLMANN
FRAU HELLMANN
CHARLOTTE RHEINBERG ⎱ *their daughters*
HERMINE SAMUEL ⎰
HERR SAMUEL
FRAU SAMUEL
JACOB SAMUEL
FRITZ RHEINBERG
EMANUEL WASSERSTEIN
COUNT VON SCHRAMM, CAPTAIN, CAVALRY (*Retired*)
DR. BICHLER
FRANZ WURZLECHNER
PETER VEDNIK
CLERK
FIRST MAID
SECOND MAID
COOK
BUTLER

Place: Vienna.   Time: 1893

ACT I

A drawing room, elegantly furnished in the style of the late seventies, with much gilt. The main door is on the right. Upstage center, an open door, giving on a wide, narrow balcony. *Upstage left, a broad archway leading to the dining room, with part of a sideboard visible. Downstage left, another open door. Many wedding gifts are on display and there is a profusion of flowers.*

[*As the curtain rises, the servants of the Hellmann household are expecting the return of the family and its guests from the synagogue, where the marriage of the younger daughter, Hermine, to a rising young attorney, Jacob Samuel, has been solemnized.*]

Scene 2

WASSERSTEIN, SECOND MAID.

WASSERSTEIN. (*Enters from the right, dressed in a neat but threadbare suit. His silk hat is worn but carefully brushed.*) A good day to you. Folks haven't returned yet?

SECOND MAID. No. What do you want?

WASSERSTEIN. What do you mean, what do I want? I want to pay my respects. I'm a guest, that's what I am. Name of Wasserstein.

SECOND MAID. Well, you'll just have to wait.

WASSERSTEIN. (*Looks about; aside.*) Really something! (*Sighs.*) Real class! (*Wanders about, examining the furnishings like a buyer.*) Real style! Not quite new, of course, but I'd still offer 800 gulden for the lot—well, let's say 750. Easily worth it. (*Sighs.*) Well, it's just my luck! (*Looks at a drapery.*) Real top quality! (SECOND MAID *watches him suspiciously, trails him by three paces.* WASSERSTEIN *noticing; aside.*) Aha! Doesn't trust me! (*Sighs.*) Wasserstein, that's you all over; you've really come down in the world! (*Takes a chair.*) If you please, Miss! I tell you, I'm a guest! (*Catches sight of the display of wedding gifts.*) Oh, the wedding gifts, Miss?

SECOND MAID. (*With growing suspicion.*) What did you think they were?

WASSERSTEIN. (*Approaches the table.*) Some stuff! . . . Well, my luck! (SECOND MAID *keeps close to him.*) Centerpieces!

Silverware—service for twenty-four! Look at those candlesticks! Solid! Fine stuff, silver, even though it doesn't cost a lot. (*Picks up a candlestick.*)

SECOND MAID. Put it down!

WASSERSTEIN. Don't talk to me that way, girl; I'm a guest, I tell you!

SECOND MAID. Put it down, I say!

WASSERSTEIN. If you put it like that . . . very well! You don't mind if I look, do you? I can't carry anything off with my eyes, young lady. (*Puts his hands behind his back and bends over the table.*)

Scene 3

WASSERSTEIN, SECOND MAID, DR. BICHLER.

DR. BICHLER. (*Enters from the left.*) The real thing, Herr Wasserstein!

WASSERSTEIN. (*Startled.*) Doctor Bichler! I am honored, Doctor, that you should recognize me.

DR. BICHLER. What's strange about that?

WASSERSTEIN. Oh, well, when a man's down on his luck, you find that people don't know him any more. They're all suddenly nearsighted. It's like an epidemic of blindness—that's what it is.

DR. BICHLER. (*Sits down.*) Why don't we sit down?

WASSERSTEIN. Why not? (*To Second Maid.*) You see, Miss, I'm really a guest! (*To Dr. Bichler.*) She has her suspicions about me. (*Sits down.*)

DR. BICHLER. (*Laughs.*) I'll vouch for him.

SECOND MAID. (*Embarrassed.*) Well, how was I to know? (*Exits upstage left.*)

DR. BICHLER. Down and out, my friend?

WASSERSTEIN. Lower than that, right down in the basement —a flooded basement, at that.

DR. BICHLER. The market?

WASSERSTEIN. Lost every penny. Oh, I paid up, right down to the last copper and now . . .

DR. BICHLER. No more speculating?

WASSERSTEIN. What an idea! Sure, I have debts, and I can't go on the floor of the exchange. . . .

DR. BICHLER. Tough! And what are you up to now?

WASSERSTEIN. Playing the market, of course.

DR. BICHLER. I see, on the curb?

WASSERSTEIN. No, I still get inside the building. Rheinberg —you know, he married the other Hellmann girl—settled up for me. (*Sighs.*) He got a bargain. I work for him now. I really came here today only to give him the closing quotations. What else would I be doing in this house?

DR. BICHLER. How's that?

WASSERSTEIN. Don't you know that . . . I, I was to marry Miss Hermine? It was all set.

DR. BICHLER. I can't believe it!

WASSERSTEIN. As I live and breathe! Or rather, as I lived and breathed a year ago, when this suit was still brand-new. In a way, she's the cause of my downfall.

DR. BICHLER. What? Miss Hermine?

WASSERSTEIN. Of course! It takes a lot of money to marry one of the Hellmann girls.

DR. BICHLER. Herr Hellmann isn't that rich!

WASSERSTEIN. Well, I wouldn't exactly rate him A 1. Let's say, a hundred thousand gulden, most of it tied up in his business. If he should die—which I hope won't ever happen. . . . (DR. BICHLER *laughs.*) In a nutshell, not much money, but a high scale of living. The girls were brought up to marry millionaires. When I fell in love with Miss Hermine, I said to myself, Wasserstein, I said, you'll have to become a millionaire! I took Rheinberg as a model—he's the other son-in-law, married Miss Charlotte three years ago. I went out with blood in my eye to win Miss Hermine. I went sweet on Portuguese debentures.

DR. BICHLER. You went sweet on what?

WASSERSTEIN. It's a manner of speaking. It means to be on the long side. I bought and bought. And the bottom promptly dropped out of the Portuguese market. Oh, I fought . . .

DR. BICHLER. And lost the battle?

WASSERSTEIN. Like a general.

DR. BICHLER. (*Rises and paces.*) Ah, the ways of love! Romeo, trying to corner the market!

WASSERSTEIN. My dear Doctor, I was in such a state, I could hardly add up two and two! All I could think about was her. I was crazy about that girl! She's the loveliest thing, hair like spun gold.

DR. BICHLER. You're waxing quite lyrical.

WASSERSTEIN. I'm waxing what?

DR. BICHLER. I mean you talk like a poet.

WASSERSTEIN. And now I've lost everything—my money and the girl. If I'd at least hung on to the money! But to lose both! My tough luck!

DR. BICHLER. If you were more of a philosopher, Herr Wasserstein, you'd realize that your case evens up the score. It restores the balance.

WASSERSTEIN. How's that again?

DR. BICHLER. If a lucky break in the market can win the grand prize, why, then a bad break must carry its penalties. Rheinberg made it—you failed. Poetic justice.

WASSERSTEIN. Say, that's pretty good!

DR. BICHLER. Well, it's the way a philosopher would look at it.

WASSERSTEIN. I'm no philosopher—not me! My heart almost broke just now at the Temple. Seeing her there beside young Samuel—she all in white, he in black! And I thought to myself, Wasserstein, I thought, if you'd only sold those Portuguese debentures short! (*Wipes a tear from his eye.*) My tough luck! Well, I just sneaked away, so people wouldn't see me in my misery. I was desperate, so I went over Aspern Bridge.

DR. BICHLER. Not really!

WASSERSTEIN. On my way to the exchange, of course. There's a bull market in Turkish lottery shares.

DR. BICHLER. Oh! And here I was afraid you were going to commit suicide.

WASSERSTEIN. What? Listen, I have other troubles.

DR. BICHLER. It's strange, the way things happen. If you had been luckier playing the market, three lives would have been changed.

WASSERSTEIN. What do you mean, three lives?

DR. BICHLER. Yours, Miss Hermine's, and young Samuel's.

WASSERSTEIN. Do you know him?

DR. BICHLER. Why, I was the one who introduced him into this house!

WASSERSTEIN. You don't say! And I thought it was a marriage broker!

DR. BICHLER. Young Samuel? Not a chance—he's not the type. Haven't you ever heard about him?

WASSERSTEIN. I heard—oh, sure! He's a lawyer, isn't he? Has he got much business?

DR. BICHLER. So, so. Not too much. He's determined to represent only honorable clients.

WASSERSTEIN. Can a man make a living that way?

DR. BICHLER. He gets along.

WASSERSTEIN. I mean a *good* living. Remember, Miss Hermine will want to live in the same style as her sister, Frau Rheinberg. Fine clothes, jewelry, the theater, concerts. That means a lot of money. Do you think an attorney can sweat that out? . . . But what am I saying? Rheinberg will take care of him all right. A brother-in-law like that is worth his weight in gold. Rheinberg will get him in with the banks, as a consul.

DR. BICHLER. You mean a consultant.

WASSERSTEIN. Have it your way. Anyway, Rheinberg is sure to give him a hand.

DR. BICHLER. If young Samuel stands for it, that is.

WASSERSTEIN. What do you mean? He'd be crazy not to stand for it. What would be the sense of that?

DR. BICHLER. I'm afraid you wouldn't understand, Herr Wasserstein.

WASSERSTEIN. May be, but he isn't that much of a . . . a man as lucky as that!

DR. BICHLER. I suppose you must be quite envious of him.

WASSERSTEIN. Who, me? To tell you the truth, no. Emanuel Wasserstein isn't envious of anybody. I'm only sorry for myself. I was so sorry for myself I had to leave the Temple.

DR. BICHLER. Were there many people?

WASSERSTEIN. The whole textile trade, in honor of Hellmann.

Quite a few lawyers, of course. . . . Why? Weren't you there,
Doctor?

DR. BICHLER. (*Smiles.*) What do you think?

WASSERSTEIN. Oh, I forgot. You're a convert, aren't you?

DR. BICHLER. The Rabbi isn't very well disposed toward me,
I know that much. With good reason, from his point of view.
And I didn't wish to give offense to the devout Jews by my
presence. . . . (*Sound of a carriage approaching.*)

WASSERSTEIN. Tell me, why did you have yourself baptized
anyway?

DR. BICHLER. It's really none of your business, my good fellow. But I won't evade the question. Mine was the solution
of the problem on an individual basis.

WASSERSTEIN. Indivi—I don't quite follow you.

DR. BICHLER. (*Sighs.*) Let's say it was an attempt at a solution. . . . For, between you and me, it solves nothing.

FIRST MAID. (*Crosses, left to right.*) Here they come! (*Exits
right.*)

[*The young couple, the family, and the guests arrive, and
the wedding reception gets under way. Among the guests is
Franz Wurzlechner, a close Gentile friend of Jacob Samuel,
who has never witnessed Jewish customs at first hand before.
The bridegroom's mother offers good matriarchal advice to both
her son and her new daughter-in-law.*]

Scene 5

CHARLOTTE, HERMINE, RHEINBERG, JACOB, THEN WASSERSTEIN,
WURZLECHNER, LATER COUNT VON SCHRAMM.

CHARLOTTE. (*To Hermine.*) Did you see Frau Schlesinger at
the synagogue? That was a Paris model.

HERMINE. It's scarcely something I'd notice in the Temple.

CHARLOTTE. Oh my! What sentiment!

HERMINE. Charlotte!

CHARLOTTE. I tell you, sleeves that big! It was really a sight. (*They move upstage and sit down at the balcony door.*)

RHEINBERG. (*There is nothing Jewish in his appearance. He wears a reddish cavalry mustache. Confronts Jacob.*) My new brother!

JACOB. Brother! (*They clasp hands firmly.*)

RHEINBERG. No need to make a speech. We'll stick together! (*Glances about.*)

JACOB. Agreed! You're looking for someone?

RHEINBERG. An agent of mine, fellow by the name of Wasserstein—do you know him?

JACOB. I don't think so. . . . Oh, you mean that funny little man! (*Laughs.*) He was here a while ago. (WASSERSTEIN *enters upstage left, a glass of champagne in one hand, a sandwich in the other, munching heartily.*)

RHEINBERG. (*Imperiously.*) Wasserstein!

WASSERSTEIN. (*Comes up hastily, speaks with his mouth full.*) 370, 266, 281, 498. (WURZLECHNER *enters upstage left, joins Jacob, and listens in amazement.*)

JACOB. Now I can pay some attention to you.

WURZLECHNER. (*Under his breath.*) What's going on?

JACOB. (*Shrugs his shoulders.*) Stock market quotations! . . . Come, let's smoke a cigarette. (*They find chairs downstage left and light up.*)

RHEINBERG. What about Berlin?

WASSERSTEIN. 99, 82, 75, 109—the Sultan is supposed to have sprained a foot.

RHEINBERG. That's an old one.

WASSERSTEIN. Mines are down.

RHEINBERG. And Paris?

WASSERSTEIN. Reacting badly to London.

RHEINBERG. What's the gossip?

WASSERSTEIN. Coal shares being unloaded in Berlin. Someone here is buying heavily. Schlesinger is believed to be behind it.

RHEINBERG. (*Laughs.*) Wasserstein, you're a fool!

WASSERSTEIN. (*Obsequiously.*) Why am I a fool, Herr von Rheinberg?

RHEINBERG. You want to know who's selling in Berlin and buying here? I am!

WASSERSTEIN. (*With an injured air.*) Are you using some other agent, Herr von Rheinberg?

RHEINBERG. Well, everyone knows you're working for me. Actually I'm ready to tip my hand in this coal business. If I had seen you in the synagogue—I wanted to give you instructions. It's too late now.

WASSERSTEIN. My luck! I had to get away from there. Who thinks of business in the Temple?

RHEINBERG. Wasserstein, you're a . . .

WASSERSTEIN. A fool. I know. Herr von Rheinberg. . . . So you're behind that coal deal! Then it must be true that you plan to incorporate Captain von Schramm's colliery.

RHEINBERG. Who says so?

WASSERSTEIN. It's all over the floor.

RHEINBERG. It's a lie!

WASSERSTEIN. Well, Herr von Rheinberg. You've been seen in the company of Count von Schramm several times.

RHEINBERG. (*Flattered.*) Is that so? Well, I do see him occasionally. The Count is an old friend of mine.

WASSERSTEIN. You don't say! A real pal, Herr von Rheinberg?

RHEINBERG. (*Condescendingly.*) My dear Wasserstein, I know a lot of people in high places.

WASSERSTEIN. He actually appears in public with you?

RHEINBERG. What do you mean? If I want him to! . . . You don't seem to realize that a great many celebrities come to my parties.

WASSERSTEIN. How should I? You never invite me, Herr von Rheinberg.

RHEINBERG. (*Evasively.*) As I was saying, you can pass it around that there isn't a word of truth in it. I'm not going to incorporate the mine!

FIRST MAID. (*Enters hurriedly from the right, approaches Hermine and Charlotte.*) Count von Schramm, Ma'am!

JACOB. (*Overhearing, rises precipitately; under his breath.*) What? Schramm?

WURZLECHNER. What's the matter with you? (RHEINBERG

moves toward the door at right, extends his hand to Schramm who enters. SCHRAMM *is a horsy type in smart street clothes, aged 42. Together with Rheinberg he approaches the ladies who rise. Silent exchange of greetings.*)

WASSERSTEIN. (*Aside.*) What does he mean, not a word of truth? If it isn't so, why should I have to disclaim it? Well, we'll see what kind of a fool Wasserstein is! But first I think I'll get me a few more sandwiches. . . . (*Sidles upstage left, his bows to right and left being ignored; exits.*)

WURZLECHNER. Did you have run-in with that chap?

JACOB. Yes. Some years ago. A most unpleasant incident.

RHEINBERG. I don't think you've met my wife's parents.

SCHRAMM. (*In a Prussian tone of voice.*) Haven't had the pleasure! . . . Only met Miss Hermine—ha ha, beg pardon, *Madam* Hermine. (*Turns to the ladies with a trace of condescension.*) Just dropped in for a moment to pay my respects.

CHARLOTTE. Charming of you, as usual.

SCHRAMM. Don't mention it! (*To Hermine.*) Haven't met the groom yet.

HERMINE. (*Takes a step forward.*) Jacques, let me introduce you. Count von Schramm, my husband.

SCHRAMM. (*Steps forward, his arm raised as though to shake hands with Jacob, then starts as he recognizes Jacob, drops his hand, and bows smartly.*) Delighted!

JACOB. (*He too has taken a couple of steps forward, looks Schramm in the eye and bows politely.*) How do you do?

SCHRAMM. (*Aside.*) So that's the fellow! (*Turns back to the ladies.*) If you'd be so kind as to present me to your parents.

CHARLOTTE. A privilege.

RHEINBERG. (*Walks ahead officiously.*) At your service. (*Exits upstage left.* SCHRAMM *exits upstage left, following* CHARLOTTE *and* HERMINE.)

Scene 6

(JACOB *looks after them.*)

WURZLECHNER. That was a funny look you gave him, not a bit polite.

JACOB. If you only knew how it still haunts me! Five years ago it was.

WURZLECHNER. What happened? Can't you tell me!

JACOB. You? I can tell you anything. . . . Remember when my father was so ill, five years ago?

WURZLECHNER. Of course I do. That's when I first grew so fond of you, watching you worry about your father, waiting on him day and night.

JACOB. That was just it! I was all worn out, run down from sitting up nights. Well, I let my mother send me off once. I went downtown and into a café. I sat down at a table—a man I didn't particularly notice was already sitting there. A paper was lying on the table and I picked it up. Evidently I must have irritated him. "That's my newspaper," he said roughly. "What do you mean, your newspaper? It's mine now," I said. He raised his voice: "Put it down!" "I haven't the slightest intention of putting it down," I replied in kind. He grew threatening: "Do you know to whom you're talking?" "You're scaring me out of my wits," I said mockingly. "I dare you to say that again," he shouted. "I'll say it as often as you please, my dear sir," I said. He lost his temper completely: "Don't you dear sir me! Do you know who I am?" "I'm sure you'll tell me, all in good time," I said contemptuously. "Here, my card," he said, tossing it on the table. I gave him mine and off I went.

WURZLECHNER. Silliest challenge I ever heard of!

JACOB. The card said: "Count von Schramm, Captain, Cavalry, Retired." When I got home my father was worse, my mother beside herself. I was in a bad state myself. It was certainly no time to be fighting a duel, even though it probably wouldn't have amounted to much—a nick on the finger or across the arm, first blood. My father seemed to be on his deathbed. I—I simply couldn't face it! When Schramm's seconds called on me the next day, I—I apologized. (*Covers his eyes.*)

WURZLECHNER. (*Warmly.*) Poor fellow!

JACOB. I didn't tell you at the time—I was so ashamed. Will you still give me your hand?

WURZLECHNER. (*Protests.*) Look here! . . . (*Presses his hand.*)

No man in his right mind would fight a duel over a thing like that. The whole thing is stupid from beginning to end! You shouldn't have given it a thought!

JACOB. I haven't been able to forget it. Not I—you see, I'm a Jew! You and your kind can take that kind of thing in stride. When you, Franz Wurzlechner, settle such a run-in peaceably, that makes you a solid, clear-headed chap. Me—me, Jacob Samuel—it makes a coward!

WURZLECHNER. Rubbish! . . . You don't mean to say the Captain called you a coward after you had apologized!

JACOB. (*Flares up.*) If he only had! He didn't do anything. For him the matter was settled, according to the code of chivalry. (*Grinds his teeth.*) Not much honor, at that, dueling with a Jew! I ran into him several times on the street. He looked straight through me. Oh, if he had blinked even an eyelash, I would have torn him limb from limb. . . . But no, he was as bland as can be. I tell you, there were times when I deliberately tried to jostle him.

WURZLECHNER. What idiocy to go looking for a brawl!

JACOB. He simply stepped aside. I couldn't very well collar him like a tough. (*Lowers his voice.*) So you see, Franz, there's at least one man of honor who has the right to hold me in contempt!

WURZLECHNER. Go on, you're out of your mind!

[*Captain von Schramm superciliously takes leave, pleading that he must visit his sister, Countess Wülckenau, which properly impresses the guests. Charlotte Rheinberg self-importantly gives him a message to the Countess. The Captain scarcely disguises his contempt for the Jewish company.*]

Scene 8

RABBI FRIEDHEIMER, FRAU SAMUEL, HERR HELLMANN, HERR SAMUEL, OTHERS AS BEFORE, EXCEPT FOR SCHRAMM.

HERR HELLMANN. Jacques! The Rabbi wants to see you. (JA-COB *leaves Franz, goes to meet the Rabbi.* RABBI FRIEDHEIMER *enters upstage left with* FRAU SAMUEL *on his arm. The guests open a passage for him. He nods to some of them full of dignity.*)

WASSERSTEIN. (*Pushes himself forward.*) A great honor, Rabbi!

RABBI FRIEDHEIMER. (*Shakes Wasserstein's hand in passing, continues his stately progress downstage center, where Rheinberg stands; in a booming voice.*) Herr Rheinberg, I hear the market is down.

RHEINBERG. It's not likely to be much of a slump.

WURZLECHNER. (*Stands with Dr. Bichler downstage left; under his breath.*) I say! Does the Rabbi play the market too?

JACOB. (*To the Rabbi.*) I can hardly believe my ears, Rabbi! Are you interested in the stock market?

RABBI FRIEDHEIMER. (*Calmly.*) Not on my own account, my young friend; on account of our poor. (*He seats Frau Samuel downstage right and takes a chair beside her. The guests gradually gather around, listening to him respectfully, those in the back peering over the shoulders of those in front. Wasserstein is on the fringe of the group, farthest toward the center, cupping his ear. Wurzlechner and Dr. Bichler stand apart downstage left.* JACOB *stands immediately facing Rabbi Friedheimer.* RABBI FRIEDHEIMER *speaks somewhat unctuously.*) Yes, indeed, when the market is good I have money for my poor. The stock exchange can be generous.

WASSERSTEIN. In a bull market.

RHEINBERG. (*Turns his head in annoyance.*) Sh-sh!

RABBI FRIEDHEIMER. We need a lot of money right now, for the Russian emigrants we're sending overseas. Those poor people! Yes my friends, we are not nearly so badly off as our coreligionists. We at least can stay in our homeland.

JACOB. On sufferance!

RABBI FRIEDHEIMER. We enjoy the protection of law. It's true, we are looked down upon once again, just as in the old days, when we lived in the ghetto. But the walls have come down.

JACOB. The *visible* walls.

RABBI FRIEDHEIMER. Antisemitism isn't all bad. As the movement gains force, I observe a return to religion. Antisemitism is a warning to us to stand together, not to abandon the God of our fathers, as many have done. (*Bends forward slightly to peer at Dr. Bichler.*)

DR. BICHLER. (*To Wurzlechner.*) Touché! (*Several guests glance surreptitiously at him.*)

RABBI FRIEDHEIMER. Our God always delivers us from bondage. And because we trust in him, we have preserved ourselves with all our ancient virtues.

JACOB. And our ancient faults.

FRAU SAMUEL. (*Reprovingly.*) Jacob!

RABBI FRIEDHEIMER. True, the ghetto was crowded and dirty, but the virtues of family life flourished there. The father was a patriarch. The mother . . . (*lays his hand lightly on that of Frau Samuel*) lived only for her children, and they honored their parents. Don't belittle the Jewish quarter, my dear friend! Poor it is, but it's our home.

JACOB. I don't belittle it. I only say we must get out of it.

RABBI FRIEDHEIMER. (*Rises.*) And I tell you we cannot do it! When there was still a real ghetto, we were not allowed to leave it without permission, on pain of severe punishment. Now the walls and barriers have become invisible, as you say. Yet we are still rigidly confined to a moral ghetto. Woe unto him who would desert! (*Walks away.*)

JACOB. (*Escorts the Rabbi to the door. The guests again respectfully open a passage.*) Rabbi, these new barriers we must break down after some other fashion than we did the old ones. Outward barriers had to be cleared away from without, but the inner barriers we must clear away ourselves. We ourselves! On our own!

FRAU SAMUEL. (*Puts her hand on her heart.*) God in heaven! (RABBI FRIEDHEIMER *shrugs his shoulders and walks toward the door, nodding to several guests with amiable dignity.*)

DR. BICHLER. (*Downstage, to Wurzlechner.*) Well, what do you say to all this, Gentile?

WURZLECHNER. (*Muses.*) It's another world! . . . (*He and* DR. BICHLER *turn upstage.*)

(Curtain.)

ACT II

Office-study in Jacob Samuel's home. The main entrance is in the center. There are doors on the right and left. The walls are covered with books. There is a window downstage right. At a distance from the window stands a large desk with a lamp burning on it.

Scene 1

JACOB, THEN WURZLECHNER.

(JACOB *sits at the desk, pondering, writing, consulting books.*)

WURZLECHNER. (*Enters, calls out softly.*) Hello, Jacob!

JACOB. Franz! (*Looks up in surprise, greets him.*) What brings you here so early?

WURZLECHNER. It's not as early as all that! Ten o'clock.

JACOB. (*Consults his watch.*) Good heavens! Let me draw the curtains. (*Goes to the window, draws back the draperies and glances outside.*) Why, the sun's shining!

WURZLECHNER. (*Reaches for the desk lamp.*) Shall I turn off the light?

JACOB. If you please.

WURZLECHNER. (*Turns it off.*) You must have been up pretty early.

JACOB. Since five o'clock. . . . It's been going on for days.

WURZLECHNER. As busy as all that?

JACOB. Not with the practice of law—that isn't going so well. (*Paces the floor.*)

WURZLECHNER. My dear fellow, nobody would mourn if I closed my office either.

JACOB. (*Stops before him.*) You're single—you don't need very much. But a household—it's a lot of responsibility. It's not much fun, keeping a bride of six months on short purse-strings. I'm afraid I've had to go into debt.

WURZLECHNER. Oh, oh! Are they dunning you?

JACOB. Rather!

WURZLECHNER. Look, I've just come into a small inheritance
—three thousand gulden. I can lend it to you.

JACOB. Do you mean it? You've no idea how much it would
mean to me. I don't like to go to my father. He's not doing too
well with his jewelry shop. . . . I would have to speak to my
wealthy brother-in-law, and I . . .

WURZLECHNER. (*Nods.*) Don't like the idea?

JACOB. Oh, he's nice enough. He'd help me in a moment. But
. . . I don't know. I'd rather it were you.

WURZLECHNER. Let's not even discuss it. You'll have the
money before the morning's over.

JACOB. Wonderful! You my creditor! I've been dreaming of
that sort of thing, Gentiles lending money to Jews—at outrageous interest!

WURZLECHNER. (*Laughs.*) I'm not going to charge you any
interest.

JACOB. (*Laughing.*) And I was counting on it . . . (*Rubs his
hands.*) Franz, now I can get on with my work. Now I won't
have to worry about these wretched money matters.

WURZLECHNER. (*Points to the desk.*) What on earth were
you up to? Writing?

JACOB. Something big, Franz—really big. You may have
heard that I was assigned to defend some Socialists—poor
devils! Well, I got to know them quite well, and I've been
thinking about them.

WURZLECHNER. (*Genially.*) Don't tell me you've become a
Socialist!

JACOB. Of course not! Perhaps they are right, but I don't
see it. I'm certainly not in favor of uprooting capital. Too much
would go by the board—too many cultural values. I don't want
to see thrift and incentive banished. And useful enterprise
is entitled to handsome rewards—up to a certain limit!

WURZLECHNER. Yes, where is the limit?

JACOB. That's what I'm trying to find out.

WURZLECHNER. I see!

JACOB. There must be a way of setting it. Look, I've been

studying a number of industries, from the bottom up. I've concentrated on ten large firms—I'll spare you the details. Do you want to know what I'm finding out? The river has overflowed its banks. Today's accepted business morality was considered dishonest only yesterday. We shall have to build new levees. I really haven't thought this thing out yet, but you're my friend and I can talk to you about it. . . .

WURZLECHNER. No, you can't!

JACOB. What do you mean?

WURZLECHNER. (*Lowers his eyes.*) Because we'll have to break up.

JACOB. I don't know what you're talking about!

WURZLECHNER. That's why I came. I don't think we'll be seeing each other any more.

JACOB. (*Upset.*) Franz!

WURZLECHNER. I'm sorry. (*Firmly.*) But I can't help it.

JACOB. What on earth has happened?

WURZLECHNER. It's you—you've changed. Your environment is different—the company you keep. I don't belong there —with these Rheinbergs, Wassersteins, the whole lot of them. Can't you see? I can't take them—they rub me the wrong way. And since your marriage I'm likely to run into them at any time in your home—there's no escaping them. It's not your fault—they're your people—though I must say, sometimes I do get a little angry at you. Somehow it doesn't seem quite fair. Anyway, let's call it quits! Let's not just drift apart bit by bit, with pretended misunderstandings. Let's make it a clean break! My feelings about you haven't changed. I'll be at your service whenever you need me, as I know you'll be at mine. But no more social meetings! Here, let's shake hands!

JACOB. (*Offers his hand.*) I thank you for being so frank. I'm sure you must have thought it over very carefully before you made up your mind to hurt me like this. I thank you also for your friendship all these years. I've learned a good deal from you.

WURZLECHNER. (*Taken aback.*) You're joking! . . . You learned from me?

JACOB. It's true—though at first without quite knowing it. I learned big things and little—inflections, gestures, how to bow without being obsequious, how to stand up without seeming defiant—all sorts of things.

WURZLECHNER. You really think I'm such a paragon?

JACOB. To tell the truth, what I really admired in you was your family background, just as you now despise mine.

WURZLECHNER. I never said any such thing!

JACOB. Your people have been free citizens for hundreds of years, while we . . . (*Smiles wryly.*) Well, if I've managed a few steps beyond the Jewish quarter, it was with your guidance. Now I'll be able to go on alone. . . . We're talking as friends for the last time, so let me give you something on your way. You studied law, Franz, because the Wurzlechners have always been lawyers or doctors in Vienna. Wasserstein too is what his ancestors made him—what their destiny made him. It may not be to his credit. But it's not his fault. Moral values don't come into being until instinct gives way to awareness. In our case it wasn't even nature that made us what we are, but history. It was your people who rubbed our noses in money—but now we are told to despise it! For a thousand years you kept us in bondage—and now we're to acquire the souls of free men, from one day to the next! Who is really free in his heart? Are you? *We're* not even permitted to have everyday human foibles. We're dirty Jews!

WURZLECHNER. (*With compassion.*) Jacob!

JACOB. Yes, it's over between us, Wurzlechner. Even if you had given me a choice between you and Wasserstein—well, I've already made it. My place is with Wasserstein, rich or poor. I can reproach him no more than I can praise you. You each stand where history has placed you. But we must move on— onward and upward! You must understand that. Only then do we become men!

WURZLECHNER. (*Shaken.*) Jacob, believe me, I can't help it. I wish I could tell you. I—well, I plan to go into politics.

JACOB. Antisemitism should be a sure thing!

WURZLECHNER. Don't be unfair! Why should I play into the

hands of my opponents—too many Jewish friends, brokers, speculators? I'd be branded a tool of the Jews first thing!

JACOB. (*Resigned.*) It's true. You're right.

[*Jacob's parents arrive, full of innocent praise for Wurzlechner, whom they have long known as their son's friend. Taking him to the door, Jacob now refuses to accept the loan. The parents have come at Hermine's behest, because of family concern with Jacob's overwork. He tells them and his wife of the break with Wurzlechner and how much the friendship meant to him. Hermine appeals to her husband to ask Rheinberg's help.*]

Scene 6

JACOB, HERMINE, RHEINBERG, WASSERSTEIN

RHEINBERG. (*Enters.*) May I come in?

HERMINE. Fritz! (*Goes to meet him.*)

WASSERSTEIN. (*Smartly dressed, with a new silk hat. His bearing is calm and assured.*) A great honor, Madam!

HERMINE. (*Smiles.*) Well, if it isn't Herr Wasserstein!

WASSERSTEIN. Yes, it's me—begging your pardon for the intrusion. (*Aside.*) That woman always throws me off!

HERMINE. (*In an undertone, to Rheinberg.*) Your shadow!

RHEINBERG. (*Chuckles.*) Can't do without him!

WASSERSTEIN. (*Has greeted Jacob obsequiously; in an undertone.*) She's always laughing at me, your wife, I mean.

JACOB. (*Smiles and pats him on the shoulder.*) Nothing of the kind!

WASSERSTEIN. I'm telling you. I give her the giggles. (RHEINBERG *turns to Jacob and shakes hands. They walk upstage.* HERMINE *takes a seat downstage left.* WASSERSTEIN *approaches her.*)

JACOB. (*In an undertone, to Rheinberg.*) It's damn awkward —so I'll give it to you straight.

RHEINBERG. Go ahead. (*They continue to talk in an undertone.*)

WASSERSTEIN. That's a pretty robe you're wearing, Madam!

HERMINE. (*Laughs.*) You like it?

WASSERSTEIN. (*Aside.*) Whatever I say, she laughs!

RHEINBERG. (*Pulls out his wallet.*) I haven't got quite enough on me. (*Turns.*) Herr Wasserstein!

WASSERSTEIN. Herr Rheinberg!

RHEINBERG. Can you lend me fifteen hundred gulden?

WASSERSTEIN. Can I! (*He pulls a roll of bills from his vest pocket, peels off a few, and passes them over.*)

RHEINBERG. I'll give it back to you in half an hour, Herr Wasserstein.

WASSERSTEIN. (*Magnanimously.*) No hurry, Herr Rheinberg! (*Glances at Hermine to observe the effect.*)

RHEINBERG. Hermine, we have some business to discuss.

HERMINE. (*Rises.*) That means I'm to . . . (*Whispers to Rheinberg in passing.*) Too bad—that Wasserstein does make me laugh!

RHEINBERG. (*Whispers back.*) Watch yourself! He made a hundred thousand gulden in a week speculating on coal.

HERMINE. No wonder you're impressed! . . . (*Goes to Jacob who is just pocketing Rheinberg's money.*) Jacques!

JACOB. Yes? (RHEINBERG *crosses over to Wasserstein.*)

HERMINE. Please give me some of it.

JACOB. (*Gives her money.*) Here you are.

HERMINE. You aren't angry because I like to dress up?

JACOB. (*Smiles.*) Spendthrift!

HERMINE. I have a wonderful idea for a winter dress. Plaid trimmed with red! I'll surprise you! (*Exits right, laughing.*)

Scene 7

JACOB, WASSERSTEIN, RHEINBERG

JACOB. (*To Rheinberg, in an undertone.*) I hope to be able to pay you back soon. Can you give me three months?

RHEINBERG. My dear Jacques, I won't let you pay me back at all!

JACOB. What do you mean?

RHEINBERG. It's an advance on a fee I expect you to earn.

JACOB. (*Suspiciously.*) A legal fee?

RHEINBERG. Yes indeed! Earn and let earn—that's my motto. Live and let live.

WASSERSTEIN. All of us—and good health too!

RHEINBERG. Let me explain the deal to you.

JACOB. But I'm not a businessman!

RHEINBERG. Will you let me finish? . . . You'd better sit down at the desk. You'll have to take some notes to draw up the contract.

JACOB. (*Reassured.*) Oh, a contract! (*Sits down.*)

Scene 8

AS BEFORE. CLERK.

CLERK. (*Enters at center.*) There's a man to see you, sir.

JACOB. Who is he?

CLERK. His name is Vednik or Vyednik—he's a Slovak.

JACOB. I don't think I know him. Ask him to wait.

CLERK. Yes, sir. (*Exits.*)

JACOB. (*To Rheinberg.*) Let's get to the point.

RHEINBERG. (*Oratorically.*) As you may be aware, this is the age of coal.

WASSERSTEIN. The golden age of coal!

RHEINBERG. I've been the first here to take advantage of it.

WASSERSTEIN. And I the second.

RHEINBERG. (*Courteously.*) Please, Herr Wasserstein, don't interrupt me. (*To Jacob.*) Long before anyone saw the possibilities in coal-mining stock, I was buying it up secretly— great blocks of it. Then I had Wasserstein sell it for me, quite openly. Well, they all fell for it.

WASSERSTEIN. Except me. . . . Well, am I still a fool, Herr Rheinberg?

RHEINBERG. (*Respectfully.*) No, you aren't, Herr Wasserstein. . . . (*To Jacob.*) More than that, I got an option on the Dubnitz pit from Schramm.

JACOB. (*Winces.*) Count von Schramm?

RHEINBERG. Yes. There's quite a story to his coal mine. Old Man Schramm came from Laibach and made his fortune from the Dubnitz pit. His two children inherited it after his death. But the son is a gentleman and the daughter married to one. The Captain keeps an expensive racing stable, and his brother-in-law, Count Wülckenau, gambles away what the chorus girls leave him. For ten years they've been milking the pit, without putting a penny in it. It's badly run, the equipment is old. There's just about everything wrong with it you can think of. Still, it shows an excellent yield.

JACOB. I see. And now you plan to put everything back in order.

RHEINBERG. (*In surprise.*) I?

WASSERSTEIN. Why should he do such a thing?

RHEINBERG. No, I want to incorporate the mine. The time is ripe. There's a bull market in coal stocks. And the Count would thank his lucky stars if he could get rid of the mine.

JACOB. Why should he feel that way if the yield is so good?

RHEINBERG. If he wants to hang on to it, he has to put up a lot of money. A run-down mine is bad business. To make up for past neglect costs twice as much now, four times as much tomorrow. To make the necessary repairs he would have to sell his stable. And he's deep in debt already, as is Wülckenau. They're both anxious for me to incorporate the mine.

JACOB. Did they come to you?

RHEINBERG. Of course they did. I have a reputation.

JACOB. And just what am I to do in the matter?

RHEINBERG. You're to draw up the incorporation papers.

JACOB. Does Count von Schramm know about it? Did you mention my name to him?

RHEINBERG. Certainly.

JACOB. And he offered no objection?

RHEINBERG. None.

WASSERSTEIN. Why should he object?

JACOB. I thought . . . Well, after all I'm your brother-in-law, and I might be more concerned with your interests than his.

RHEINBERG. His attorney will check everything.

JACOB. Right!

RHEINBERG. Besides, the whole thing's settled. The capital will be three million. Schramm, Wülckenau, and I will form the syndicate. Each of us gets one third of the stock.

JACOB. You too? In return for what?

RHEINBERG. For money—for good money! I'm putting up a million in cash—that is, provided I exercise my option to buy the stock.

JACOB. And on what does that depend?

RHEINBERG. On how the stock does on the market.

WASSERSTEIN. Let me explain—I can see you aren't familiar with stock promotions.

JACOB. No, I'm not.

WASSERSTEIN. Strange! . . . Listen: Schramm and Wülckenau will give Rheinberg, as compensation . . .

JACOB. As compensation for what?

WASSERSTEIN. For floating the stock! . . . Do you think that's child's play? For his pains he gets an option to buy one third of the stock.

RHEINBERG. Two thousand shares, at five hundred per.

WASSERSTEIN. So the issue is floated. . . . Now listen carefully. If the stock rises, Rheinberg exercises his option. If it falls, he doesn't.

RHEINBERG. However, I must decide within two weeks after the issue. If the stock rises fifty gulden, I stand to make fifty times two thousand.

WASSERSTEIN. In other words, a hundred thousand gulden.

RHEINBERG. If it falls even one gulden below par, I forfeit my option, make nothing and lose nothing.

WASSERSTEIN. Schramm comes out ahead anyway.

RHEINBERG. My services cost him nothing. The commission is paid by the exchange, and he gets three million for Dubnitz, which isn't worth two million.

JACOB. Isn't it true that he comes out ahead only if the stock is sold at par value?

WASSERSTEIN. Of course. But there's a bull market in coal stock. . . . Why do you make such a face?

JACOB. To tell you the truth, I don't like such deals.

WASSERSTEIN. What do you mean, you don't like them?

RHEINBERG. I see! You're down on the brokerage business?

JACOB. (*Calmly.*) I didn't say that. I'm well aware of the services the stock market performs. It enables the government to finance long-range undertakings. It builds railroads, stimulates enterprise, exports surpluses to foreign markets.

WASSERSTEIN. (*With enthusiasm.*) Say! I didn't even know that!

JACOB. (*Smiles.*) Indeed, Herr Wasserstein, you don't know the good you do—nor the harm.

WASSERSTEIN. How can I do harm when I do good?

JACOB. You harm yourself.

WASSERSTEIN. I don't get you.

JACOB. No, you don't understand me! You harm us, the Jews! There are always people who are ruined in these big deals. And the victims blame the Jews. Not everyone has insight enough to see the whole picture. People think in terms of other people. That's why I'm sorry our people are so deeply involved in the stock market.

RHEINBERG. (*Sneeringly, to Wasserstein.*) I think I'll just go out of business . . . after such a fine sermon!

JACOB. I'm not blaming anyone.

RHEINBERG. Why don't you just say you don't want any part of my deal? I'll go and find another attorney.

JACOB. No, that's not what I want.

WASSERSTEIN. (*Chuckling, in an undertone to Rheinberg.*) He wouldn't let such a fat fee get away from him!

JACOB. There's a special reason—a personal reason—why I want to fix up your deal with Schramm.

RHEINBERG. Very well.

JACOB. Let him realize that he's dealing with decent people.

RHEINBERG. Schramm knows that.

JACOB. People who won't take advantage of him.

RHEINBERG. Right.

JACOB. I'll go right down the line with you!

RHEINBERG. (*Offers him his hand.*) Agreed!

WASSERSTEIN. (*Looks at his watch.*) For God's sake!

RHEINBERG. What's up?

WASSERSTEIN. I'm overdue on the floor! Haven't we anything better to do than argue? I'm leaving. I'm a trader—that's my profession. You can stay here, if you want. I've been buying, and I'm on pins and needles. . . . Goodbye, sir! (*Hastens off.*)

RHEINBERG. Wait for me, Herr Wasserstein! (*Nods to Jacob, follows.*)

Scene 9

JACOB, CLERK, VEDNIK

JACOB. (*Alone.*) I'll see to it that nothing happens to the Count! . . . (*Sits down at the desk.*)

CLERK. (*Enters at center.*) Shall I send the man in now?

JACOB. Oh! Of course! At once! (CLERK *opens the door, waves in Vednik, and exits.* VEDNIK, *a toil-worn miner, stands uncertainly, twisting his cap in his hands. He has a Slavic accent.*)

JACOB. (*Genially.*) What can I do for you?

VEDNIK. (*Gutturally.*) The workers of Dubnich—they send me.

JACOB. (*Pricks up his ears.*) What was that name?

VEDNIK. Dubnich, the coal pit.

JACOB. The one that belongs to Count von Schramm?

VEDNIK. Aye, sir!

JACOB. Sit down!

VEDNIK. Vednik, Peter, is name. They send me on account I speak German. Bad trouble—bad, bad! We decide, must go to big town lawyer. Is mention your name, on account you help workers. No much money in treasury. (*Suspiciously.*) Is cost much?

JACOB. My advice? Not a penny.

VEDNIK. Good, very good! Is mention, you no charge. We chip in for trip. Cost seven gulden, the ticket, pay for whole week. I report sick. I sick often. (*Slyly.*) They believe, no go to Old Dubnich for check-up. Boss, he not know of trip, or *kaputt!*

JACOB. Well, they aren't going to find out from me.

VEDNIK. Boss, he bad man! Real tough! All time dock pay. Fire for nothing. Then children got no food, big people too.

JACOB. Have you complained to Count von Schramm?

VEDNIK. No good! Lordship, he send pe-ti-shun to boss, he trust boss. Boss like wild man. No good! Lordship, he good man, always send money when is accident. Me too, get thirty gulden when hoist fall, bust my arm. Lordship, he good man, we know. Boss bad man.

JACOB. You'll have to tell me the whole story if you want me to advise you. (*Sighs.*) *If* I can help at all.

VEDNIK. (*Scratches his head.*) How to start? Me, I get up four o'clock in morning, walk two hours from Old Dubnich to mine. Is shift from six to six, many times longer. Then two hours back to Old Dubnich.

JACOB. And how much pay do you get?

VEDNIK. One gulden, twelve kreuzer a day. Me pickman, get more than trolleyman. We no kick about pay. . . .

JACOB. What is your complaint then?

VEDNIK. Fines very bad! Dock us fifteen, twenty kreuzer for nothing. Foreman, he no give us quarter hour for eat lunch. Foreman, his name Kremenzak! (*Rises in agitation, shakes his fist.*) He dirty dog!

JACOB. Sounds pretty grim. But what am I supposed to do?

VEDNIK. Kremenzak, he worse than boss. . . . Drive, all time drive! No time for shoring, whole business maybe come down on top of us.

JACOB. If I understand you correctly, not enough is being done to safeguard the miners.

VEDNIK. Right! Mine no safe. Ven-ti-la-shun very bad. No give us enough timber. Rosamunde worst of all!

JACOB. Who's that?

VEDNIK. Rosamunde, name of one pit. . . . Last accident happen there. They patch up a little—not enough. Now no dare blast in Rosamunde. (*Ominously, with lowered voice.*) Only use pick, or bad trouble. Now boss, he give order to blast. We no come out any more!

JACOB. (*Leaps up.*) You mean you're working in danger of your lives?

VEDNIK. All time. . . . We complain to boss, he show us order from Lordship, "Blast!" Lordship, he not know about Rosamunde. He good man, never come Dubnich. Boss, he say, must make much coal, Lordship, he sell Dubnich!

JACOB. (*Laughs disdainfully.*) Of course, to make a good showing. (*Paces the room.*) Go on, go on!

VEDNIK. No more! All *kaputt;* if blast in Rosamunde, we die. No dare strike now, on account winter coming. We all starve, freeze.

JACOB. How dreadful! . . . I don't know yet what I'll do, but something will be done, you can depend on me!

VEDNIK. I go back today. How I answer my people?

JACOB. When does your train leave?

VEDNIK. Seven o'clock tonight.

JACOB. Wait for me at the station. I'll help you!

VEDNIK. God bless you, Mister. (*Tries to kiss his hand.*)

JACOB. (*Tears his hand away.*) Go on! I'll meet you! (VEDNIK *exits.*)

[*In a rage, Jacob retrieves Rheinberg's money from Hermine and dispatches the bills to her brother-in-law. He is off for Dubnitz as the curtain falls.*]

A C T   I I I

Small drawing room at the home of the Rheinbergs. Tastefully furnished without ostentation. The style is Empire. There are some fine wall-hangings and objêts d'art. *A valuable painting stands on an easel. In the background a conservatory. There are three doors.*

[*As the curtain rises, Wasserstein is seeking to impress Charlotte and Hermine with his regained wealth. Dr. Bichler brings the latest news of the mine disaster that has meanwhile occurred in Dubnitz, following a strike which rumor falsely credits Jacob with instigating.*]

Scene 3

CHARLOTTE, HERMINE AND WASSERSTEIN AT THE TEA TABLE; LATER, BUTLER.

HERMINE. Jacques hasn't been himself since all this happened. He thinks of nothing else, day and night.

CHARLOTTE. Your husband is a strange man! I think I may say that, even in Herr Wasserstein's presence.

WASSERSTEIN. Please, don't mind me in the least! (*Drinks his tea nosily.*)

HERMINE. You call it strange, if anyone takes pity on the wretched?

WASSERSTEIN. Let me tell you, this mine accident did something to me. I was so upset I went and sold all my coal shares. I don't want to have anything to do with coal if it costs people's lives. As it happened, my good heart paid off. I sold at top prices—immediately afterward the bottom dropped out of the coal market. So that's the way it is, I said to myself! And lost no time going over to the short side. I sold and sold. I must say, it was pretty good. May I have another liverwurst sandwich?

BUTLER. (*Enters from the left.*) Count von Schramm is here, Ma'am.

CHARLOTTE. Please show him in.

BUTLER. If you please, Ma'am, he says he's come to see the Master.

CHARLOTTE. (*Irritated.*) Herr Rheinberg is not at home!

BUTLER. I took the liberty of so informing the Count. He was—er—rather loud with me and ordered me to look again. He said if Herr Rheinberg really isn't at home, he'll call again in an hour.

CHARLOTTE. (*Shrugs her shoulders.*) That suits me. (BUTLER *exits.*)

WASSERSTEIN. (*Scratches his head.*) I don't think Rheinberg is going to like it.

CHARLOTTE. Why not?

WASSERSTEIN. Haven't you heard?

CHARLOTTE. My husband never discusses his business affairs with me. Anything wrong with Schramm?

WASSERSTEIN. He's ruined—that's all.

CHARLOTTE. You don't mean it!

HERMINE. The disaster at the mine?

WASSERSTEIN. Not exactly, though that has something to do with it. . . . Schramm and his brother-in-law needed money. When the Rosamunde stock was issued . . .

CHARLOTTE. They sold theirs?

WASSERSTEIN. No. It was agreed that they wouldn't sell right off—that would have sent the stock down. They put up the stock as collateral.

HERMINE. What does that mean?

WASSERSTEIN. They secured a loan with it—a quarter of a million—and used the money to pay off their debts. Then came the strike and suddenly there was no market for Rosamunde stock. Oh, we kept the price up, Rheinberg and I. But then, bang! the accident! Well, I threw in my hand, and I'm pretty sure Rheinberg did the same. The stock tumbled. The bank no longer had its security and called Schramm's note. He couldn't pay, of course, so they sold his stock for a song. Now he hasn't got the stock, and he hasn't got the mine either.

CHARLOTTE. Dear me!

WASSERSTEIN. Well, it isn't my hide! . . . Would you please pass the caviar?

HERMINE. Does my husband know about this?

WASSERSTEIN. Why shouldn't he? It's common knowledge.

Scene 4

AS BEFORE, JACOB, RABBI FRIEDHEIMER.

JACOB. (*Enters at left.*) Come with me, Rabbi, we don't have to be announced.

CHARLOTTE. Rabbi! (*Goes to meet him.*) You don't visit us often enough! (*They all rise.* RABBI FRIEDHEIMER *shakes hands with Charlotte.*)

WASSERSTEIN. An honor, Rabbi!

RABBI FRIEDHEIMER. (*Nods to him, then to Charlotte.*) Herr Rheinberg isn't home?

CHARLOTTE. Not yet.

WASSERSTEIN. Probably at the club. Shall I call him?

JACOB. Please do.

CHARLOTTE. The butler can take care of it.

JACOB. (*Aside, to Charlotte.*) Please let Wasserstein do it. We want to be among ourselves.

WASSERSTEIN. Well, shall I telephone him?

CHARLOTTE. If you please.

WASSERSTEIN. No sooner said than done. (*Exits right.*)

HERMINE. (*Tenderly.*) Jacques, you didn't even kiss me!

JACOB. Forgive me, my dear! (*Kisses her on the forehead.*)

HERMINE. Something in the wind? I can see it by your face.

JACOB. Do me a favor and keep Wasserstein outside, or send him away.

CHARLOTTE. I'm afraid that won't do. Fritz is expecting him.

HERMINE. (*Aside to Jacob.*) I'm worried. Something has happened to you.

JACOB. (*Aside, to Hermine.*) Please don't worry. Nothing has happened to me personally. I give you my word!

WASSERSTEIN. (*Returns.*) Well, I got him on the phone. He's coming.

CHARLOTTE. Thank you. . . . Would you like a cigar?

WASSERSTEIN. I smoke! . . . I don't smoke! . . . Just as you please.

CHARLOTTE. Let's go outside.

WASSERSTEIN. To the conservatory? Delighted! (*Exits with Charlotte at center.*)

JACOB. (*To Hermine.*) Darling, run along with them! (*Escorts her to the glass door, which he closes behind her.*)

RABBI FRIEDHEIMER. As bad as all that?

JACOB. (*Comes back; quietly.*) Indescribable, beyond words. When I got there, they were just bringing up the bodies. Outside the pit entrance the women stood weeping and moaning. Some of them never said a word. I could hardly look at them. I tell you, I'll remember the scene as long as I live. Everything black in black, as though in mourning. The tattered clothes, all black with coal dust, and a sharp autumn breeze making the thin bodies shiver under the rags. Even the sky was leaden. And the children—enough of them to wring your heart. Tiny ones with grave wizened faces. They seemed to be looking with terror at the black hole that would engulf them too some day. They'll ride down just like their fathers who were being brought up—they'll push the iron trolleys before they're in their teens, for forty-five kreuzer a day! . . . Later on, when they become pickmen, they'll lie on their sides in the holes, hacking away at the seam in the dark. One slip with the lamp, and the firedamp comes crashing about their ears. This time it was the water. It was a holocaust! . . . (*Covers his eyes.*) Yet tomorrow, down they'll go again. If they don't they'll just starve to death up above.

RABBI FRIEDHEIMER. My son, no one suffers more than he can bear. God in his wisdom has so ordained it. Whoever goes barefoot grows callus on his sole.

JACOB. Is that all the solace you offer?

RABBI FRIEDHEIMER. Poverty and misery are no greater today than in the past. On the contrary, things are getting better.

JACOB. (*Sits down.*) You mean, we must stand idly by and do nothing?

RABBI FRIEDHEIMER. Patience. I approve of what you plan to do with Rheinberg. That's why I came along. But your task ends there.

JACOB. And I tell you, it only begins there!

RABBI FRIEDHEIMER. Foolishness! Be glad they're leaving you alone! You want to look after other people—but tell me, who will look after you, my son?

JACOB. I'm not concerned with that.

RABBI FRIEDHEIMER. By what right do you meddle in the affairs of the miners?

JACOB. I'm a lawyer!

RABBI FRIEDHEIMER. Let me tell you a story—I found it in the ancient Jewish chronicle of Rabbi Joshua of Speyer. It was written somewhere on the road, after one of the many expulsions of the Jews from the Rhineland. As early as the month of Ab of the year 5143, the fourteenth century as the Gentiles reckon, there were signs and portents of trouble in Mainz. One case was that of Moses Ben Abraham, a worthy youth, son of a merchant, who wanted to be a scholar. One summer evening he sat studying the ancient books of our sages. Suddenly he heard cries for succor in the night. He leaned out the window, but the sound came from outside the Ghetto. The screams grew more and more desperate. Moses was moved in his heart and left the house. His mother stopped him and asked him where he was going so late at night. "Mother, I hear someone cry for help," he said and vanished into the dark. When he failed to return, his mother grew more and more anxious until at last she went after him. She too did not return. The next morning Moses was found stabbed to death just outside the open gate of the Ghetto. By his side sat his mother, an unearthly smile on her lips. She had gone mad. Well, what do you say to that story?

JACOB. I say that my heart goes out to Moses of Mainz, that I am proud of him. All of us should take him as an example. The cry for help is sometimes genuine.

RABBI FRIEDHEIMER. But we're too weak!

JACOB. What merit is there when the strong show compassion? (RABBI FRIEDHEIMER *shrugs his shoulders, spreads his hands, and drops them again.*)

Scene 5

AS BEFORE, RHEINBERG.

RHEINBERG. (*Enters from the left, goes straight to the Rabbi.*) I only just heard that you'd come to call, Rabbi! (*Shakes hands with him and nods curtly to Jacob.*) Where's Wasserstein?

JACOB. Over there. (RHEINBERG *hastens to the glass door.*) *I* came to talk to you, *not* Wasserstein.

RHEINBERG. You? . . . Just let me say hello to him. (*Opens the door halfway and says in a honey-sweet voice.*) Good evening, Wasserstein!

WASSERSTEIN. Evening, Rheinberg.

RHEINBERG. Was there anything you wanted of me?

WASSERSTEIN. Nothing. I called you only to deliver the message.

RHEINBERG (*Sweetly.*) It was nice of you to go to so much trouble.

JACOB. (*Dryly.*) Come on! Shut the door!

RHEINBERG. (*Does so and comes downstage.*) And to what do I owe this honor?

RABBI FRIEDHEIMER. (*In an undertone.*) We have a very serious matter to discuss with you.

RHEINBERG. We? . . . Both of you?

JACOB. Yes. . . . I'll put it in a nutshell. (*Softly but insistently.*) You have ruined Count von Schramm. You must undo the damage.

RHEINBERG. (*In the same tone.*) I've ruined him? (*Breaks into a nervous laugh.*) You're insane! The man ruined himself! (*He draws Jacob a few steps away from the Rabbi and whispers into his ear.*) And he's ruined me along with himself!

JACOB. (*Startled.*) What?

RHEINBERG. I'm in a desperate situation—it's absolutely between ourselves. No one must know! (*Looks about carefully.*) Least of all Wasserstein, otherwise it will be all over the floor tomorrow. Then I *would* be lost.

JACOB. What happened?

RHEINBERG. I've been cornered. I'm short on Rosamunde stock and can't get hold of any. It has suddenly disappeared from sight. I have my head in a noose, and he can pull it any time he pleases.

JACOB. Who?

RHEINBERG. That's just what I don't know! It's a weird situation. There's someone, somewhere, who can do with me as he pleases. He can force me to pay any price. If I knew who he was I could go to him and offer him half my fortune. He might very well ask for all of it, and I would have to give it to him. He could take the shirt off my back—and I would have to be grateful if he didn't have me barred from the exchange.

JACOB. (*Gravely.*) The chickens have come home to roost.

RABBI FRIEDHEIMER. (*He has risen and now takes a few steps toward Jacob.*) Well, do you still need my support, or have you managed to convince Herr Rheinberg?

JACOB. I don't think I've succeeded.

RABBI FRIEDHEIMER. (*To Rheinberg.*) Please listen to your brother-in-law! He asked me to accompany him because he thought my moral support might carry weight with you.

RHEINBERG. (*Confused.*) Of course, of course!

RABBI FRIEDHEIMER. I'm sure you are taking no unfair advantage of the Count, as the customs of the brokerage business go. If he were a businessman himself, he would have no reason to complain. But you know infinitely more about the market than he does. That imposes an obligation on you to make amends.

RHEINBERG. I can't agree with you. I have no obligation whatever toward him. My brother-in-law only *thinks* I have. He's on Schramm's side, I can't imagine why.

RABBI FRIEDHEIMER. Because he believes, quite properly, that our enemies will once again exploit a case like that against us Jews. I share his opinion. That's why I'm here to ask you to help Schramm.

RHEINBERG. You're mistaken. Schramm doesn't deserve any help. He behaved stupidly and utterly irresponsibly. (*Stamps his foot.*) Why didn't he hang on to his stock? Why did he have to borrow on it? Quite apart from the fact that mismanagement at his mine was the cause of the whole mess—the pit wasn't worth two million but he was drooling to get three million for it. Now he has ruined himself and others, and he's screaming for help. Ask Wasserstein if it was I who did him out of his money! It was an accident. (*In a labored voice.*) A dreadful mischance! (*Hastens to the door and cries through it.*) Wasserstein!

WASSERSTEIN. (*From outside.*) Rheinberg? (*Enters.*) What do you want?

RHEINBERG. Tell them whether I engaged in any manipulations to ruin Count von Schramm!

WASSERSTEIN. What do you mean, manipulation? You sold when there was a selling trend! I sold, you sold, everybody sold! When the merchandise is no good, you sell. Rosamunde turned sour, so we sold. Where's the manipulation? If you can't sell worthless securities, there's no more business. I myself did a lot of selling. (HERMINE *and* CHARLOTTE *have entered from the conservatory.*)

RHEINBERG. Are you covered, Wasserstein?

WASSERSTEIN. Naturally, Rheinberg. How about yourself?

RHEINBERG. (*With forced nonchalance.*) Of course.

WASSERSTEIN. Well, what do we care about the Count. Do you know him? Do I know him?

[*The butler announces Captain von Schramm. Rheinberg cravenly refuses to see him and Jacob agrees to act on his behalf. Wasserstein arranges to have the butler stand by in case of trouble. The ladies retire.*]

Scene 7

JACOB, SCHRAMM, RABBI FRIEDHEIMER, WASSERSTEIN.

SCHRAMM. (*Bows as before and waits until the ladies have left; then, to Jacob.*) You are informed—about the fraud?

JACOB. (*Quietly.*) I would advise you to be a little more careful in your choice of terms.

SCHRAMM. (*Provocatively.*) Or else?

JACOB. I might find it necessary to forego this discussion, much as I desire it. The point is to establish the facts.

SCHRAMM. What is there to establish?

JACOB. In the first place, there's no question of fraud.

SCHRAMM. That's what you say!

JACOB. Anyone would.

SCHRAMM. (*Inspects Wasserstein from head to toe.*) Who's that?

WASSERSTEIN. (*Courteously.*) Name of Wasserstein.

SCHRAMM. (*Turns his back; to Jacob.*) I've been done out of everything I owned. Don't try to tell me that was on the up and up!

JACOB. I shall try to do just that.

SCHRAMM. Oh, I suppose a lawyer can do almost anything.

JACOB. (*Controls himself.*) Count, let us be calm. It was indeed an ill-fated venture, but it wasn't Rheinberg's fault you were sold out.

WASSERSTEIN. Why did you have to go and mortgage the stock?

SCHRAMM. (*Bridling.*) Shut up!

WASSERSTEIN. (*Injured.*) Well, I declare! (*Walks aside.*)

JACOB. If you had held on to the stock, you could have weathered the panic and the price fall that followed the accident. Even today the stock is up a good bit.

SCHRAMM. (*Laughs grimly.*) Yes indeed! The dirty work is done. My pockets have been picked.

RABBI FRIEDHEIMER. (*In an undertone to Jacob.*) Please keep your temper!

JACOB. I will. . . . (*To Schramm.*) I'm determined to see that you get the facts and I intend to finish it. It's your own fault twice over that you've lost your fortune. In the first place, you borrowed on your stock, and your ignorance of business betrayed you. I'm very sorry about that, as Rabbi Friedheimer here can attest.

SCHRAMM. The Rabbi! You don't say!

JACOB. But you're much more to blame in another way, and there you don't deserve *any* sympathy.

SCHRAMM. All right, my friend, I'm going to let you have your say. I want to see just how brazen a man can be.

JACOB. I'm brazen enough to speak the truth. You're to blame for the neglect at your mine. The slipshod way it was being run . . .

SCHRAMM. (*Beside himself.*) How dare you!

JACOB. (*Heatedly.*) Your mismanagement not only destroyed your property but the lives of many people. While you indulged your aristocratic pastimes, your slaves drudged for you underground.

WASSERSTEIN. (*With enthusiasm, to Rabbi Friedheimer, in an undertone.*) That's telling him!

JACOB. Men, women, and children toiling in peonage in the bowels for the earth—for a pittance!

SCHRAMM. (*Gasps.*) Go on!

JACOB. I intend to! That's the way it went, year after year. No thought was wasted on safety measures, until the inevitable collapse came. And you really have the audacity to complain that the ground water washed away your ill-gotten wealth too! What will you do with the bodies? I've seen them with my own eyes. I've seen the widows too, and the orphans, who must go hungry now, because their fathers died for the Honorable Count von Schramm! I don't think you even attended the funeral!

SCHRAMM. I know you did. I have it on good authority.

JACOB. I was there.

SCHRAMM. Yes, for the strike too! It was because the miners refused to go down that the water backed up. At first I didn't understand what you were after. What's the Jew up to, I asked myself?

JACOB. The Jew was doing his Christian duty.

SCHRAMM. Your fine brother-in-law told me you were a fool. He said he was at odds with you. . . . But now I understand it all. You were hand in glove with him.

JACOB. That's a lie!

SCHRAMM. You're just another dirty Jew!

JACOB. You'll take that back!

WASSERSTEIN. (*In an undertone, to Friedheimer.*) I'll have him thrown out. (*Rings the bell.*)

SCHRAMM. And if I don't—you'll crawl, as you did once before? (BUTLER *enters.*) I know your kind! You'll crawl for your brother and for yourself. You dirty Jews are all the same! (JACOB *has flinched on hearing the words:* "As you did once before." *Now he hurls himself at Schramm and strikes him in the face.* SCHRAMM *staggers back, his hat falling to the ground. He utters a hoarse cry and is about to attack Jacob, when* RABBI FRIEDHEIMER *and* WASSERSTEIN *step between them. The* BUTLER *seizes him by the arms from behind and pushes*

*him out the door at left, despite his furious struggles. The whole
scene takes only a moment.*)

WASSERSTEIN. (*Picks up Schramm's hat and throws it out
the door, which he closes, turning the key twice.*) Now that's
what I call a real treat! And it all happened in front of witnesses! He won't be able to deny it. (*Rubs his hands.*)

JACOB. (*He has stood rooted to the floor ever since striking
Schramm. Now he shivers slightly.*) No, he won't deny it.

RABBI FRIEDHEIMER. (*Sinks into a chair; in a worried tone.*)
Like Moses of Mainz!

(Curtain.)

ACT IV

*The scene is the same as in Act II. It is three o'clock in the
afternoon.*

[*As the curtain rises, Wasserstein is ushered in by the Hellmann maid, who is now in Hermine's service. Despite the way
she has treated him before, he offers her a tip, which she takes
as an improper advance. Hermine, in considerable perturba-
tion, tells him that her husband is absent with Wurzlechner,
following a visit from two officers.*]

Scene 3

HERMINE, WASSERSTEIN. RHEINBERG

RHEINBERG. (*Enters at center.*) Anyone home? . . . Ah, Herr
von Wasserstein, what a privilege!

WASSERSTEIN. (*Carelessly.*) Hello, Rheinberg! . . . I think I'll
have to go now.

RHEINBERG. (*Presses Hermine's arm; in an urgent undertone.*)
Please don't let him get away!

HERMINE. (*Aside.*) Why not?

RHEINBERG. (*As before.*) You simply must help me! (*Aloud.*) Herr von Wasserstein!

WASSERSTEIN. (*Pauses at the door.*) What is it?

RHEINBERG. Won't you wait for me a few minutes?

WASSERSTEIN. Why?

RHEINBERG. You could take me along in your carriage. I saw it downstairs.

WASSERSTEIN. (*With a note of irony.*) Oh yes! . . . But I've already taken leave.

HERMINE. (*Smiles.*) Don't be so formal!

WASSERSTEIN. Oh, very well! (*Turns and sits down downstage left.*)

RHEINBERG. I'll be done in a moment, Herr von Wasserstein! (*To Hermine.*) Isn't your husband home? (*Draws her downstage right.*)

HERMINE. He's at a meeting. (*With returning worry.*) He should be back by now. . . . What do you want of him?

RHEINBERG. (*In a whisper.*) Nothing. It's only an excuse. . . . You simply must ask Wasserstein to go easy on me! He won't turn you down. He used to be mad about you—still is!

HERMINE. What on earth is it?

RHEINBERG. He's got it in his power to throttle me. He owns Rosamunde stock which I owe. I've just found out about it. If he decides to corner me, I'm lost. . . . Ask him for mercy!

HERMINE. Very well. (*Turns to the left.*)

RHEINBERG. (*Aloud.*) I'll tell you what, Hermine, I think I'd better leave a note for Jacques. . . . (*Sits down at the desk.*) You might forget some of the details. (*Pretends to write as he listens.*)

HERMINE. (*Walks over to Wasserstein.*) My dear Herr Wasserstein, I come to you on a diplomatic mission.

WASSERSTEIN. (*Rises.*) Really? On whose behalf?

HERMINE. On Fritz's behalf. He's told me his situation. You can ruin him.

WASSERSTEIN. I? You're joking!

HERMINE. I don't quite understand it myself. He says he's cornered.

WASSERSTEIN. (*A light dawns on him.*) Coal! Rosamunde!

HERMINE. That's it.

WASSERSTEIN. And I thought all the time it was Schlesinger! . . . So it's him!

HERMINE. (*Pleading.*) Please don't ruin him! Shall I leave you alone with him? (WASSERSTEIN *nods.* HERMINE *exits at left.*)

WASSERSTEIN. (*Goes to the right, pats Rheinberg on the shoulder.*) Rheinberg, you're a fool!

RHEINBERG. (*Rises; humbly.*) Why am I a fool, Herr von Wasserstein?

WASSERSTEIN. Because you allow yourself to be cornered.

RHEINBERG. I'm at your mercy.

WASSERSTEIN. And because you're afraid of me—of Emanuel Wasserstein! You really have it coming to you—you pushed me around often enough . . . but . . . (*with a glance to the left*) I'm going to let you off the hook!

RHEINBERG. (*Seizes both his hands.*) Wasserstein, you're a prince!

[*Wurzlechner brings the news that Jacob has been gravely wounded in a pistol duel with Captain von Schramm and is on the way home. Wasserstein goes to summon Jacob's parents, while Rheinberg and Wurzlechner apprise Hermine.*]

Scene 7

AS BEFORE. SECOND MAID, THEN DR. BICHLER, JACOB, TWO AID MEN.

SECOND MAID. (*Dashes in.*) The Red Cross men are bringing the Master!

RHEINBERG. Quiet! Quiet!

DR. BICHLER. (*Enters at center.*) Please have a bed fixed up.

RHEINBERG. (*To Second Maid.*) Quick, the bed! (SECOND MAID *exits at right, wringing her hands.* JACOB, *unconscious, is carried in at center on the arms of two* AID MEN.)

HERMINE. (*Wants to go to him.*) Jacques!

WURZLECHNER. (*Restrains her.*) Hush!

DR. BICHLER. He's only unconscious! . . . (*To the Aid Men.*) On the couch. (AID MEN *carefully put Jacob down, then exit at center.* DR. BICHLER *bends over Jacob; then, to Hermine.*) Towels, water, ice!

RHEINBERG. I'll get it. (*Exits right.* DR. BICHLER *adjusts Jacob's bandage.*)

JACOB. (*Opens his eyes; softly.*) You're hurting me, Bichler. Thank you. Hermine! (HERMINE *totters over to him.*)

SECOND MAID. (*Enters at right, whispers to Dr. Bichler.*) The bed is all made. (*Exits right.*)

DR. BICHLER. We're going to put you to bed.

JACOB. (*Feebly.*) No! Here! Where is—Franz?

WURZLECHNER. (*Moves to his side.*) Here I am.

JACOB. Thank you. . . . Franz! I want to stay here . . . with my books. Remember what I wanted? . . . Fellowship!

DR. BICHLER. Don't talk so much!

JACOB. (*Caresses Wurzlechner's hand.*) Good old Franz! . . . Tell the Rabbi . . . like Moses of Mainz. (*Mumbles.*) And by the side of the body sat his mother, an unearthly smile on her lips. (*Lapses into unconsciousness.*)

RHEINBERG. (*Enters at right with jug, basin, and towels; to Bichler in an undertone.*) Ice is coming up.

HERMINE (*Softly, to Dr. Bichler.*) Can't I help?

DR. BICHLER. (*Sadly.*) I'm afraid not.

Scene 8

AS BEFORE. HERR AND FRAU SAMUEL, WASSERSTEIN.

(FRAU SAMUEL, *pale and dry-eyed, her face a mask, between* HERR SAMUEL *and* WASSERSTEIN *who lead her by the arms.*)

HERR SAMUEL. (*Moaning.*) Where's my Kobi?

WURZLECHNER. (*Goes to meet them.*) He's unconscious. We must be quiet. (FRAU SAMUEL *stares ahead.*)

JACOB. (*Comes to.*) Tell the Rabbi!

WURZLECHNER. (*Softly, to Wasserstein.*) What does he want the Rabbi for? The last sacraments?

WASSERSTEIN. (*Shakes his head.*) No, we Jews die without sacraments. . . .

JACOB. (*Cries out weakly.*) Father! Mother!

HERR SAMUEL. (*Leads Frau Samuel to the couch.*) Kobi, here we are.

JACOB. (*Tries to sit up.*) Help me up! (WASSERSTEIN *weeps softly.*)

RHEINBERG. Get hold of yourself, old man!

WASSERSTEIN. Why does it have to be him? Why not us? (DR. BICHLER *helps Jacob sit up with Rheinberg's help.*)

JACOB. (*Takes his mother's hand and kisses it.*) Forgive me this sorrow, Mother. . . . (*Kisses his father's hand.*) You can understand, Father! You're a man! . . . (*Raises his voice.*) O Jews, my brethren, they won't let you live again—until you . . . Why do you hold me so tight? (*Mumbles.*) I want to— get—out! (*Louder.*) Out—of—the—Ghetto! (*Flails both arms, falls back, and dies.* FRAU SAMUEL *utters a piercing scream, throws herself to the floor, and beats her head against it repeatedly.*)

DR. BICHLER. (*To the others.*) Dead!

HERR SAMUEL. (*Erect, in a firm voice.*) The Lord hath given, the Lord hath taken away, blessed be the name of the Lord!

WURZLECHNER. Amen!

(Curtain.)

(Paris, 1894)

THE DREYFUS AFFAIR

PARIS, November 1 [1894.]—The ugly story of Captain Dreyfus is the talk of the day. It is not yet fully established whether Dreyfus is indeed guilty. But the arrest of the General Staff officer has been officially confirmed, and the Minister of War placed the matter before today's Cabinet session. These circumstances lend support to the presumption that Dreyfus has in fact committed his shameful deed. For the past year he has been assigned to the *Premier Bureau* of the General Staff, where the most important documents relating to the national defense are kept. All documents on mobilization and the order of battle originate here, and top-echelon orders are kept ready for instant dispatch in the event of a declaration of war. The *Premier Bureau* also designates Army concentration points in case of war, and if an enemy were to be informed of these matters he might conceivably prevent the deployment of the French Army. Just what documents Dreyfus has stolen has not yet been made public, any more than the identity of the power to which they were sold. It is rumored to be Germany, though Dreyfus himself is said to have had dealings only with Italians. He has been under close surveillance for some time and is reported to have been observed in conversation with an Italian colonel at Monte Carlo. This locale may also furnish the first hint of a motive that could have led a promising officer of wealthy family, heretofore of unblemished reputation, into a crime of particular gravity, in view of his position. Dreyfus was a gambler. Born in 1859 in Mülhausen, the son of a well-to-do manufacturer, he entered the Polytechnic School in 1876, became a second

Selections from Herzl's dispatches in the *Neue Freie Presse*.

lieutenant of artillery in 1880, was promoted to first lieutenant in 1882 and to captain in 1889. Five years ago he married the daughter of a Paris diamond merchant. He lived with his wife and two children in an attractive apartment near the Trocadero. His arrest two weeks ago was kept a close secret until yesterday. To prevent the news from coming out, he was committed to the Military Prison under a false name. An authoritative source reports that Dreyfus was intrusted with foreign intelligence on behalf of the French Ministry of War. The acquaintances he cultivated in this connection led him astray. His arrest took place in the following manner: Ordered to guard duty with several other officers, he was detained by the general, who put a number of questions to him and then had him taken into custody. Dreyfus is said to have denied his guilt for several days but later to have confessed. Treason on the part of an officer is punishable by death. A number of jurists have voiced the opinion that this applies only in time of war.

Paris, November 5—New versions of the Dreyfus Affair keep cropping up. It is now said that Dreyfus fell victim to the wiles of an Italian woman spy. She is supposed to have turned his head to such an extent that his infatuation led him to throw all caution to the winds and finally to betray national defense secrets. The Captain's family stoutly maintains his innocence and reports that he had twice been provided with a loaded revolver so that he might shoot himself. The accused declined to kill himself, insisting that he could prove his innocence.

Paris, December 19—The trial of Captain Dreyfus began today and within a short time the mystery that has been stirring up violent passions for many weeks is expected to be solved. Whether Captain Dreyfus has betrayed his country or whether it is possible, without sufficient proof, to arrest and publicly dishonor an officer on the most heinous of charges—these are more than military questions. Counsels for the defense and prosecution have for weeks issued statements in the most intemperate language. The case has been discussed in newspaper

articles marked by a degree of excitement rare even here. And
General Mercier, Minister of War, was represented in Saint
Genest's well-known article in *Figaro* as the great antagonist
of the accused. Other papers have responded with sharp appeals
to the people and the Army to rally behind the Minister of
War. The events have created a state of brooding dissatisfaction
in Parliament, and if this has not yet found expression from
the rostrum, it is because the circumstances are unknown—
all has been mystery and agitation. During the first few days,
demands for the accused officer's head were voiced in many
quarters. Subsequently, doubts of his guilt were heard from
many other sources, which served only to deepen unrest. Most
recently, argument has raged about the question of whether the
trial proceedings should be public or secret. In political circles
the death of President Burdeau only momentarily halted discussion of the mysterious case. Today all eyes are again turned
toward the court-martial that is to render the verdict.

The trial is to get under way at one o'clock in the afternoon.
As a precautionary measure, since admission to the proceedings
is very difficult, we set out for the remote Rue du Cherche
Midi as early as eleven o'clock. The court-martial is to sit in a
building far from the city's main traffic arteries, over on the
left bank of the Seine. It is a quiet street, calling to mind a
sleepy little provincial town. At this hour it shows no signs yet of
the great impending event. Outside the court building the street
is deserted, except for policemen in uniform and plain clothes.
No one is permitted to loiter. Now one notices several groups
at the far street corners. Small merchants stand before their
shops, craning their necks with curiosity. Opposite the courthouse a high wall surrounds the Military Prison. The accused
will have to cross the street—indeed, already had to do so
during the preliminary examination. This is what caused the
matter to leak out, for initially the arrest had been kept a close
secret. Newspaper reporters got wind of the fact that an officer
whose name no one knew was being mysteriously detained in
the Prison in the Rue Cherche Midi. The military courthouse
is an ancient, dilapidated palace that has nothing in common

with the majestic splendor of the Palais de Justice. A courtyard, still and deserted as we arrive, separates the building from the street. Two guardsmen march to and fro on the uneven cobblestones. Another is posted at the gate with fixed bayonet, while still others stand about in the guardroom. Everyday life shows its familiar traces—a servant girl comes to the well; a baker's boy delivers bread; and a sudden chirping is heard from a cage in the concierge's second-floor flat, a bird singing into the sunshine of the full day. Several journalists now arrive, then some veteran officers in civilian dress and others in uniform, a few in full dress. They are either judges or witnesses.

We now ascend the fine wide flight of stone steps leading up to the courtroom. We must wait for admission in a small lobby. There is a small room where the accused wait for the verdict. The grimy walls are covered with prison legends. Some have noted their name, guilt, and penalty—three years on such-and-such a date. We are admitted, eighteen at a time. The tiny hall is cluttered with benches and wooden partitions. In the middle stands a huge iron stove, radiating insufferable heat. Two iron columns bear up the plain yellow ceiling. The walls are wainscoted to more than six feet in height, and a few gas lamps with green paper shades hang from the ceiling. The judges' table, covered with green baize, stands on a raised platform. It is surrounded by seven chairs, upholstered in red velvet. Behind the table is a large picture of Christ and on the wall behind the defense attorney's seat an ordinary round wall-clock. The seat looks like a large wooden chicken-roost. Before it, three steps up, stands a rude bench inside a wooden compartment. This is where the accused will sit, facing the public prosecutor. Many officers and a few ladies are already in the hall. Several artists for illustrated journals are sketching rapidly. The witnesses arrive, most of them officers in full-dress uniform, all of them stiff and solemn. Behind the press benches a guard is mounted, erecting a hedge of bayonets against the rest of the public. A few ladies now emerge behind the judges' table, feathers nodding gaily from their hats. There is a sudden stir and commands ring out as the court is an-

nounced. The officer of the guard sings out: *"Garde à vous!*
Portez armes! Présentez armes!" Everyone rises, the officers
salute, the members of the court-martial enter.

Colonel Maurel, President of the Court, and the six assessor
judges take their stand at the table. They have their kepis on.
Maurel announces in a firm voice: "This court is now in session.
Call the defendant." Several minutes elapse. The hall is deathly
quiet. All heads turn toward the small doorway and now the
accused man makes his public appearance. Although the crime
with which he is charged is punishable by death, he is un-
shackled, with only a lieutenant as an escort. An extraordinary
feeling of tension grips us all as we gaze at him. Somewhat
above average height, he cuts a smart figure in the trim, dark
uniform of an artillery officer, the three gold stripes of a captain
on his sleeves. Dreyfus walks with lowered head through the
crowd, climbs the three steps to the prisoner's dock, comes to
attention facing the court, and bows smartly. Then he sits
down. His face can now be seen. He looks ten years older,* his
hair is grizzled and has receded from his forehead, his nose
is sharply aquiline, his ears prominent, his cheeks and firm chin
shaven, his thick mustache close-trimmed, his mouth twisted
as though in pain. Surmounting his nose is a pince-nez. His
bearing is firm and calm.

Colonel Maurel orders the case to be called and the officer-
clerk, seated beside Major Brisset, the Government Commissioner, rises to read the brief official docket and the names of the
judges. Colonel Maurel speaks: "The defendant will rise. What
is your name?" The accused: "Alfred Dreyfus." The President
of the Court: "How old are you?" Dreyfus: "Thirty-five."
President: "Where were you born?" Dreyfus: "In Mülhausen,
Alsace." President: "What is your occupation?" Dreyfus: "Captain in the artillery." The accused speaks in a firm voice, only
slightly strained. President: "Please follow the proceedings
carefully." Dreyfus sits down. Commissioner Brisset, a veteran
officer with white mustache and imperial, at once takes the
floor and says: "Article 113 of the Military Penal Code pre-
scribes secret proceedings whenever publicity may be harmful

* The photostat of the newspaper clipping, made in Berlin, omits a line here.

to public order. This applies in the present case. I therefore request that the public be excluded."

Counsel for the defense Demange has appeared in barrister's robes. He seeks to reply to the Commissioner, but Colonel Maurel interposes: "In granting you the floor, I urgently request you to confine yourself to the question of secret proceedings. This is the sole question presently before us." Counselor Demange: "I have the honor to offer the following motions." He reads from a written brief, to the effect that each case must be individually examined as to whether open proceedings should constitute a clear danger of harm to good morals and public order. Actually the only documentary evidence of the prosecution—The President brusquely interrupts him: "I repeat my urgent request not to mention a single document relating to the trial." Counselor: "I am reading my motions in order to set forth my views on the question of secret proceedings. They do not discuss the substance of any documents. Nevertheless, it seems to me absolutely essential to discuss—" President (interrupts): "I deem it unnecessary to cite even a single piece of evidence, otherwise the request of the Commissioner would become illusory." Counselor (with raised voice): "I request the court-martial to examine the documentary evidence. I shall disclose none of their contents. I do not exceed my prerogatives when I touch upon facts and circumstances on which members of the court-martial must be fully informed in order to know whether secret proceedings are necessary. You will see that I mention nothing. In view of the fact that the sole piece of evidence—" Commissioner Brisset pounds the table with his fist and the President cuts off the Counselor: "I shall not permit you to continue along this line."

Brisset: "You are permitted only to make remarks, not to offer motions." Counselor: "I ask that the record show that I am denied the right to offer motions." President: "It shall be so recorded." Counselor: "Clerk, please take it down!" Brisset: "No, no! You cannot mention any documents!" Counselor: "The interests of the defense demand that I set this forth." Brisset: "Interests other than those of the defense and even the prosecution are involved. The President, moreover, will submit the entire file to the judges." Counselor: "The President is acquainted with the file. I regret that not all the judges know it. I wish to prove that there is no case for secrecy." President: "An opinion of the Court of Cassation of 1883 holds that secrecy may be imposed for overriding reasons, without even consulting the accused. I do not wish you to go into the merits." Counselor: "I wish to make it known that I have been forbidden to offer my motions. I shall place them on the table without having read them." Commissioner Brisset: "For half an hour you have done nothing but read. You have read everything." Counselor: "How do you know that?" Brisset: "You have read the most important part." Counselor: "Who has told you that? You do not know my brief, yet you assert this was the most important part." The objection of counsel for the defense is hereupon made a matter of record.

Demange now cites decisions of the Court of Cassation under which counsel seeking to speak against secrecy must be heard. "Gentlemen," he says, "you may decide on the advisability to the best of your knowledge and belief, but only after you know the circumstances." President: "You are not to discuss the circumstances." Counselor: "Very well, but there are material and moral elements which I must clear up. When I mention moral elements, I include background and motivations that have nothing to do with public order." President: "You are beginning your plea." Counselor: "Certainly not. As for the material elements, there is no possible danger when I point to a piece of evidence in the files, only a single document." President (angrily): "In view of your persistence I shall order the court to take a recess." He rises. Counselor (quickly): "One more word." The President resumes his seat and says: "Very well, one word." Counselor: "If the defendant and I demand a public trial, it is not, we wish you to believe, because we think your verdict will be in any manner subject to public influence. The defendant and I know that you will judge conscientiously, that your impartiality is beyond the reach of either secret or public proceedings. Yet no one will contradict me when I say that for seven weeks the honor of an officer of the French Army has been at the mercy of the scandal-mongers." The President snaps shut his portfolio: "By virtue of the discretionary power vested in me, I order this court now to stand in recess."

Counselor: "I request that it be made a matter of record that I was interrupted." The court retires, the guard presents arms, commands ring out as before.

Dreyfus rises and glances about the hall without a trace of embarrassment. Then he calmly sits down, twirls his mustache, and speaks a few words to the lieutenant by his side. The hum of conversation rises in the hall, there is loud talk and laughter, and the ladies stare at the defendant curiously. A quarter-hour elapses, then *"Garde à vous!"* again rings out. The court returns. All the judges keep their kepis on. All rise as the President reads the decision: "Having taken note of the defense motions, the court has decided—the last appointed lowest ranking member voting first, the President last—that proceedings will be held in secret, since public order would be otherwise endangered. The court's verdict will be made public. No reports of the case may be published, with the exception of the verdict. I order the hall to be cleared immediately. Nothing of what is said here may go beyond these walls. Please leave."

All spectators now retire, only the witnesses remaining. Witnesses summoned by the prosecution include General Gonse, several colonels and majors and a few captains, four handwriting experts, and Police Commissioner Cochefert. Witnesses for the defense are Grand Rabbi Dreyfus, several Alsatians, including Koechlin, several captains and majors, and Colonel Clément. The court-martial remained in session until half past six in the evening, at which time it adjourned to one o'clock tomorrow. So far only five of thirty-five witnesses have been heard—General Gonse, a colonel, two captains, and Major du Paty. Upon leaving the session, the witnesses were ringed by journalists and showered with questions. None gave any information, secrecy being maintained with great strictness. Each witness was required to depart immediately after examination. None of them learned what any of the others testified. The trial is expected to last three days. Dreyfus is reported to be maintaining his firm composure.

Paris, December 22—As on preceding days, Captain Dreyfus was escorted from prison across the street to the courthouse this morning at seven o'clock, in civilian clothes. He habitually dons the uniform only when he reaches the guardroom. The trial resumed at one o'clock, in a courtroom that remains rigidly barred, as before. Admission is forbidden even to the courtyard. Police Prefect Lepine is again on hand. Counselor Demange took the floor as soon as the court was in session. He spoke until three o'clock, then asked for a brief respite.

Eight o'clock P.M.—A huge crowd occupied the vicinity of the military courthouse during the evening hours. Even those with cards of admission were not permitted to approach the gate before six o'clock. At six Counselor Demange at long last finished his plea. The court-martial retired to consider its verdict. The public was admitted to the courtroom, pushing its way inside tumultuously. An hour of breathless expectancy followed. At seven the court reappeared, to the customary command: *"Garde à vous!"* Amid a profound silence Colonel Maurel announced in a firm voice: "The court-martial has unanimously found Dreyfus guilty." (Cries of "Ah!" from among the spectators.) Colonel Maurel declares further that Dreyfus has been sentenced to deportation for life and to military degradation. A voice in the courtroom cries out: *"Vive la France!"* Some spectators immediately begin to push their way outside, to spread the sensational news in the city as swiftly as possible.

Nine o'clock P.M.—When the court-martial originally retired, Dreyfus was escorted downstairs and taken to the guard room where he remained thenceforth, since under the Military Penal Code the defendant is not present when the verdict is rendered. It is communicated to him later. This is to prevent condemned soldiers from abusing the court. Colonel Maurel, President of the Court, used the following words: "A single question was before the court-martial: 'Is Captain Dreyfus guilty of having delivered to a foreign power or its representatives, in Paris in the year 1894, documents relating to the national defense, and has he thereby committed acts, or maintained communications with this foreign power, for the purpose of persuading it to commit hostile acts against France, or calculated to furnish it the means toward that end?' The question was unanimously answered in the affirmative." A few minutes later, Government Commissioner Brisset went to the courtyard of the palace. Dreyfus was produced by the guard, stood in the light of a few gas lanterns, and listened as the verdict was read to him. When the clerk had finished, Brisset addressed Dreyfus: "You have twenty-four hours to file an appeal." Dreyfus intends to appeal. The crowd before the courthouse has meanwhile grown to many thousands. Everyone who emerges is bombarded with questions. The news has spread through the city like wildfire. The first extras were on the street at 8:29 P.M., only to be gobbled up on every hand. All they are able to print is a brief summary of the verdict.

Half past ten o'clock P.M.—Dreyfus wept when the verdict was read to him. Gauthier de Clagoy, a member of the Boulangist party, will put a question on the Dreyfus affair in Parliament on Monday. Other Deputies are said to be planning to press for reintroduction of the death penalty for similar cases of treason.

Paris, December 24.—Captain Dreyfus has appealed his case, which will consequently come before the Paris Appellate Council. Dreyfus' appeal is reported to be based on alleged violations of trial procedure. If the verdict is set aside, a second court-martial will meet in Paris. There is no expectation that the appeal will prevail, and the public is convinced that Captain Dreyfus is guilty. The trial was closed to the public, but the verdict was unanimous. It is believed that the foreign power for which Dreyfus is said to have spied would not have stood by to see an innocent man accused and convicted without declaring publicly that it had no relations with him. Hence the general belief in Dreyfus' guilt. On Saturday his place was set at the family table. The family expected his acquittal, but instead came the news of his conviction. Military degradation, to which Dreyfus was sentenced, is an extremely humiliating ceremony. The condemned man, in full-dress uniform with saber, is conducted to a parade ground. Until 1886 this was the Champ du Mars, since then it has been the great courtyard of the École Militaire. The interment of Dreyfus' honor is to take place on the great esplanade before the Invalides. Detachments from the entire Paris garrison will be on hand. At the center will stand a general chosen by the Military Governor. He will order the sentence to be read to the condemned man by the clerk of the court-martial. When this has been done, in a loud voice the general will proclaim: "Dreyfus, you are unworthy to bear arms. We degrade you in the name of the French people!" Thereupon the adjutant will step forward, unsheathe Dreyfus' saber, which has been previously filed down in the middle, and snap it with his foot. The buttons, pipings, and sleeve insignia on Dreyfus' uniform have likewise been previously half-severed, and they are now torn off. In this state the condemned man must then march past the entire line of troops, a custom that harks back to the ancient penalty of running the gantlet. Dreyfus, no longer a soldier, will then be taken to a civilian prison. From there he will be taken to the Island of Ré and will remain in the port fortress, awaiting the departure of the next steamer for New Caledonia. There he will be interned in a fortress on Ducos Peninsula, under no compulsion to work or engage in any occupation. His wife and children will be permitted to join him. After five years of exemplary conduct, he may become a free colonist and even purchase a piece of land. However, he will never be permitted to leave New Caledonia.

After midnight today a rumor spread that Dreyfus had committed suicide in prison, but this was denied. The Dreyfus case has revived memories of other treason trials of French officers, from Marshal Bazaine to Triponet, associate of Turpin.

Paris, December 27—Captain Dreyfus, upon denial of his appeal, will be stripped of his military status on the barracks ground of the École Militaire. Failure of the appeal is held to be certain. Even Dreyfus has now given up all hope. Until the last he had been in the habit of telling the sergeant who guards him: "You see, I am the victim of personal vengeance. I am persecuted, because I am a Jew.* At the trial the charges against me will collapse like a house of cards." Dreyfus' wife still believes in his innocence and is determined to go to New Caledonia with him. His brothers who live in Mülhausen and send their sons to school in Belfort have been unofficially requested to take the boys out of school.

Paris, December 31—The Appellate Council of the Court-Martial, presided over by General Gossard, met to consider Captain Dreyfus' appeal. The proceedings took place in the same courtroom where Dreyfus was convicted. No attorney appeared for him. Defense counsel had merely notified the court in writing that he reposed full confidence in the appeals tribunal and would not appear to offer any further motions. After studying the complaint briefly, the President of the Council announced that the appeal was denied.

Paris, January 5 [1895]—On this gloomy winter morning the degradation of Captain Dreyfus brought a large crowd of curiosity-seekers to the vicinity of the War College, located behind the site of the World's Fair of 1889. Many officers were in evidence, some with their ladies. Admission to the courtyard of the École Militaire was limited to officers and a handful of journalists. The gawking crowd, of the kind that usually attends executions, was kept outside. The police were present in force. By nine o'clock the huge courtyard was filled with troop detachments which formed a hollow square. Some 5,000 men were on hand. A mounted general held the center. A few minutes after nine Dreyfus, wearing captain's uniform, was conducted to the scene. Four guards led him before the general who addressed him in these words: "Alfred Dreyfus, you are unworthy to bear arms. In the name of the French people, I degrade you. Let the judgment be done." Dreyfus raised his right hand and exclaimed: "I swear and declare that you are degrading an innocent man. *Vive la France!*" A

* This is the first mention that Dreyfus was a Jew. Earlier references may have been cut by the editor.

roll of drums sounded at this instant. A military court official began to rip away from the condemned man's uniform the buttons and insignia that had been previously loosened. Dreyfus maintained his composure. It was all over in a matter of minutes.

Now began the review of the troops. Dreyfus strode past the ranks like one who is sure of his innocence. Cries of "Judas! Traitor!" came as he passed one group of officers. Dreyfus cried back: "I protest your insults!" By 9:20 the review was completed. Dreyfus was shackled and turned over to the gendarmes. Henceforth he will be treated as a civil prisoner. When he had been led away, the troops began to march off. The crowd massed at the gates to see the prisoner leave. Angry words were heard—"If they bring him out here, he'll be torn limb from limb." But the crowd waited in vain. The witnesses to the ceremony departed in a strange state of agitation. The oddly* firm bearing of the dishonored officer had registered a deep impression on many.

Paris, January 5—Further details of Dreyfus' degradation: while he passed in review he repeatedly called out to the soldiers, many of them young recruits, "I am innocent!" When he reached a group of journalists, he halted and said: "Tell all France that I am innocent!" Several responded with abuse. The crowd outside the iron gate was able to witness part of the degradation ceremony and repeated cries were heard:** "Death to the traitor!" An interesting rumor, much in need of confirmation, is presently making the rounds. In the waiting room, just before his degradation, Dreyfus is supposed to have told his guards: "I am innocent. If I delivered documents abroad, it was as bait, in order to secure important documents. Within three years the truth will be out. The Minister himself will take up my case." An evening paper reports that Dreyfus

* Here is early evidence that Herzl entertained serious doubts of Dreyfus' guilt.
** This passage was probably edited. In later years Herzl always related that the crowd had cried: "*À la mort les juifs!*" ("Death to the Jews!"), and that it was this cry that had struck him so deeply. See also the dispatch of December 27.

told the captain who awakened him in the Military Prison this morning: "Captain, you are the instrument of one of the greatest injustices of the century." After his degradation Dreyfus was taken to civil prison in an ordinary police van. There he was subjected to all the procedures applied to common criminals. He was photographed in his tattered uniform.

Paris, April 6—Captain Dreyfus arrived at Cayenne on March 13. He was transferred to Devil's Island, where he is guarded day and night by five soldiers. He can move only within a radius of 500 feet from his hut. The topography prevents anyone from approaching him by sea or land. On admission Dreyfus again protested his innocence. He said he would wait patiently until the truth is known.

CONDITIONS IN FRANCE

BY BENJAMIN SEFF*

A FEW upright and valiant men have tried to roll away the stone that lies over his crypt. But a rabble swarmed over the liberators and bore them down. The stone is in the old place and the living dead man remains buried. Such is the state of the case that has achieved a sorry renown throughout the world as the "Dreyfus Affair." The people of France—greathearted, loving justice, the nation of human rights, that is continually reviewing all verdicts, never likes to regard any case as closed—that nation refuses to have the guilt of the Jewish captain called into the slightest question. There have been tumultuous demonstrations in the streets, patriotic oratory in the Chamber, yellow journalism, and all these have but one purpose: to keep the Jew overseas on Devil's Island. They keep on beating him to death, even though he is as good as buried. One is reminded of their adage: *Quand on est mort, c'est pour longtemps.* How true, especially for one who is still alive! He is indeed a long time dead.

Yet in the hearts and minds of many, and by no means the worst, nor Jews alone, the thought has lodged that this unhappy Jew on the equatorial isle is innocent—this Jew whose insignia were stripped from his sleeve on the ceremonial occasion when his honor was interred. Gutter fury and newspaper campaigns can no longer banish that thought, and those who harbor it join the mourners for the living dead man. The reticent and contradictory attitude of the French Government, evi-

---

* Herzl's *nom de plume*, based on his Hebrew given name, Binyamin Ze'ev.

Herzl's later articles on the Dreyfus Affair; from the *Welt*, Vol. 1, No. 30, December 24, 1897.

dently dictated by self-preservation, has scarcely served to dispel doubt. In any other case the new facts that have become known would have resulted in further proceedings. True, a second trial might conceivably bring another conviction, but it would at least serve to allay the qualms of justice. Yet there's the rub. They do not dare revive the case, for Captain Dreyfus must on no account have been innocent. That would leave the people with a sense of having been cheated. They would regard another trial and an acquittal as a pretense, veiling the influence of Jewish financiers. A furious popular upheaval would have to be reckoned with. These may have been the reasons of state that led to the glossing over of the attempt at review. Matters had reached such threatening proportions that the "Méline" Cabinet probably had no other recourse, government being so often no more than a choice among different brands of wrong. It is even conceivable that some French Jews prefer to see the tragedy end with only one casualty. Matters might have been worse. The shirt is closer than the vest. Poor Dreyfus!—he's lost! Let's not have any more victims!

But that line of reasoning is not only cold-blooded; it is useless. The Dreyfus case won't be settled when the poor fellow on his faraway isle has slowly succumbed to the fever. The bitter ordeal of one man has long since posed a much larger question. For whom is he serving as scapegoat?

We do not mean the scoundrel, as yet unidentified, who committed the treason ascribed to Dreyfus—if indeed there was treason rather than forgery, as in the notorious Norton Affair. We mean the people or groups to whom he owes his agony. For such there are, without a doubt. Let us assume for a moment that he really committed the crime with which he was charged. Such villainy was perpetrated by others before him; indeed, there were several similar cases in the French Army shortly before his conviction. So far as is known, none of these culprits was ceremoniously dishonored with fiendish shrieks of glee. Yet on Dreyfus an almost voluptuous fury was vented. They would have dearly loved to tar and feather him, wreak unmentionable atrocities on his person. Why? This was no longer retribution for the betrayal of military secrets. As the other cases prove, that does not arouse insensate fury in time of peace. No, this rage was of a different stripe, closer to the excesses of a mob uprising. And the wholesale charge was not long wanting. The mob did not cry "Down with Dreyfus!" It howled "Down with the Jews!" That was the keynote from the first moment, and that is the keynote today. Oh yes, Captain Dreyfus was summoned before a tribunal of seven gentlemen of the French Army, on the basis of a single document, the famous *"bordereau"* now suspect throughout the world. But his officer judges were under terrific pressure. Precisely because the proceedings were held in secret, the pressure of public opinion was enormous. Those seven stalwarts, never afraid of their lives, may have been more greatly afraid of their reputation. For outside the courthouse in the streets lurked slander, ready to pounce. From the very outset the foul and crafty rumor of Jewish gold that would free the traitor showed its fangs.

Poor Jew, laden with the curse of money, the curse of wealth others owned! He had nothing to do with them, nor they with him, yet instantly kinship was established between him and them. When one cannot lay hold of the hated, one hates those near at hand. The Dreyfus case bared an accumulated hatred of the Jews far beyond the measure we had suspected in France. Whose fault is it? Surely not the worthy artillery captain's—the Alsatian who was prepared to give his life for France on the battlefield. One deputy in the republican Chamber of this country has risen to move that henceforth no Jew should be permitted to hold public office. A similar bill, a little more subtle, was proposed several years ago, after the Panama Affair, enlisting some 160 votes. How many would it command today? France today is antisemitic to the core, no doubt about it. *Le Figaro*, one of the richest and most powerful newspapers, tried to champion Dreyfus' cause for a while. Public opinion forced it to capitulate. The editor-in-chief had to withdraw, lest he imperil its continuance. Yet a journalist at the head of *Le Figaro* has greater independence than a representative of the people. A legislator's popularity is a hand-to-mouth affair, so to speak. Parliamentary scandals of recent years have already severely shaken the reputation enjoyed by deputies. Even if they knew better, would they dare oppose passions? The elections are at hand and it is readily foreseeable that antisemitism will become a campaign issue. From the extreme right to the extreme left a single cry sounds through the land: "Curb the Jews!"

The temper is one of rebellion. Yet those concerned are stricken deaf and blind. They still think it will all blow over. Indeed it will, as does everything. The question is, how?

Does anyone think the Jew-baiters, just having tested their strength on the hapless Dreyfus, will rest content with a single victim? They have tasted blood and will clamor for more, all the more greedily and confidently, since they have come to know the irresistible quality of their appeal. This entire case has revealed the startling weakness and confusion that afflict governmental authority in France. The flood is ever ready to go on a rampage when the dam weakens. In France conservative interests do not coincide with those of the government, though the conservatives always "rally around" any stable government. Now the widely hailed speech of Count Mun has shown that even those who rally are against the Jews. It is only the opportunists who still offer the Jews a support scarcely worth having, for the opportunists are silent and intimidated. It is commonly said that opportunism has declined because of the Jews. It would be more correct to say that the Jews have declined because of opportunism. The radicals and reactionaries are against them and the parties of the middle can save themselves only by deserting the Jews. It will be seen that the situation in France is grave enough.

Even now it is no longer a matter of a wretched, degraded captain whose worst enemies cannot claim that he enriched himself by his alleged crime. But what if enrichment itself is arranged? There will be no question of guilt or innocence, nor even the shadow of due process. Passion will render the verdict.

THE REVISION

BY BENJAMIN SEFF

The most gripping drama staged in the nineteenth century is moving toward its final curtain. It is the kind of happy ending old-fashioned storytellers of a simpler age were fond of tacking on. At long last, after bitter tribulations, innocence comes into its own. A wreath of flowers is pressed upon the blood-stained brow of virtue. The sinner gets his just deserts—unless, of course, he has already escaped his unpleasant due by a verdict that must be allowed to stand, by the operation of the statute of limitations, or by some other pettifoggery. Now Du Paty de Clam is delivered to the pangs of his conscience in the very cell where Dreyfus and Picquart languished. Few can have failed to feel at least a small thrill at this dramatic reversal of fate. There is, after all, retribution down here below. Evil cannot in the end prevail. The day of justice dawns, perforce, because a society that can no longer tell right from wrong must otherwise perish of its own ruthlessness, as of shameful sickness. With a sigh of relief we ring down the curtain on the play that has given us so much anguish. The last act has made up for much that went before. It was majestic and exalted, showing that mankind can cleanse itself, if it but have the will.

Yet this was no dream the poet's hand wove about our terrified souls. It was real. For five years the burden lay upon France, like a noisome stench that rises from the herded throng, only to reach down again with its poisonous touch. That is what gives us pause, as we look back on this closed chapter in the history of a great nation—a nation all of us loved when

From the *Welt*, Vol. 3, No. 23, June 9, 1899.

it was a nation of lofty thought and humanitarian aspiration— the splendid laboratory of freedom. Will those days come again? It is a question that haunts us all. Why us, the spectators at long range? What more is there than the ordeal of one man, perhaps a family or a faction, at best a foreign land? Ah, there was more at stake in this fierce rift. Perhaps it did begin as the misfortune of one man; but it grew and spread, overflowing the borders of his country, becoming a poignant cause that affected the whole civilized world. And perhaps we who watched the fearsome events unfold step by step as yet fail to appreciate how later ages will read in them vital clues to the current state of our morality.

An innocent man, of blameless reputation, is snatched from his profession and his family at one fell swoop. He is a soldier without reproach, honorable, hard-working, conscientious. These very qualities arouse the envy and resentment of some of his colleagues. Perhaps his sense of duty was a little too uncompromising, too self-righteous. He becomes unpopular. And because his fellows dislike him, malevolent prejudice seeks for justification. Prejudgment, preceding judgment, sought to be executed. A miscarriage of justice is an evil thing; but even the most outrageous and contradictory judicial verdict pales before the power of prejudice. This is the very core of the Dreyfus case, and because of it the figure of the hapless captain looms large in the history of our times. This is the vital point, if we would understand the whole sorry case. Judicial error, persecution of the innocent, these are, alas! part and parcel of human frailty. Legal language itself recognizes this with covert honesty and instinctive doubt when it speaks of "trial" and "jeopardy" and "reasonable doubt." Coincidence, too, plays its part in jurisprudence, as every wise judge will admit. Even legislators have faced up to the dreadful chance that the innocent may be adjudged guilty, as witness modern laws providing indemnities for such victims. Error is the chance we take as long as we want our judges to be men to whom nothing human is alien.

And we may well believe that from every place of judgment rise the unheard pleas of the innocent. Judge Lynch, running riot in the Wild West, may be no less at fault than a stiff-necked bench blinded by the inflexible paragraphs of a legal code history has left behind. But the plea that was to be stifled within the walls where the French court-martial met in secret, the plea that miraculously reached out to gain such power as made the whole world tremble—that was a very special plea. Behind it was prejudice rather than a verdict without justice.

True, the suffering on Devil's Island was bad enough. But then, countless men suffer. Life is full of plots in which the innocent and good suffer much wrong. Judgment and punishment are not always the worst of it. There is more torment in everyday life than ever echoed in the most ingenious torture chambers of medieval Spain. Banishment to a desert island is not the ultimate cruelty our imagination can picture. Even had the victim died on that far shore, his destiny would not have been fulfilled; for from the outset his case transcended his physical identity. It had become an abstract issue.

Again, it would be doing the degraded Captain Dreyfus a curious injustice to represent him as a tragic hero or martyr. For he championed no cause, suffered for no belief. From his point of view, the whole incident was no more than a wretched mischance, even though he did display much strength of character and nobility in the face of adversity. One cannot even say with assurance that he would have sided with the victim, had it all happened to another. Some who knew the prisoner of Devil's Island of old were fond of describing him as one whose whole background and cast of mind would have made him an anti-Dreyfusard. When the blessed vessel that bears him homeward nears the shores of France, his first cry of delivery may be: *"Vive la France!"*; and surely his second: *"Vive l'Armée!"* From his own heart, the very slogans that served to justify his five years of ostracism and exile! It sounds paradoxical, yet it is true: none is intellectually less involved in the battle of ideas that raged so violently around the name of Dreyfus than the victim who bears that name.

To limit the whole affair to the conviction, banishment, and return of a French artillery captain would be a meaningless belittlement. Much more was in the background, and it may not yet be ended. The name and person of Dreyfus are no more than the name and location of some previously unknown hamlet about which raged a historic battle. For that is what it was—one of the greatest political battles of our times. The glorious banner of liberty and justice carried the day. Under that banner, so often in peril of being struck, are to be found the true tragic heroes and sacrificial blood witnesses. And if France today can boast not only a Court of Cassation that will not be intimidated but a public opinion that is sound to the core, it must recognize as its finest sons the writer Zola, who lives in hiding, and the soldier Picquart, housed in a prison cell.

Has it come to this in the land of Voltaire, champion of Calas? The revision, that triumph of reason and truth, was not won as forthrightly as might have been desired. The rulers of France who have now shown their leadership on the side of good may not have been too sure of success. They felt they had to resort to a stratagem, to creep up on public opinion, so to speak. No one at first appreciated the significance of the piecemeal revelations in *Le Figaro* which, oddly formulated as they were, appealed to the sense of curiosity rather than justice. It was a brilliant move, no doubt, but in addition to other secrets it revealed the leaders' awareness that the French people, once so lucid and generous, were undergoing a crisis. Like an ailing tyrant, the sovereign people had to be prepared for the truth by means of a clever side show, else they might have resentfully rejected it.

But these considerations need not long detain us. It is enough that France shows the will to recover. Even in error it showed signs of marvelous vitality. The crisis seems to have passed, and all for the good. Even now another question emerges. What benefit can morality in general derive from the struggle and settlement in France? For a hundred years France has been the fire that warmed all mankind. Surely these five years of haggling over Dreyfus must hold a lesson for history. The fear and trembling and now the joy among all civilized men have created an obligation to guard against the possibility that everything will simply revert to the status quo. It would be absurd, and a great pity, if the titanic struggle resulted only in Captain Dreyfus' sewing the stripes back on his dishonored uniform and being promoted to major at the next turn, while the Marquis du Paty de Clam now languishes in jail. We expect something more from these volatile events which have taken on a rich symbolic significance by virtue of the ideological struggles they precipitated. They must yield something more exalted and universal than the blissful return of an innocent man. That is a sign that an unquenchable yearning for justice dwells in the hearts of all men—or at least most of them; that they do not despair of a better future for mankind; that the intricate destiny of one man may hold an enduring lesson in loving-kindness; and that we must strive for the eradication of prejudice even more than for the revision of unjust verdicts. That is the true meaning of the message that today crackled over the wires to the far corners of the inhabited world; and that is the reason why so many people greeted the news of the revision of the Dreyfus Affair as though something wonderful had happened to them personally. All men are bidden to the table where humanity feasts.

FIVE AGAINST TWO

BY BENJAMIN SEFF

A STRANGE discovery was made in the evening hours of September 9, 1899; nor has it failed to excite interest in all those parts of the world to which telegraph cables run. What was discovered is that it is possible to deny justice to a Jew, for no other reason than that he is a Jew. It was discovered to be possible to torture a Jew as though he were not a human being at all, to sentence him to infamous punishment even though he be innocent.

This rather surprising discovery was widely made when the new verdict of guilty was pronounced over Dreyfus. The assimilated Jews particularly were greatly astonished. Yes, Alfred Dreyfus, captain in the French artillery which he loved so much, has again been convicted. True, this time the sentence is not deportation to Devil's Island, which must have lost its terrors for him, since he first got to know his comrades in arms in the courtroom at Rennes. This time they merely sentenced him to ten years in prison. Merely! What leniency! What has happened? Has compassion suddenly invaded those doughty soldiers' hearts? Have they become softer than the inexorable honor of the officer allows, more indulgent than love of country dictates? Is treason no longer a crime that brings banishment? Is ten years' incarceration enough to expiate a guilt the convicted man never shared? Perhaps these puzzling questions are resolved when one considers that the "proof" was not sufficiently authentic to warrant another term of exile on Devil's Island. But since one of the circumstances was that the defendant was a Jew, the forgeries constituted enough evidence

From the *Welt*, Vol. 3, No. 37, September 15, 1899.

for the honorable generals to assess a sentence of ten years in prison. The sentence, moreover, is only a scrap of paper. The valiant President of the Court-Martial merely pronounced guilt and sentence from behind a wall of stern-faced gendarmes. No one dreams of keeping the hapless Dreyfus much longer behind lock and key. Soon he will be free to depart. No one will stay him, least of all his fellow officers, who are glad to get rid of the insolent Jew. Needless to say, he will have no further business on the General Staff or in the Army. Among the members of the court were found five, full five stout-hearted men to cleanse the French uniform of the stain of being worn by a Jew. Five against two! A fine, memorable, instructive figure for our contemporary civilization.

As already mentioned, the discovery that such a feat is possible today has created a painful stir. Are these the achievements of culture? inquire the true friends of progress. Is this how human rights are respected? complain the constitutionalists, citing the immortal principles of the great Revolution. Are not all citizens equal before the law? moans the Council of French Jews. Oh yes, indeed! All citizens are equal in the eyes of the law, with a single, trifling exception—the Jews. But of course, everyone knows that the exception only serves to prove the rule. Hence there is no reason for any real apprehension.

One really must read the newspapers published beyond the borders of France. They covered the proceedings at Rennes in long daily dispatches and thus had proclaimed the defendent's innocence far and wide. Only the members of the court-martial remained in ignorance that Esterhazy had written the *bordereau*, had acknowledged authorship of the sole document that led to Dreyfus' conviction, then as now. Only the members of the court did not know that on the day before the conviction the German government declared officially that it had never maintained any relations with Dreyfus. In publishing this statement, it declared it was obeying the dictates of humanity. Well, what may affect the archenemy need scarcely detain French patriots when they sit in judgment over a Jew. These and other reproaches were to be found in all the papers, except those suffering from the disease of antisemitism. Comment on the sentence was entirely in the same vein. In Berlin and Rome, London and New York, there were only outcries of indignation. It was a relief to be able to read, in the same papers that had first expressed wonderment at the unfair treatment of a Jew and then their confidence in an acquittal, that all of Europe and Asia and even Polynesia were angry at the discovery to which we have referred. Even a newspaper correspondent can succumb to illusions—indeed, can spread them by wire. But let us assume that these well-meant reports reflect no error. Do they hold anything beyond the mood of the moment? Keep in mind what has happened. After five years of the utmost torment, an innocent man is dragged through another thirty days in court. Not even a shadow of evidence is produced against him; indeed, reputable officials of foreign governments testify to his innocence; yet he is convicted. Is it any wonder that the reaction throughout the world is one of resentment? If a dumb beast were tortured in public, would not the crowd send up a cry of indignation? This is the meaning of the pro-Dreyfus sentiment in non-French countries, if indeed it is as widespread as many Jews estimate, perhaps wishfully rather than by the evidence of their eyes. To put it in a nutshell, we might say that the injustice committed against Dreyfus is so great that we forget we are dealing with a Jew. It would take considerable ingenuity to read more than that into the "general indignation." Is it really as general, even beyond France? He was convicted by a vote of five against two. Is the proportion in favor of the Jews more favorable elsewhere? Who could be so blind and obstinate, so unfamiliar with the facts of life, so enthralled with error as to assume such a thing? Those seven have been represented as responsible solely to their superiors. Actually they were exposed to the pitiless control of public opinion. Each of their utterances and gestures was scrutinized and judged before they themselves judged. They had to base their verdict on witnesses, even though perjured, on evidence, even though forged. These liars and forgeries were the tribute the judges had to pay to the public. But what about the views and verdicts and prejudices that keep on being quietly pronounced against Jews everywhere, day after day? Is anyone presumptuous enough to claim that of any seven people two, or even one, favor the Jews? Everything considered, the situation was relatively favorable to the accused at Rennes.

Our smug Jews, blinded to the truth, will soon close their eyes again. The discovery at Rennes may have startled and dazzled them, but only for seconds. Soon we shall rationalize the thing in one way or another, say what is acceptable, believe what we like to believe. The whole world is indignant. Dreyfus receives messages of sympathy from the best people. And after all, he will soon be a free man, even though stripped of his uniform. There is no rule that everyone must serve with the artillery or on the General Staff. The argument is reassuring, but it has a flaw. It does not answer the hard figures: five against two!

Poor Dreyfus! He is no longer a man, he is an issue. There has been a sentimental approach to his case—people who try to plumb what he must have suffered on the desolate island during years of which each day was a decade. Such musings are childish, exaggerated, and inadequate. The human suffering in this case is simply beyond measurement. It can be calculated no more than the sufferings of a patient on whom the surgeons have operated for five years on end. Does he still have the power of feeling? When did a sense of numbness supervene? To look at the case like that is to trivialize it. All that is left of Dreyfus is an abstraction. He represents the Jew in modern society—the Jew who tries to adapt himself to his environment, to speak its language, to think its thoughts, to sew its insignia on his sleeves—only to have them ruthlessly ripped away. Dreyfus represents a bastion that has been and still is a point of struggle. Unless we are deceived, that bastion is lost!

DIARIES OF THEODOR HERZL

[*The Diaries of Herzl open with a sort of prelude, or invo-
cation. He is in the grip of an inspiration, unable to foresee
to what lengths he will be carried and what forms he will
use for its expression. But that this is something outside the
range of all previous experience is quite clear to him.*]

Begun in Paris, Shavuot, 1895

I HAVE been occupied for some time past with a work which
is of immeasurable greatness. I cannot tell today whether I
shall bring it to a close. It has the appearance of a gigantic
dream. But for days and weeks it has filled me, saturated even
my subconsciousness; it accompanies me wherever I go, broods
above my ordinary daily converse, looks over my shoulder and
at my petty, comical journalistic work, disturbs me, and in-
toxicates me.

What it will lead to it is impossible to surmise as yet. But
my experience tells me that it is something marvelous, even
as a dream, and that I shall write it down—if not as a memorial for mankind, then for my own delight or meditation in
later years. And perhaps for something between both these
possibilities: for the enrichment of literature. If the romance
does not become a fact, at least the fact can become a romance. Title: The Promised Land!

Today I really no longer know whether it was not the romance that I first had in mind. In any case it was not to be something belletristic for its own sake, but something serving a purpose.

When was it I began to occupy myself with the Jewish question? Probably since it first arose. Assuredly ever since I read Dühring's book. In one of my old notebooks, packed away somewhere in Vienna, are some of my first observations on Dühring's book and the question. At that time I had not yet found a publication for my literary work—it was, I believe, in 1881 or 1882—but I know that even today I often say things that are written down there. As the years went on that question ate its way deeper into me, tormented me and made me very unhappy. In actual fact I returned to it again and again whenever I translated my own personal experience, pain, and joy into general terms.

[*From the foregoing and from what follows we see that, in spite of frequent reports to the contrary, Herzl was involved in the Jewish question long before he ever dreamed of responding to its pressure even in literary form. Eugene Karl Dühring (1833–1901), German philosopher with antisemitic leanings, was among the first to establish a rationale of antisemitism*]

The Jewish question lay in ambush wherever I went. I sighed and derided and was wretched. But I would not let it truly lay hold upon me, although even before I came here I already wanted to write a Jewish novel. I was going to compose it during my travels in Spain, in 1891. The central figure was to be my dear friend Heinrich Kana, who shot himself in Berlin in February, 1891. I believe that I wanted to exorcise his ghost in the writing of that novel. Naturally I wanted to place the poor, despised, and fine groups of Jews in contrast to the rich Jews. The latter feel nothing of that antisemitism for which they in reality are chiefly responsible.

Then the *Neue Freie Presse* called me to Paris as its correspondent. In Paris I entered—at least as an observer—political life. I saw how the world is ruled. I also stood at gaze before the phenomenon of the crowd, for a long time without understanding it. Here I also knew a freer and higher relationship to antisemitism, from which I at least did not have to suffer directly. In Austria or Germany I had always to tremble lest some one shout Hep! Hep!* after me. Here I passed "unrecognized" in the crowd.

In that word "unrecognized" lies a terrific reproach against the antisemites.

That Hep! Hep! has come to my own ears only twice. The first time in Mainz, when I traveled through the city in 1888. In the evening I came to a cheap concert hall, drank my beer there, and as I stood up and made my way toward the door through the noise and smoke a young fellow called after me: Hep! Hep!

The second time it was in Baden, when somebody called "Jew-Pig" after me as I went by in a carriage.

From the beginning I understood the emptiness and futility of efforts to "combat antisemitism." With paper declamations or arguments moving in a vicious circle nothing at all can be done. In fact, the effect is comical. You may find—among pushers and cranks—very honest people on such "relief committees." They resemble the "relief committees" which follow —and precede!—floods, and are about as far-reaching in effect. The noble Bertha von Suttner is in error—an error, indeed, which does her all honor—when she thinks that such a committee can be of help. Exactly the case of the peace societies. A man who invents a terrible explosive does more for peace than a thousand mild apostles.

This was the answer which I gave casually to Baron Leitenberger when he asked me, three years ago, what I thought of the *Freie Blatt* for the "combating, etc." I thought nothing of it . . .

Since that day antisemitism has grown, keeps on growing— and I with it.

I still remember two different approaches to the question

* Hep! Hep! is the cry which comes down from the Jew-baiting mobs of the Middle Ages. Its origin is said to be the first letters of the three Latin words: *Hierosolyma est perdita*, Jerusalem is lost.

and its solution which I tried within the last few years. About two years ago I wanted to solve the Jewish question, at least in Austria, with the help of the Catholic Church. I wanted to get entree to the Pope, not without having assured myself in advance of the assistance of the Austrian upper clergy, and to say to him: "Help us against antisemitism, and I shall lead a great movement for the free and decent conversion of the Jews to Christianity."

Free and *decent* because the leaders of this movement—and I above all—would remain Jews and would propagate the idea as Jews. The conversion was to take place in broad daylight, at twelve o'clock on Sunday, in the San Stefan Cathedral of Vienna, in festive processions and to the sound of bells. Not in shame, as single ones have done hitherto, but with proud gestures . . .

> [*Herzl tells how he tried to win the editor-in-chief of the* Neue Freie Presse *to the idea and failed. His second approach to the question of antisemitism was—the turning of the Jews to the professions. But this, too, was nothing more than a conversation. And then, finally, while he sat for the sculptor Beer, in Paris, the inspiration came.*]

The conversation turned to the fact that it did not help the Jews at all if one were an artist untainted by money. The curse clung. I became greatly excited in my talk, and I was still glowing after I left. With the swiftness of that dream in the Arabian fairy story rose the plan for this work. I think I had scarcely gone the distance from the Rue Descombes to the Place Péreire, and it was complete in my mind.

The next day I sat down. Three wonderful weeks of excitement and work.

I thought that through this dramatic eruption I should write myself free. On the contrary, I was drawn in deeper and deeper. The thought grew ever stronger that I had to do something for the Jews.

For the first time I went to the Temple in the Rue de la Victoire, and again I found the services festive and touching.

There was much to remind me of my youth, the Temple on the Tabakgasse in Pest . . .

Did it happen then? Or had I conceived before that time the plan to write "The Situation of the Jews"?

Now I remember that it was before. I had already spoken of it the fall before in Vienna . . .

[*The "literary" prelude to the Diaries takes up thirteen out of nearly two thousand pages. Suddenly, without understanding why, Herzl writes a letter to Baron de Hirsch, the famous philanthropist, asking for an interview. De Hirsch turns out to be in London. After some correspondence they meet in Paris, on June 2, 1895. Herzl lays his plans for a Jewish State before the Baron—and here follows the result.*]

The Baron said, benevolently, as if I were asking him for a position in his banking house: "I observe that you are an intelligent man."

I smiled inwardly. Such a project as I have in mind lifts one above conceit. I shall yet see and hear diverse things.

And de Hirsch continued his praise with: "But you have such fantastic ideas."

I stood up. "Yes. Did I not tell you that it would sound either too simple or too fantastic to you? You do not know what the fantastic is, and that the only way to get the large lines of mankind is from a great height."

He answered: "Emigration is the only thing. There is land enough to be bought."

I almost shouted. "But who tells you that I do not want to emigrate? Here it is, in my notes. I shall go to the German Kaiser—and he will understand me, for he has been brought up to understand big things . . . "

[*Herzl makes no direct entry into his diary, after this interview, for nearly a whole year. He keeps only scattered notes. He cannot sit down to make coherent entries. He explains why.*]

I wrote walking, standing, lying down, on the street, at table, by night when I was driven forth from my sleep.

Every note bears its date. I no longer have the time to copy the notes. I have begun the second book, so as to put down daily what is worth putting down. And thus the notes accumulate. Now I shall ask my good father to enter these in the book, in their proper order, as they were written.

[*Among the first entries is the letter he wrote de Hirsch after the unsuccessful interview. In part he says:*]

"You are the big money Jew, I the Jew of the spirit. Hence the divergence between our means and methods. Naturally you took up an attitude of gentle irony. I expected it. I told you so at the beginning. That is the way new ideas are received.

"Do you know that you are fearfully reactionary in your politics—worse than the most absolutist autocracies? Fortunately your powers do not extend far enough. You mean well, *parbleu, je le sais bien*. That is why I should like to give the right turn to your intentions. Do not hold it against me that I am a young man. At thirty-five one is a minister in France and Napoleon was emperor. . . .

"Believe me: the politics of an entire people—particularly when it is scattered throughout the whole world—can be made only with imponderabilia, which float in the air . . . What? You do not understand the imponderable? And what is religion? . . .

"Yet the national fantasy must have firm ground beneath. But who says that I have not thoroughly practical ideas as to the detailed method?

"Will you make a bet with me? I shall create a national loan for the Jews. If you will undertake to provide fifty million marks, I shall create the first hundred million. In exchange, I shall make you the commander.

"What are ten billion marks for the Jews? They are richer than the French were before 1870—and how many Jews there were among them! As a matter of fact, under pressure of necessity we could start off with one billion. For it will be working capital, the foundation of our later railways, our immigration fleets, and our war fleet. With this we shall build houses, palaces, workers' dwellings, schools, theatres, museums, government houses, hospitals, lunatic asylums—in brief, cities.

"You will find Jewish money in heavy quantities for a Chinese loan, for Negro railways in Africa, for most adventurous enterprises—and for the deepest, most immediate and most tormenting needs of the Jews shall you find none?"

[*As is well known, the negotiations with de Hirsch came to nothing. The next section of the Diaries is constituted by a series of* Gedankensplitter, *fragments of ideas, which Herzl intends to integrate with the* Judenstaat. *Part of them follows here.*]

We shall unite all the Zionists.

General sanitary measures must be taken before masses entrain. We shall have emigrant hospitals (quarantines), baths, clothing institutes before emigration.

To try to prepare, artificially, a historic peasantry is like equipping a modern army with bows and arrows.

I am so filled with this idea that I refer everything to it, as a lover refers everything to his beloved. . . . I went to see *Tannhäuser* in the evening. We too shall have the same splendid showrooms, the gentlemen in frock coats, the ladies as luxurious as can be. Yes, I shall make use of Jewish luxuriousness, as of everything else.

We shall have to face great fights: with retracting Pharaohs, enemies, and above all with ourselves. The golden calf!

The army must be kept well in hand!

All officials must be uniformed handsomely, neatly, but not absurdly.

Prizes for all sorts of virtues.

Tobacco plantations, silk factories.

Have the Wonder Rabbi of Sadagora migrate, to be a sort of provincial bishop. In fact, win the entire clergy over.

Order of procedure:
1. Creation of means (the syndicate).
2. Beginning of publicity (which costs nothing, for the anti-semites will be happy, and I shall break the opposition of liberals by threat of competition).
3. Engagement of land prospectors.
4. Continuation of publicity on a grand scale. Let Europe laugh at it, swear at it—as long as it talks about it.
5. Negotiations with Zion.
6. Marking out of territorial points to be acquired.
7. Purchase of first lands (one billion).
8. Purchase and construction of ships.
9. Continuous enrollment of all who report; recruiting, division, direction. . . .
Etc.

June 7, 1895.
De Hirsch, who eight days ago was the keystone of my plans, has today become a *quantité negligeable.*

I am the man who manufactures aniline dyes from waste products.
I must use a variety of similes, for this thing is without parallel.

I tried de Hirsch, now I am going to Rothschild, as von Moltke went from Denmark to Prussia.

The cowardly, assimilated, baptized Jews may remain. Even they will come in useful—they will be proud of their relationship with us, of whom they are now ashamed. But we, the faithful Jews, will again become great.

For all that, if I get the Rothschilds, I do not want to repulse poor de Hirsch.

I shall make him Vice-President (in recognition of his meritorious work till now and because he knows the plan).

My removal from Vienna to Paris was historically necessary, so that I might learn the meaning of migration.

Güdemann! I shall make you the first bishop of the capital.

The exodus under Moses will bear the same relation to this thing as a *Fastnachtsingspiel* by Hans Sachs to an opera by Wagner.

After one hundred years we shall have general military duty; but who knows how far civilization will have advanced by then?

Circenses as soon as possible.

German theater, international theater, opera, operetta, circus, *café-concert*, café Champs Elysées.

Our High Priest will wear imposing ceremonial dress: our cuirassiers will have yellow trousers, white tunics. Officers, silver cuirasses. . . .

For rewards to my brave soldiers, striving artists, faithful and gifted officials, I shall use the dowries of rich girls.

I must conduct marriage politics.

I shall punish suicide: an unsuccessful attempt by long incarceration in a lunatic asylum, a successful attempt with refusal of honorable burial.

I need the duel, in order to have proper officers, and in order to refine the tone of good society on the French model.

[Page after page these random ideas continue. They touch on every imaginable theme. Prizes for large families, disposition of unskilled labor, its organization into an army; architecture, introduction of Viennese cafés for the homesick, luxury taxes, amnesties, punishments, a House of Lords, general parliamentary organization, entertainment on the transports of returning Jews, etc., etc. He also considers South America as a possibility. Ships will have three classes. Jewish consular employees can be taken over usefully, etc., etc. Then follows a purely personal note:]

Much that is set down in these notes will appear ridiculous, exaggerated, crazy. But if I were to exercise self-criticism, as in my literary works, the thoughts would become crippled.

Artists will understand why, amid my practical, political, and law-creating ideas I, who am for the rest clear in my logic, permit these exaggerations and dreams to sprout like green grass between cement stones. I must not force myself downward into a state of sober carefulness. This light intoxication was necessary.

Yes, artists will understand it completely. But there are so few artists.

[In the midst of these reflections he writes, on June 11, 1895, to Rabbi Güdemann of Vienna, without unfolding his plan, but mentioning that he is about to start an important movement. He only asks Güdemann for a general report on Jewish conditions in Austria-Hungary, Germany, Russia, etc. He wants Güdemann to meet him in Caux—there he will speak to him in detail. Another Jew, the businessman Salo Cohn, was also invited but did not reply. Herzl enjoins Güdemann to strictest secrecy. The meeting in Caux never took place.

Then the reflections continue in the same irregular

stream. Universal insurance; organization of Russian Jews into a labor army; question of tobacco monopoly, whisky monopoly, establishment of branches of the Neue Freie Presse, *the* New York Herald, *etc., over there; transformation of the Society of Jews into the Jewish State; religious toleration; banking questions for the Society of Jews; prevention of land-speculation "over there"—he does not say Palestine or any other specific place; building credits; architectural conferences; possibility of purchasing South American republics; which of the Rothschilds should he approach now that de Hirsch is out of it? Question of prostitution; the seven-hour day, etc. Much of this material found its way into the* Judenstaat.]

London, July 15, 1896. After a mass meeting in the East End.

On Sunday, while I sat on the platform I was in a curious mood. I saw and heard the rising of my legend. The people are sentimental; the masses do not see clearly. I believe that even now they no longer have a clear idea of me. A light mist has begun to beat about me, which will perhaps deepen into a cloud in the midst of which I shall walk. But even now if they no longer see my outline clearly, at least they understand that I mean well by them, I am the man of the poor.

August 23, Baden.

Long conversation with the electrotechnician Kremenetzky. He is a good Zionist with modern ideas. Great chemical industries might be set up around the heavily salt-laden Dead Sea.

The rivers feeding it now with sweet water would be diverted and used for drinking water. They would be replaced by a canal from the Mediterranean, part of which would have to be made as a tunnel because of the mountains (a tourist spectacle), and the difference between the levels of the two seas (water-fall) could be utilized to drive machines. Many thousands of horsepower.

And even besides this there is enough water power in Palestine which can be converted into electricity.

We must found a national Arbor Society for the reforestation of the land. Every Jew to plant one or more trees!

Ten million trees.

THE JEWISH STATE

THE idea which I have developed in this pamphlet is an ancient one: it is the restoration of the Jewish State.

The world resounds with clamor against the Jews, and this has revived the dormant idea.

I claim no new discoveries; let this be noted at once and throughout my discussion. I have discovered neither the Jewish situation as it has crystallized in history, nor the means to remedy it. The materials for the structure I here sketch exist in reality, they are quite tangible; this anyone can establish to his own satisfaction. Hence, if this attempt to resolve the Jewish Question is to be described by a single word, let it be labeled not a "fantasy," but at most a "construction."

I must first of all defend my sketch from being treated as "Utopian." To do this is simply to protect superficial critics from committing a foolish error. Though, indeed, it would be no disgrace to have written an idealist Utopia. And very likely I could also assure myself easier literary success while avoiding all responsibility, if I were to offer this plan in the form of romantic fiction to a public that seeks to be entertained. But this is no amiable Utopia such as have been projected in abundance before and since Sir Thomas More. And it seems to me that the situation of the Jews in various lands is grave enough to make quite superfluous any attention-getting tricks.

An interesting book, *Freiland*, by Dr. Theodor Hertzka, which appeared a few years ago, may serve to illustrate the distinction I draw between my construction and a Utopia. His is the ingenious invention of a modern mind thoroughly schooled in the principles of political economy; it is as remote from actuality as the equatorial mountain on which his dream state lies. "Freiland" is a complicated mechanism with numerous cogs and wheels that even seem to mesh well; but I have no reason whatever to believe that they can be set in motion. Even if I were to see "Freiland societies" come into being, I should regard the whole thing as a joke.

The present scheme, on the other hand, involves the use of a motive force which exists in reality. In view of my own limitations, I shall do no more than suggest what cogs and wheels constitute the machinery I propose, trusting that better mechanics than myself will be found to carry the work out.

The decisive factor is our propelling force. And what is that force? The plight of the Jews.

Who would dare to deny that this exists? We shall discuss it fully in the chapter on the causes of antisemitism.

Now everyone knows how steam is generated by boiling water in a kettle, only rattling the lid. The current Zionist projects and other associations to check antisemitism are tea-kettle phenomena of this kind. But I say that this force, if properly harnessed, is powerful enough to propel a large engine and to move passengers and goods, let the engine have whatever form it may.

I am profoundly convinced that I am right, though I doubt whether I shall live to see myself proved so. Those who today inaugurate this movement are unlikely to live to see its glorious culmination. But the very inauguration is enough to inspire in them a high pride and the joy of an inner liberation of their existence.

To avoid all suspicion of utopianism, I shall also be very sparing of picturesque details in my exposition. I expect, in any case, that unthinking scoffers will caricature my sketch in an attempt to vitiate the whole idea. A Jew, of excellent judgment in other respects, to whom I explained my plan, remarked that "It is the hallmark of Utopias to present facets of the future as facts in present reality." This is a mistake. Every finance minister bases his budget estimates on future figures, and not only on projections of the actual average returns of previous years, or on previous revenues in other states, but sometimes on figures for which there is no precedent whatever; as, for example, in instituting a new tax. Anyone who has examined a budget knows that this is so. But is such a financial draft considered Utopian, even when we know that the estimates will never be rigidly adhered to?

But I expect far more of my readers. I ask the cultivated men whom I address to set aside many preconceptions. I shall even go so far as to ask those Jews who have most earnestly tried to solve the Jewish Question to look upon their previous attempts as mistaken and impracticable.

There is one danger I must guard against in the presentation of my idea. If I am restrained in describing all these things that lie in the future, I may appear to be doubting the possibility of their ever being realized. If, on the other hand, I speak of them quite unreservedly as realized, I may appear to be building castles in the air.

I therefore state, clearly and emphatically, that I believe in the achievement of the idea, though I do not profess to have discovered the shape it may ultimately take. The world needs the Jewish State; therefore it will arise.

The plan would seem mad enough if a single individual were to undertake it; but if many Jews simultaneously agree on it, it is entirely reasonable, and its achievement presents no difficulties worth mentioning. The idea depends only on the number of its adherents. Perhaps our ambitious young men, to whom every road of advancement is now closed, and for whom the Jewish State throws open a bright prospect of freedom, happiness and honor—perhaps they will see to it that this idea is spread.

I feel that with the publication of this pamphlet my own task is done. I shall not again take up my pen unless the attacks of serious opponents force me to do so, or it becomes necessary to meet objections and errors not already dealt with.

Is what I am saying not yet true? Am I ahead of time? Are the sufferings of the Jews not yet acute enough? We shall see.

It depends on the Jews themselves whether this political document remains for the present a political romance. If this generation is too dull to understand it rightly, a future, finer, more advanced generation will arise to comprehend it. The Jews who will try it shall achieve their State; and they will deserve it.

CHAPTER I. INTRODUCTION

The understanding of economics among men actively engaged in business is often astonishingly slight. This seems to be the only explanation for the fact that even Jews faithfully parrot the catchword of the antisemites: "We live off 'Host-nations'; and if we had no 'Host-nation' to sustain us we should starve to death." This is one case in point of the undermining of our self-respect through unjust accusations. But how does this theory of "Host-nations" stand up in the light of reality? Where it does not rest on narrow physiocratic views, it reflects the childish error which assumes that there is a fixed quantity of values in continuous circulation. But it is not necessary to be Rip van Winkle, and wake from long slumber, in order to realize that the world is considerably altered by the continuous production of new values. The technical progress achieved in our own wonderful era enables even the dullest of minds with the dimmest of vision to note the appearance of new commodities all around him. The spirit of enterprise has created them.

Without enterprise, labor remains static, unaltering; typical of it is the labor of the farmer, who stands now precisely where his forebears stood a thousand years ago. All our material welfare has been brought about by men of enterprise. I feel almost ashamed of writing down so trite a remark. Even if we were a nation of entrepreneurs—such as absurdly exaggerated accounts make us out to be—we should require no "Host-nation." We are not dependent upon the circulation of old values; we produce new ones.

We now possess slave labor of unexampled productivity, whose appearance in civilization has proved fatal competition to handicrafts; these slaves are our machines. It is true that we need workmen to set our machinery in motion; but for this the Jews have manpower enough, too much, in fact. Only those who are ignorant of the condition of Jews in many countries of Eastern Europe would dare assert that Jews are unfit or unwilling to perform manual labor.

But in this pamphlet I will offer no defense of the Jews. It would be useless. Everything that reason and everything that sentiment can possibly say in their defense already has been said. Obviously, arguments fit to appeal to reason and sentiment are not enough; one's audience must first of all be able to understand or one is only preaching in a vacuum. But if the audience is already so far advanced, then the sermon itself is superfluous. I believe that man is steadily advancing to a higher ethical level; but I see this ascent to be fearfully slow. Should we wait for the average man to become as generously minded as was Lessing when he wrote *Nathan the Wise*, we would have to wait beyond our own lifetime, beyond the lifetimes of our children, of our grandchildren, and of our great-grandchildren. But destiny favors us in a different respect.

The technical achievements of our century have brought about a remarkable renaissance; but we have not yet seen this fabulous advance applied for the benefit of humanity. Distance has ceased to be an obstacle, yet we complain of the problem of congestion. Our great steamships carry us swiftly and surely over hitherto uncharted seas. Our railways carry us safely into a mountain-world hitherto cautiously scaled on foot. Events occurring in countries undiscovered when Europe first confined Jews in ghettos are known to us in a matter of an hour. That is why the plight of the Jews is an anachronism—not because over a hundred years ago there was a period of enlightenment which in reality affected only the most elevated spirits.

To my mind, the electric light was certainly not invented so that the drawing rooms of a few snobs might be illuminated, but rather to enable us to solve some of the problems of humanity by its light. One of these problems, and not the least of them, is the Jewish Question. In solving it we are working not only for ourselves, but also for many other downtrodden and oppressed beings.

The Jewish Question still exists. It would be foolish to deny it. It is a misplaced piece of medievalism which civilized nations do not even yet seem able to shake off, try as they will. They proved they had this high-minded desire when they emancipated us. The Jewish Question persists wherever Jews live in appreciable numbers. Wherever it does not exist, it is brought in together with Jewish immigrants. We are naturally drawn into those places where we are not persecuted, and our appearance there gives rise to persecution. This is the case, and will inevitably be so, everywhere, even in highly civilized countries—see, for instance, France—so long as the Jewish Question is not solved on the political level. The unfortunate Jews are now carrying the seeds of antisemitism into England; they have already introduced it into America.

Antisemitism is a highly complex movement, which I think I understand. I approach this movement as a Jew, yet without fear or hatred. I believe that I can see in it the elements of cruel sport, of common commercial rivalry, of inherited prejudice, of religious intolerance—but also of a supposed need for self-defense. I consider the Jewish Question neither a social nor a religious one, even though it sometimes takes these and other forms. It is a national question, and to solve it we must first of all establish it as an international political problem to be discussed and settled by the civilized nations of the world in council.

We are a people—*one* people.

We have sincerely tried everywhere to merge with the national communities in which we live, seeking only to preserve the faith of our fathers. It is not permitted us. In vain are we loyal patriots, sometimes super-loyal; in vain do we make the same sacrifices of life and property as our fellow citizens; in vain do we strive to enhance the fame of our native land in the arts and sciences, or her wealth by trade and commerce. In our native lands where we have lived for centuries we are still decried as aliens, often by men whose ancestors had not yet come at a time when Jewish sighs had long been heard in the country. The majority decide who the "alien" is; this, and all else in the relations between peoples, is a matter of power. I do not surrender any part of our prescriptive right when I make this statement merely in my own name, as an individual. In the world as it now is and for an indefinite period will probably remain, might takes precedence over right. It is without avail, therefore, for us to be loyal patriots, as were the Huguenots, who were forced to emigrate. If we were left in peace . . .

But I think we shall not be left in peace.

Oppression and persecution cannot exterminate us. No nation on earth has endured such struggles and sufferings as we have. Jew-baiting has merely winnowed out our weaklings; the strong among us defiantly return to their own whenever persecution breaks out. This was most clearly apparent in the period immediately following the emancipation of the Jews. Those Jews who rose highest intellectually and materially entirely lost the sense of unity with their people. Wherever we remain politically secure for any length of time, we assimilate. I think this is not unpraiseworthy. Hence, the statesman who would wish to see a Jewish strain added to his nation must see to it that we continue politically secure. But even a Bismarck could never achieve that.

For old prejudices against us are still deeply ingrained in the folk-ethos. He who would have proof of this need only listen to the people where they speak candidly and artlessly: folk-wisdom and folklore both are antisemitic. The people is everywhere a great child, which can be readily educated; but even in the most favorable circumstances its education would be such a long-drawn-out process that we could far sooner, as already mentioned, help ourselves by other means.

Assimilation, by which I understand not only external conformity in dress, habits, customs, and speech, but also identity of attitude and deportment—assimilation of Jews could be achieved only by intermarriage. But the need for intermarriage would have to be felt by the majority; mere legislative sanction would never suffice.

The Hungarian Liberals, who have just legalized intermarriage, have placed themselves in a thoroughly false position. The doctrinaire character of this legislation is well illustrated by one of the earliest cases: it was a baptized Jew who married a Jewess. At the same time the conflict which arose in the course of enacting the new form of marriage has aggravated the differences between Jews and Christians in Hungary, thus hindering rather than furthering the amalgamation of the races.

Those who really wish to see the Jews disappear through interbreeding can hope to see it come about in one way only. The Jews must first rise so far in the economic scale that old social prejudices against them would be overcome. How this might happen is shown by the example of the aristocracy, with whom the highest proportion of intermarriage occurs. The old nobility has itself refurbished with Jewish money, and in the process Jewish families are absorbed. But what form would this process take in the middle classes, where (the Jews being a bourgeois people) the Jewish question is mainly centered? The prerequisite growth in economic power might here be resented as economic domination, something which is already falsely attributed to the Jews. And if the power Jews now possess evokes rage and indignation among the antisemites, to what outbursts would a further increase lead? The first step towards absorption cannot be taken, because this step would mean the subjection of the majority to a recently despised minority, which, however, would possess neither military nor administrative authority of its own. I, therefore, hold the absorption of Jews by means of their prosperity to be unlikely. In countries which now are antisemitic my view will be seconded. In others, where Jews are for the moment secure, it will probably be passionately challenged by my coreligionists. They will not believe me until they are again visited by Jew-baiting; and the longer antisemitism lies dormant, the more violently will it erupt. The infiltration of immigrating Jews attracted to a land by apparent security, and the rising class-status of native Jews, combine powerfully to bring about a revolution. Nothing could be plainer than this rational conclusion.

Yet, because I have drawn this conclusion with complete indifference to everything but the truth, I shall probably be opposed and rejected by Jews who are in comfortable circumstances. Insofar as private interests alone are held by their anxious or timid possessors to be threatened, they may safely be ignored, for the concerns of the poor and oppressed are of greater importance than theirs. But I wish from the very beginning to deal with any mistaken ideas that might arise: in this case, the fear that if the present plan is realized, it could in any way damage property and interests now held by Jews. I will, therefore, thoroughly explain everything connected with property rights. If, on the other hand, my plan never becomes anything more than literature, things will merely remain as they are.

A more serious objection would be that I am giving aid and comfort to the antisemites when I say we are a people—*one* people. Or that I am hindering the assimilation of Jews where there are hopes of achieving it, and endangering it where it is already an accomplished fact, insofar as it is possible for a solitary writer to hinder or endanger anything.

This objection will be especially brought forward in France. It will probably also be made in other countries, but I shall first answer only the French Jews, who afford the most striking example of my point.

However much I may esteem personality—powerful individual personality in statesmen, inventors, artists, philosophers, or leaders, as well as the collective personality of a historic group of human beings, which we designate "nation"—however much I may esteem personality, I do not mourn its decline. Whoever can, will, and must perish, let him perish. But the distinctive nationality of the Jews neither can, will, nor must perish. It cannot, because external enemies consolidate it. It does not wish to; this it has proved through two millennia of appalling suffering. It need not; that, as a descendant of countless Jews who refused to despair, I am trying once more to prove in this pamphlet. Whole branches of Jewry may wither and fall away. The tree lives on.

Hence, if any or all of French Jewry protest against this scheme, because they are already "assimilated," my answer is simple: The whole thing does not concern them at all. They are Israelitic Frenchmen? Splendid! This is a private affair for Jews alone.

However, the movement for the creation of the State which I here propose would harm Israelitic Frenchmen no more than it would harm those who have "assimilated" in other countries. It would, rather, be distinctly to their advantage. For they would no longer be disturbed in their "chromatic function," as Darwin puts it, but would be able to assimilate in peace, because present-day antisemitism would have been stopped for all time. For it would certainly be believed that they are assimilated to the very depths of their being if they remained in their old homes, even after the new Jewish State, with its superior institutions, had become a reality.

The departure of the dedicated Jews would be even more to the advantage of the "assimilated" than of the Christian citizens; for they would be freed of the disquieting, unpredictable, and inescapable competition of a Jewish proletariat driven by poverty and political pressure from place to place, from land to land. This drifting proletariat would become stabilized. Certain Christians today—whom we call antisemites —feel free to offer determined resistance to the immigration of foreign Jews. Jewish citizens cannot do this, although it affects them far more severely; for it is they who first feel the competition of individuals who engage in similar fields of enterprise, and who besides give rise to antisemitism where it does not exist, and intensify it where it does. This is a secret grievance of the "assimilated" which finds expression in their "philanthropic" undertakings. They organize emigration societies for incoming Jews. The ambiguous character of this project would be comical if it did not involve human suffering. Some of these charity institutions are created not for but against the persecuted Jews: Remove the paupers as quickly and as far away as possible. And thus, many an apparent friend of the Jews turns out, on closer examination, to be no more than an antisemite of Jewish origin in philanthropist's clothing.

But the attempts at colonization made even by truly well-meaning men, interesting attempts though they were, have so far been unsuccessful. I do not think that one or another person took up the matter merely as an amusement, that they sent Jews off on their journeys in the same spirit as one races horses. The matter was too grave and too painful for that. These attempts were interesting, to the extent that they may serve on a small scale as an experiment foreshadowing the Jewish State Idea. They were even useful, for out of their mistakes we may learn how to proceed in a large-scale project. They have, of course, also done harm. The transplantation of antisemitism to new areas, which is the inevitable consequence of such artificial infiltration, seems to me the least of these aftereffects. Far worse is the fact that the unsatisfactory results inspire among the Jews themselves doubt as to the capacity of Jewish manpower. But the following simple argument will suffice to dispel this doubt for any intelligent person: What is impractical or impossible on a small scale need not be so on a larger one. A small enterprise may result in loss under the same conditions that would make a large one pay. A rivulet is not navigable even by boats; the river into which it flows carries stately iron vessels.

No human being is wealthy or powerful enough to transplant a people from one place of residence to another. Only an idea can achieve that. The State Idea surely has that power. The Jews have dreamt this princely dream throughout the long night of their history. "Next year in Jerusalem" is our age-old motto. It is now a matter of showing that the vague dream can be transformed into a clear and glowing idea.

For this, our minds must first be throughly cleansed of many old, outworn, muddled, and short-sighted notions. The unthinking might, for example, imagine that this exodus would have to take its way from civilization into the desert. That is not so! It will be carried out entirely in the framework of civilization. We shall not revert to a lower stage; we shall rise to a higher one. We shall not dwell in mud huts; we shall build new, more beautiful, and more modern houses, and possess them in safety. We shall not lose our acquired possessions; we shall realize them. We shall surrender our well-earned rights for better ones. We shall relinquish none of our cherished customs; we shall find them again. We shall not leave our old home until the new one is available. Those only will depart who are sure thereby to improve their lot; those who are now desperate will go first, after them the poor, next the well-to-do, and last of all the wealthy. Those who go first will raise themselves to a higher grade, on a level with that whose representatives will shortly follow. The exodus will thus at the same time be an ascent in class.

The departure of the Jews will leave no wake of economic disturbance, no crises, no persecutions; in fact, the countries of emigration will rise to a new prosperity. There will be an inner migration of Christian citizens into the positions relinquished by Jews. The outflow will be gradual, without any disturbance, and its very inception means the end of anti-semitism. The Jews will leave as honored friends, and if some of them later return they will receive the same favorable welcome and treatment at the hands of civilized nations as is accorded all foreign visitors. Nor will their exodus in any way be a flight, but it will be a well-regulated movement under the constant check of public opinion. The movement will not only be inaugurated in absolute accordance with the law, but it can nowise be carried out without the friendly co-operation of the interested governments, who will derive substantial benefits.

To see that the idea is carried out responsibly and vigorously, the kind of guarantee is required which can be provided by the kind of corporate body which legal terminology calls a "moral" or "legal" person. I should like to distinguish clearly between these two designations, which are frequently confused. As "moral person," to deal with all but property rights, I propose to establish the "Society of Jews." As "legal person," to conduct economic activities, there will be a parallel "Jewish Company."

Only an impostor or a madman would even pretend to

undertake such a monumental task on his own. The integrity of the "moral person" will be guaranteed by the character of its members. The capacity of the "legal person" will be demonstrated by its capital funds.

These prefatory remarks are intended merely as an immediate reply to the mass of objections which the very words "Jewish State" are certain to arouse. Hereafter we shall proceed more deliberately in our exposition, meeting further objections and explaining in detail what has only been outlined as yet, though we shall try, in the interest of a smoothly reading pamphlet, to avoid a ponderous tone. Succinct, pithy chapters will best serve the purpose.

If I wish to replace an old building with a new one, I must demolish before I construct. I shall therefore adhere to this natural sequence. In the first, the general, section, I shall clarify my ideas, sweep away age-old preconceptions, establish the politico-economic premises and unfold the plan.

In the special section, which is subdivided into three principal sections, I shall describe its execution. These three sections are: The Jewish Company, Local-Groups, and The Society of Jews. The Society is to be created first, the Company last; but in this exposition the reverse order is preferable, because it is the financial soundness of the enterprise which will chiefly be called into question, and doubts on this score must be removed first.

In the conclusion, I shall try to meet every further objection that could possibly be made. My Jewish readers will, I hope, follow me patiently to the end. Some will make their objections in another order than that chosen for their refutation. But whoever finds his reservations rationally overcome, let him offer himself to the cause.

Although I speak here in terms of reason, I am well aware that reason alone will not suffice. Long-term prisoners do not willingly quit their cells. We shall see whether the youth, whom we must have, is ripe; the youth—which irresistibly draws along the aged, bears them up on powerful arms, and transforms rationality into enthusiasm.

General Section

CHAPTER II. THE JEWISH QUESTION

No one can deny the gravity of the Jewish situation. Wherever they live in appreciable numbers, Jews are persecuted in greater or lesser measure. Their equality before the law, granted by statute, has become practically a dead letter. They are debarred from filling even moderately high offices in the army, or in any public or private institutions. And attempts are being made to thrust them out of business also: "Don't buy from Jews!"

Attacks in parliaments, in assemblies, in the press, in the pulpit, in the street, on journeys—for example, their exclusion from certain hotels—even in places of recreation are increasing from day to day. The forms of persecutions vary according to country and social circle. In Russia, special taxes are levied on Jewish villages; in Romania, a few persons are put to death; in Germany, they get a good beating occasionally; in Austria, antisemites exercise their terrorism over all public life; in Algeria, there are traveling agitators; in Paris, the Jews are shut out of the so-called best social circles and excluded from clubs. The varieties of anti-Jewish expression are innumerable. But this is not the occasion to attempt the sorry catalogue of Jewish hardships. We shall not dwell on particular cases, however painful.

I do not aim to arouse sympathy on our behalf. All that is nonsense, as futile as it is dishonorable. I shall content myself with putting the following questions to the Jews: Is it not true that, in countries where we live in appreciable numbers, the position of Jewish lawyers, doctors, technicians, teachers, and employees of every description becomes daily more intolerable? Is it not true that the Jewish middle classes are seriously threatened? Is it not true that the passions of the mob are incited against our wealthy? Is it not true that our poor endure greater suffering than any other proletariat? I think

that this pressure is everywhere present. In our upper economic classes it causes discomfort, in our middle classes utter
despair.

The fact of the matter is, everything tends to one and the
same conclusion, which is expressed in the classic Berlin cry:
"*Juden 'raus!*" ("Out with the Jews!").

I shall now put the question in the briefest possible form:
Shouldn't we "get out" at once, and if so, whither?

Or, may we remain, and if so, how long?

Let us first settle the point of remaining. Can we hope for
better days, can we possess our souls in patience, can we wait in
pious resignation till the princes and peoples of this earth are
more mercifully disposed towards us? I say that we cannot hope
for the current to shift. And why not? Even if we were as near
to the hearts of princes as are their other subjects, they could
not protect us. They would only incur popular hatred by showing us too much favor. And this "too much" implies less than
is claimed as a right by any ordinary citizen or ethnic group.
The nations in whose midst Jews live are all covertly or openly
antisemitic.

The common people have not, and indeed cannot have, any
comprehension of history. They do not know that the sins of
the Middle Ages are now being visited on the nations of
Europe. We are what the Ghetto made us. We have without
a doubt attained pre-eminence in finance because medieval
conditions drove us to it. The same process is now being repeated. We are again being forced into moneylending—now
named stock exchange—by being kept out of other occupa-
tions. But once on the stock exchange, we are again objects
of contempt. At the same time we continue to produce an
abundance of mediocre intellectuals who find no outlet, and
this endangers our social position as much as does our increasing wealth. Educated Jews without means are now rapidly
becoming socialists. Hence we are certain to suffer acutely
in the struggle between the classes, because we stand in the
most exposed position in both the capitalist and the socialist
camps.

PREVIOUS ATTEMPTS AT A SOLUTION

The artificial methods heretofore employed to remedy the plight of Jews have been either too petty, such as attempts at colonization, or falsely conceived, such as attempts to convert the Jews into peasants in their present homes.

What is achieved by transporting a few thousand Jews to another country? Either they come to grief at once, or if they prosper, their prosperity gives rise to antisemitism. We have already discussed these attempts to channel poor Jews to new regions. This diversion is clearly inadequate and useless, if not actually harmful, for it merely postpones and drags out if not actually hinders the solution.

But those who would attempt to convert Jews into peasants are committing a truly astonishing error. For the peasant is a creature of the past, as seen by his style of dress, which in most countries is centuries old, and by his tools, which are identical with those used by his earliest forebears. His plow is unchanged; he sows his seed from the apron, mows with the time-honored scythe, and threshes with the flail. But we know that all this can now be done by machinery. The agrarian question is only a question of machinery. America must conquer Europe, in the same way as large landed possessions absorb small ones. The peasant is, consequently, a type which is on the way to extinction. Wherever he is preserved by special measures, there are involved political interests who hope to gain his support. To create new peasants on the old pattern is an absurd and impossible undertaking. No one is wealthy or powerful enough to make civilization take a single step backward. The mere preservation of obsolete institutions is a task vast enough to strain the capacities of even an autocratic state.

Will anyone, then, suggest to Jews, who know what they are about, that they become peasants of the old cast? That would be like saying to the Jew: "Here is a crossbow; now go to war!" What? With a crossbow, while others have small arms and Krupp cannon? Under these circumstances the Jews would be perfectly right in remaining unmoved when people try to place them on the farm. The crossbow is a pretty piece of armament, which inspires a lyrical mood in me whenever I can spare the time. But its proper place is the museum.

Now, there certainly are regions where desperate Jews go out, or at any rate are willing to go out, and till the soil. And a little observation shows that these areas, such as the enclave of Hesse in Germany and some provinces in Russia—these areas are the very hotbeds of antisemitism.

For the do-gooders of the world who send the Jews to the plow forget a very important person, who has a great deal to say in the matter. That person is the peasant. And the peasant is absolutely in the right. For the tax on the land, the risks attached to crops, the pressure of large proprietors who produce at cheaper rates, not to mention American competition, all combine to make life difficult enough for him. Besides, the duties on corn cannot go on increasing indefinitely. For the factory worker cannot be allowed to starve, either; his political influence is, in fact, in the ascendant, and he must therefore be treated with ever-increasing respect.

All these difficulties are well known; therefore I refer to them only cursorily. I merely wanted to indicate clearly how futile have been past attempts—most of them well intentioned —to solve the Jewish Question. Neither a diversion of the stream nor an artificial depression of the intellectual level of our proletariat will avail. And we have already dealt with the panacea of assimilation.

We cannot overcome antisemitism by any of these methods. It cannot be eliminated until its causes are eradicated. But are they eradicable?

CAUSES OF ANTISEMITISM

We now no longer discuss the irrational causes, prejudice and narrow-mindedness, but the political and economic causes. Modern antisemitism is not to be confused with the persecution of the Jews in former times, though it does still have a religious aspect in some countries. The main current of Jew-hatred is today a different one. In the principal centers of antisemitism, it is an outgrowth of the emancipation of the

Jews. When civilized nations awoke to the inhumanity of discriminatory legislation and enfranchised us, our enfranchisement came too late. Legislation alone no longer sufficed to emancipate us in our old homes. For in the Ghetto we had remarkably developed into a bourgeois people and we emerged from the Ghetto a prodigious rival to the middle class. Thus we found ourselves thrust upon emancipation into this bourgeois circle, where we have a double pressure to sustain, from within and from without. The Christian bourgeoisie would indeed not be loath to cast us as a peace-offering to socialism, little though that would avail them.

At the same time, the equal rights of Jews before the law cannot be rescinded where they have once been granted. Not only because their rescission would be contrary to the spirit of our age, but also because it would immediately drive all Jews, rich and poor alike, into the ranks of the revolutionary parties. No serious harm can really be done us. In olden days our jewels were taken from us. How is our movable property to be seized now? It consists of printed papers which are locked up somewhere or other in the world, perhaps in the strongboxes of Christians. It is, of course, possible to get at railway shares and debentures, banks and industrial undertakings of all descriptions by taxation; and where the progressive income tax is in force all our movable property can eventually be laid hold of. But all these efforts cannot be directed against Jews alone, and wherever they might nevertheless be made, their upshot would be immediate economic crises, which would by no means be confined to the Jews as the first affected. The very impossibility of getting at the Jews nourishes and deepens hatred of them. Antisemitism increases day by day and hour by hour among the nations; indeed, it is bound to increase, because the causes of its growth continue to exist and are ineradicable. Its remote cause is the loss of our assimilability during the Middle Ages; its immediate cause is our excessive production of mediocre intellectuals, who have no outlet downwards or upwards—or rather, no wholesome outlet in either direction. When we sink, we become a revolutionary proletariat, the corporals of every revolutionary party;

and when we rise, there rises also our terrifying financial power.

EFFECTS OF ANTISEMITISM

The pressure applied to us does not improve us, for we are no different from ordinary people. It is true enough that we do not love our enemies; but he alone who has quite mastered himself dare throw that up to us. Oppression naturally creates hostility against oppressors, and our hostility in turn increases the pressure. It is impossible to escape this vicious circle.

"No!" some soft-hearted visionaries will say. "No! It *is* possible! Possible by means of the perfectibility of man."

Is it really necessary for me, at this late stage, to show what sentimental drivel this is? He who would peg the improvement of conditions on the goodness of all mankind would indeed be writing a *Utopia!*

I referred previously to our "assimilation." I do not for a moment wish to imply that I desire such an end. Our national character is too glorious in history and, in spite of every degradation, too noble to make its annihilation desirable. Though perhaps we *could* succeed in vanishing without a trace into the surrounding peoples, if they would let us be for just two generations. But they will not let us be. After brief periods of toleration, their hostility erupts again and again. When we prosper, it seems to be unbearably irritating, for the world has for many centuries been accustomed to regarding us as the most degraded of the poor. Thus out of ignorance or ill will they failed to observe that prosperity weakens us as Jews and wipes away our differences. Only pressure drives us back to our own; only hostility stamps us ever again as strangers.

Thus we are now, and shall remain, whether we would or not, a group of unmistakable cohesiveness.

We are one people—our enemies have made us one whether we will or not, as has repeatedly happened in history. Affliction binds us together, and thus united, we suddenly discover our strength. Yes, we are strong enough to form a state, and, indeed, a model state. We possess all the requisite human and material resources.

This would, accordingly, be the appropriate place to give an account of what has been somewhat crudely termed our "human material." But it would not be appreciated till the broad outlines of the plan, on which everything depends, have first been marked out.

THE PLAN

The whole plan is essentially quite simple, as it must necessarily be if it is to be comprehensible to all.

Let sovereignty be granted us over a portion of the globe adequate to meet our rightful national requirements; we will attend to the rest.

To create a new state is neither ridiculous nor impossible. Haven't we witnessed the process in our own day, among nations which were not largely middle class as we are, but poorer, less educated, and consequently weaker than ourselves. The governments of all countries scourged by antisemitism will be keenly interested in obtaining sovereignty for us.

The plan, simple in design but complicated in execution, will be executed by two agencies: The Society of Jews and The Jewish Company.

The scientific plan and political policies which the Society of Jews will establish will be carried out by the Jewish Company.

The Jewish Company will be the liquidating agent for the business interests of departing Jews, and will organize trade and commerce in the new country.

We must not visualize the exodus of the Jews as a sudden one. It will be gradual, proceeding over a period of decades. The poorest will go first and cultivate the soil. They will construct roads, bridges, railways, and telegraph installations, regulate rivers, and provide themselves with homesteads, all according to predetermined plans. Their labor will create trade, trade will create markets, and markets will attract new settlers —for every man will go voluntarily, at his own expense and his own risk. The labor invested in the soil will enhance its value. The Jews will soon perceive that a new and permanent frontier has been opened up for that spirit of enterprise which has heretofore brought them only hatred and obloquy.

The founding of a state today is not to be accomplished in the manner that a thousand years ago would have been the only possible one. It is silly to revert to older levels of civilization, as many Zionists propose. Supposing, for example, we were obliged to clear a country of wild beasts, we should not set about it in the fashion of fifth-century Europeans. We should not take spear and lance and go out individually in pursuit of bears; we would organize a grand and glorious hunting party, drive the animals together, and throw a melinite bomb into their midst.

If we planned to erect buildings, we should not drive a few shaky piles in a marsh like the lake dwellers, but should build as men build now. Indeed, we shall build in bolder and more stately style than has ever been done before; for we now possess means which heretofore did not exist.

The emigrants standing lowest in the economic scale will be gradually followed by those of the next grade. Those now in desperate straits will go first. They will be led by the intellectual mediocrities whom we produce so abundantly and who are oppressed everywhere.

Let this pamphlet serve as the beginning of a general discussion on the question of Jewish emigration. That does not mean to suggest, however, that the question should be called to a vote. Such an approach would ruin the cause from the outset. Whoever wishes may stay behind. The opposition of a few individuals is quite immaterial.

Who would go with us, let him fall in behind our banner and fight for the cause with word and pen and deed.

Those Jews who agree with our State Idea will rally around the Society. Thereby they will give it the authority in the eyes of governments to confer and treat on behalf of our people. The Society will be recognized as, to put it in terminology of international law, a State-creating power. And this recognition will, in effect, mean the creation of the State.

Should the powers show themselves willing to grant us sovereignty over a neutral land, then the Society will enter into negotiations for the possession of this land. Here two regions come to mind: Palestine and Argentina. Significant experiments in colonization have been made in both countries, though on the mistaken principle of gradual infiltration of Jews. Infiltration is bound to end badly. For there comes the inevitable moment when the government in question, under pressure of the native populace—which feels itself threatened—puts a stop to further influx of Jews. Immigration, therefore, is futile unless it is based on our guaranteed autonomy.

The Society of Jews will treat with the present authorities in the land, under the sponsorship of the European powers, if they prove friendly to the plan. We could offer the present authorities enormous advantages, assume part of the public debt, build new thoroughfares, which we ourselves would also require, and do many other things. The very creation of the Jewish State would be beneficial to neighboring lands, since the cultivation of a strip of land increases the value of its surrounding districts.

PALESTINE OR ARGENTINA?

Is Palestine or Argentina preferable? The Society will take whatever it is given and whatever Jewish public opinion favors. The Society will determine both these points.

Argentina is one of the most fertile countries in the world, extends over a vast area, is sparsely populated, and has a temperate climate. It would be in its own highest interest for the Republic of Argentina to cede us a portion of its territory. The present *infiltration* of Jews has certainly produced some discontent, and it would be necessary to enlighten the Republic on the intrinsic difference of the new *immigration* of Jews.

Palestine is our unforgettable historic homeland. The very name would be a marvelously effective rallying cry. If His Majesty the Sultan were to give us Palestine, we could in return undertake the complete management of the finances of Turkey. We should there form a part of a wall of defense for Europe in Asia, an outpost of civilization against barbarism. We should as a neutral state remain in contact with all Europe, which would have to guarantee our existence. The holy places of Christendom could be placed under some form of international exterritoriality. We should form a guard of honor about these holy places, answering for the fulfillment of this duty with our existence. This guard of honor would be the great symbol of the solution of the Jewish Question after what were for us eighteen centuries of affliction.

NEED, ORGANIZATION, TRADE

I said in the last chapter: "The Jewish Company will organize trade and commerce in the new country." I believe I ought here to insert a few remarks on that point.

A scheme such as mine is threatened in its vital center if it is opposed by "realists." Now realists are, as a rule, nothing more than men sunk in the rut of routine, incapable of leaving a narrow circle of antiquated notions. At the same time, their adverse opinion carries great weight and can do considerable harm to a new project, at any rate until this new thing is sufficiently strong to throw the "realists" and their moldy notions aside.

At the inception of the railroad era in Europe, there were "realists" who held that the laying of certain lines was foolish "because there are not enough passengers to fill even the mail coaches." They did not realize the truth—which now seems so obvious to us—that travelers do not produce railways but, rather, railways produce travelers, the latent demand, of course, being assumed.

In a class with the doubts of those "railroad realists" may be placed the inability of some to comprehend how trade and commerce are to be created in a land that has yet to be won and developed. A "realist" would express himself somewhat as follows:

"Granted that the present situation of the Jews is in many places intolerable, and deteriorating from day to day; granted that there exists a desire to emigrate; granted even that the Jews do emigrate to the new country—how will they earn their livelihood there and what will they earn? What are they to live on, once there? The commerce of many people cannot, after all, be artificially organized overnight."

To this I reply: There is not the slightest intention of organizing trade artificially, and certainly not of doing it overnight. But, though its organization may be impossible, its promotion is not. How? Through the organization of a need. The need strives to be recognized, its organization strives to be created, and thereafter trade will come about automatically.

If there is a real and earnest demand among Jews for an improvement of their status; if the organization to be created— the Jewish Company—is sufficiently powerful, trade will expand freely in the new country.

CHAPTER III. THE JEWISH COMPANY

OUTLINES

The Jewish Company is conceived partly on the model of the great land-development companies. It might be called a Jewish Chartered Company. However, it will not exercise sovereign power, nor will it confine itself to colonization.

The Jewish Company will be set up as a joint-stock company, incorporated in England, under British laws and protection. Its principal center will be London. I cannot tell yet how large the Company's capital should be; I shall leave that calculation to our numerous financiers. But in order to be specific, let us put it at a billion marks (about £50,000,000 or $200,000,000); it may be either more or less than that sum. The form of subscription, which will be further elucidated, will determine what fraction of the whole amount must be paid in at once.

The Jewish Company is a provisional organization. It is strictly a business undertaking and must be carefully distinguished from the Society of Jews.

The Jewish Company's first task will be to convert into cash all immovables of the emigrating Jews. This will be done in such a way as to prevent crises, secure every man's rights and interests, and facilitate that inner migration of Christian citizens which has already been referred to.

IMMOVABLE GOODS

The immovable goods which come under consideration are buildings, land, and local business connections. In the beginning, the Jewish Company will simply declare itself available for negotiating the sale of these goods. At first Jewish sales will take place smoothly and without any serious fall in prices. The Company's branch establishments in various towns will become the central offices for the sale of Jewish estates. Each office will charge only so much commission on transactions as will cover its expenses.

As the movement develops, it may cause a considerable fall in the prices of landed property and eventually make it impossible to find a market. At this point the operations of the Company begin to branch out. It will take over the management of estates till such time as it can dispose of them to the greatest advantage. It will collect house rents, let out land on lease, and install business managers, wherever possible on a leasehold arrangement, too, so that there will be every incentive for careful administration. The Company will endeavor everywhere to facilitate the acquisition of the properties by the Christian leaseholders. It will, indeed, gradually replace its own officials in the European branches with Christian substitutes (lawyers, etc.); and these are by no means to act solely in the interest of the Jews. They will constitute a sort of unofficial regulative organ of the Christian population, guaranteeing that everything will be done in equity, fairness, and justice, and without imperiling the internal welfare of the people.

At the same time the Company will sell estates or, rather, exchange them. For a house, it will offer a house in the new country; and for land, land in the new country. The transfer will aim to establish in the new country, wherever possible, the conditions of the old. This transfer will be a source of great, though reasonable profit to the Company. "Over there" the houses offered in exchange will be newer, more beautiful, and more comfortably appointed, and the landed estates of greater value than those abandoned; but they will cost the Company comparatively little, because it will have bought the ground very cheaply.

PURCHASE OF LAND

The land assigned to the Society of Jews by international agreement will, of course, have to be purchased under civil contract.

Provisions made by individuals for their own settlement are not within the scope of this discussion. But the Company will require large areas for its own needs and ours, and these it must secure by centralized purchase. It will negotiate principally for the acquisition of State lands. The aim will be to acquire land "over there" without driving prices sky-high, just as it must sell here without forcing a fall in prices. Great pressure on prices need not be worried about, because the value of the land will really be created by the activities of the Company as it directs land settlement in accordance with agreed plans and under the supervision of the Society of Jews. The latter will see to it that the enterprise becomes not a Panama, but a Suez.

The Company will sell building sites at reasonable rates to its officials and grant them mortgages to build attractive homes, deducting the amount due from their salaries, or granting it in installments as supplementary pay. This, in addition to the honors they may expect, will be a reward for their services.

All the immense profits of this speculation in land will go to the Company, for it is entitled to such an unlimited premium, like any entrepreneur, in return for having borne the risk. When any undertaking involves risk, generous profits must be allowed for those who have borne it. But under no other circumstances will profits be permitted. The ethics of business consist in linking risk with profit.

BUILDINGS

The Company will thus barter houses and estates. It must be plain to anyone who has observed the rise in the value of land through its cultivation that the Company will be bound to gain on its landed property. This can best be seen in the case of the empty enclosures in town and country. Plots not built up increase in value through the development of surrounding areas. The men responsible for the extension of Paris carried out a successful speculation in land which was ingenious in its simplicity: instead of erecting new buildings in the immediate vicinity of the last houses of the town, they bought up adjacent pieces of land and began to build on the outskirts of these. This inverse order of construction raised the value of building sites with extraordinary rapidity, and, after having completed the outer ring, they built in the middle of the town on these highly valuable sites, instead of continually erecting houses at the extremity.

Will the Company do its own building or employ independent architects? It can, and will, do both. It has, as will be shown shortly, an immense reserve of working power, which, far from being exploited as a commodity, will be elevated into brighter and happier conditions of life, and yet will not prove expensive. As for building material, our geologists will have made sure it is locally available when they selected the sites of the towns.

What is to be the principle of construction?

WORKMEN'S DWELLINGS

The workmen's dwellings (which include the dwellings of all manual labor) will be erected at the Company's own risk and expense. They will resemble neither the wretched workmen's barracks of European towns, nor the squalid rows of shanties which surround factories. They will certainly present a uniform appearance, because the Company can only build cheaply if it supplies building materials by mass production—but the detached houses in little gardens will be united into attractive groups in each locality. The natural conformation of the land will rouse the ingenuity of our young architects, whose ideas have not yet been cramped by routine; and even if the people do not grasp the whole import of the plan, they will at any rate feel at ease in their loose clusters. The Temple will be visible from long distances, for it is only our ancient faith that has kept us together. There will be light, attractive, healthy schools for children, conducted along the best modern lines. There will be continuation schools for workmen, which will progressively educate them for more advanced technical functions and enable them to become familiar with the working of machinery. There will be places of popular amusement, regulated by the Society of Jews on a high moral plane.

But we are now concerned with the buildings, and not what may take place inside of them.

I said that the Company would build workmen's dwellings cheaply. Cheaply, not only because abundant building materials will be available locally, nor because the Company will own the sites, but also because the Company will not need to pay its labor for building.

American farmers have a system of mutual aid in the construction of houses. This system of simple friendship, as four-square as the blockhouses erected, can be greatly refined.

UNSKILLED LABORERS

Our unskilled laborers, who will come at first from the great reservoirs of Russia and Romania, must, also, build each other's houses. They will be obliged to build with wood in the beginning, because we cannot produce our own steel at first. Later on the original makeshift buildings will be replaced by superior dwellings.

Our unskilled laborers will first erect these shelters for each other, by prearrangement. They will acquire their houses as permanent possessions in return for their labor—not immediately, but after three years of good performance. In this way we shall secure energetic and able men, for a man with three years of good discipline behind him is well trained for life.

I said before that the Company would not have to pay these unskilled laborers. What will they live on?

Generally speaking, I am opposed to the truck system,* but it will have to be applied in the case of those first settlers. The Company provides for them in so many ways that it might as

* The practice of paying the workman's wages in goods instead of money.

well maintain them fully. In any case the truck system will be in effect only during the first few years, and it will protect the workmen from being victimized by small traders, innkeepers, etc. The Company will thus make it impossible from the outset for our poor, whom only historical necessities forced to become peddlers, to re-establish themselves in the same trades over there. And so also will the Company keep in check drunkards and dissolute men. Then will there be no payment of wages at all during the first period of settlement? There will: for overtime.

THE SEVEN-HOUR DAY

The seven-hour day is the standard working day.

This is not to say that there will be only seven hours of wood-cutting, digging, stone-breaking, and a hundred other activities each day. Indeed not. There will be fourteen hours of labor, in shifts of three and a half hours. The organization of all this will be military in character, with ranks, promotions, and pensions. We shall see later how pensions will be provided.

A healthy man can do a great deal of concentrated work in three and a half hours. After a recess of the same length of time—devoted to rest, to his family, and to his education under guidance—he is quite fresh for work again. Such labor can do wonders.

The seven-hour day thus implies fourteen hours of joint labor —more than that cannot be put into a day.

I am convinced that the seven-hour day is entirely feasible. The experiments in Belgium and England are well known. Some advanced political economists who have studied the subject declare that a five-hour day would be quite sufficient. The Society of Jews and the Jewish Company will make new and extensive experiments which will benefit the other nations of the world as well, and if the seven-hour day does prove feasible it will be introduced in our future state as the legal, standard working day.

The Company, in any event, will always grant its employees a seven-hour day; and it will always be in a position to do so.

We shall use the seven-hour day as a rallying cry for our

people in every part of the world, all of whom must come voluntarily. For ours must be truly the Promised Land. . . .

Whoever works longer than seven hours will receive additional pay for overtime in cash. Seeing that all his needs are supplied, and members of his family unable to work are provided for by philanthropic institutions, transferred and reorganized in the new country, he can save a little money. Thrift, which is already a characteristic of our people, should be greatly encouraged, because it will, in the first place, facilitate the rise of individuals to higher strata; and secondly, the money saved will provide an immense capital reserve for floating loans in the future. Overtime will be permitted only on a doctor's certificate, and must not exceed three hours. For our men will vie for work in the new country, and the world will only then see how industrious a people we are.

I shall not describe the methods used in the truck system (scrip, etc.) nor, in fact, the innumerable details of any process, for fear of confusing my readers. Women will not be allowed to perform any arduous labor, nor to work overtime.

Pregnant women will be relieved of all work and will be supplied with special rations by the truck. For we will need sturdy offspring.

We shall educate children from the first according to our ideals; but this I shall not elaborate either.

My remarks on workmen's dwellings, and on unskilled laborers and their mode of life, are no more Utopian than the rest of my scheme. Everything I have spoken of is already being put into practice, only on a pitifully small scale, unnoticed, unappreciated. The *"Assistance par le Travail,"* which I observed and studied in Paris, was of great service to me in the solution of the Jewish question.

WORK RELIEF

The system of work relief which is now applied in Paris, in many other French towns, in England, in Switzerland, and in America is a very petty affair but capable of the greatest expansion.

What is the principle of work relief?

The principle is to furnish every needy man with simple, unskilled work, such as chopping wood, cutting the *"margotins"* used for lighting stoves in Paris households. It is like penitentiary labor but assumed without any crime, done without loss of character. It is meant to prevent men from taking to crime out of want, by providing them with work and testing their willingness to do it. Starvation must never be allowed to drive men to suicide; for such suicides are the deepest disgrace to a civilization which allows rich men to throw tidbits to their dogs.

Work relief thus provides everyone with work. But the system has a great defect: there is not a sufficiently large demand for the production of the unskilled workers employed, hence there is a loss to those who employ them; though it is true that the organization is philanthropic and therefore prepared for loss. But there the donation is apparent only in the difference between the price paid for the work and its actual value. Instead of giving the beggar two sous, the institution supplies him with work on which it loses two sous. But at the same time it converts the good-for-nothing beggar into an honest breadwinner, who has earned perhaps one franc fifty centimes. One hundred and fifty centimes for ten! That is to say, the receiver of a donation in which there is nothing humiliating has increased it fifteenfold! That would mean fifteen billion for one billion!

The charitable institution certainly loses ten centimes. But the Jewish Company will not lose its one billion; it will derive enormous profits from this expenditure.

There is a moral side also. Even the minuscule system of work relief which exists now succeeds in moral rehabilitation through industry, till such time as the man who is out of work finds a post suitable to his capacities, either in his old calling or in a new one. He is allowed a few hours daily for the purpose of looking for a place, in which task the institutions assist him.

The defect of this small-scale system, so far, has been that it must not compete with timber merchants, etc. Timber merchants are voters; they would protest and would be justified in protesting. Nor may the work relief compete with State prison-labor, for the State, too, must keep its criminals fed and occupied.

In fact, there is very little room in an old-established society for the successful application of the system of *"Assistance par le Travail."*

But there is room in a new society.

For, above all, we require enormous numbers of unskilled laborers to do the first rough work of settlement, to lay down roads, plant trees, level the ground, construct railroads, telegraph installations, etc. All this will be carried out in accordance with a large-scale, predetermined plan.

COMMERCE

When we bring labor to the new country, we simultaneously create trade. At first, of course, there will be a market only for the barest necessities of life: cattle, grain, working clothes, tools, arms—to mention just a few things. These we shall be obliged at first to procure from neighboring States, or from Europe; but we shall make ourselves independent as soon as possible. Jewish entrepreneurs will soon realize the business prospects that the new country offers.

The mass of the Company officials will gradually introduce more refined requirements. (Among officials, I include officers of our security forces, to which about a tenth part of our male colonists will be assigned. This will be a large enough force to control disturbances by the disorderly, for the majority of our colonists will be peaceably inclined.)

The demand for finer things introduced by our officials in good positions will create a quality market, which will continuously expand. The married men will send for wife and children and the single for parents and relatives, as soon as a new home is established "over there." The Jews who emigrate to the United States always proceed in this fashion. As soon as one is sure of his daily bread, he sends for his people, for family ties are strong among Jews. The Society of Jews and the Jewish Company will unite in caring for and strengthening the family still more, not only morally—for this goes without saying—but materially also. The officials will receive additional pay upon marriage and upon the birth of children, for we need all who are there, and all who will follow.

OTHER CLASSES OF DWELLINGS

I spoke earlier only of workmen's dwellings, built by themselves, and omitted all mention of other classes of dwellings. These I shall now touch upon. The Company's architects will build for the lower middle class too, being paid in kind or cash; about a hundred different types of houses will be planned and built to order. These handsome models will form part of our propaganda. The soundness of their construction will be guaranteed by the Company, which will sell each at a fixed price, covering only costs. And where will these houses be situated? That will be shown in the section dealing with Local-Groups.

Seeing that the Company does not wish to earn anything on construction but only on the land, it will desire as many architects as possible to build by private contract. This system will increase the value of landed property, and it will introduce luxury, which is essential for many reasons. Luxury encourages arts and industries, paving the way for a future subdivision of large properties.

Rich Jews who are now obliged carefully to secrete their valuables, and to hold their dreary banquets behind lowered curtains, will be able to enjoy their possessions in peace, "over there." If they co-operate in carrying out this emigration scheme, their capital will be rehabilitated and will have served to promote an unexampled undertaking. If the wealthiest among the Jews in the new settlement begin to rebuild those mansions which are stared at in Europe with such envious eyes, it will soon become fashionable to move into villas over there.

SOME FORMS OF LIQUIDATION

The Jewish Company is planned as the receiver and administrator of the immovable goods of the Jews.

Its methods of procedure can be easily imagined in the case of houses and estates, but what methods will it adopt in the transfer of businesses?

Here innumerable procedures may be found practicable. We cannot survey them all in this outline. But none of them will present any great difficulties, for in each case the business proprietor, when he voluntarily decides to emigrate, will come to an agreement with the Company's officers in his district on the form of liquidation most advantageous for him.

This will most easily be arranged in the case of small businessmen, in whose trades the proprietor's own skill is the major element, while inventory and equipment are of secondary importance. The Company will secure a new occupation for the emigrant and will replace his stock with a plot of land and machinery on loan. Jews are known to adapt themselves with remarkable ease to any form of earning a livelihood, and they will quickly learn to carry on a new trade. In this way a number of small merchants will become small landholders. The Company will, in fact, be prepared to sustain what appears to be a loss in taking over the immovable property of the poorest emigrants; for it will thereby stimulate the free cultivation of tracts of land, raising the value of its adjacent tracts.

In medium-sized businesses, where inventory equals or even exceeds in importance the personal efforts of the manager, and where the firm's credit is a major imponderable factor, various forms of liquidation are possible. This is one of the important ways for carrying out the inner migration of Christian citizens into positions evacuated by Jews. The departing Jew will not lose his personal credit, but will carry it with him, and make good use of it in a new country to establish himself. The Jewish Company will open a current bank account for him. And he can sell the good will of his original business, or place it under new management, with the Company's officials exercising supervision. The managers may rent the business or buy it, paying for it in installments. But the Company acts as trustee for the emigrants, superintending, through its officers and lawyers, the administration of their affairs, and seeing to the proper collection of all payments. If a Jew cannot sell his business, or will not entrust it to a proxy, or does not wish to give up its personal management, he may stay where he is. The Jews who stay will be none the worse off, for they will be relieved of the competition of those who leave, and antisemitism with its "Don't buy from Jews!" will have ceased.

If the emigrating business proprietor wishes to carry on his old business in the new country, he can make his arrangements for it in advance. For example: Firm X carries on a large business in dry goods. The head of the firm wishes to emigrate. He begins by setting up a branch in his future place of residence, which he stocks with samples of his goods. The poor early settlers will be his first customers. Gradually new immigrants will come who require goods of better quality. X then sends out newer goods, and eventually ships his newest. The branch begins to pay while the parent firm is still in existence, so that X ends by having two going concerns. He sells his original business or hands it over to his Christian representative to manage and goes off to take charge of the new one.

An example of greater magnitude: Y and Son are large coal-traders, with mines and factories of their own. How is so huge and complex a property to be liquidated? The mines and everything connected with them might, in the first place, be bought up by the State in which they are situated. In the second place, the Jewish Company might take them over, paying for them partly in land, partly in cash. A third method might be the conversion of Y and Son into a limited company. A fourth method might be the continued operation of the business under the original proprietors, who would return at intervals to inspect their property, as foreigners, and as such, under the protection of law in every civilized State. All these suggestions are of daily occurrence. A fifth and excellent method, and one which might be particularly profitable, I shall merely indicate, because the existing examples of it are few, however ready the modern mind may be to accept it. Y and Son might sell their enterprise to their employees as a corporate body, who would form a co-operative society, with limited liability, and might perhaps pay the requisite sum with the help of a low-interest loan from the State treasury.

The employees would then gradually pay off the loan, which either the government or the Jewish Company, or even Y and Son, would have advanced to them.

The Jewish Company will be prepared to conduct the transfer of the smallest concerns equally with the largest. While the Jews quietly emigrate and establish their new homes, the Company acts as the great controlling body which organizes the departure, takes charge of possessions left behind, guarantees with its own visible and tangible property that liquidation will proceed in good order, and provides permanent security for those who have already settled.

SECURITIES OF THE COMPANY

What assurance will the company offer that the abandonment of countries will not cause their impoverishment and produce economic crises?

I have already mentioned that honest antisemites, while retaining that independence which we, too, would wish them to have, will be drawn into the project as a kind of unofficial popular regulative organ.

But the State revenues might suffer by the loss of a body of taxpayers, who, though little appreciated as citizens, are highly valued as a fiscal resource. The State should, therefore, receive compensation for this loss. This we offer indirectly by leaving in the country businesses which we have built up by means of Jewish acumen and Jewish industry, by letting our Christian fellow citizens move into our evacuated positions, and by thus facilitating a mass enrichment so peaceably and in so unparalleled a manner. The French Revolution had a somewhat similar result, on a small scale, but it was brought about by bloodshed on the guillotine in every province of France, and on the battlefields of Europe. Moreover, inherited and acquired rights were destroyed, and only those grew rich who were cunning enough to profit by the sale of State properties.

The Jewish Company will offer to the States that come within its sphere of activity direct as well as indirect advantages. It will give governments the first offer of abandoned Jewish property and allow them most favorable conditions. Governments, again, will be able to use this amicable expropriation for the purpose of certain social improvements.

The Jewish Company will give every assistance to governments and parliaments in their efforts to direct the inner migration of Christian citizens.

The Jewish Company will also pay heavy taxes. Its central office will be in London, for it must be under the legal protection of a great power which is not at present antisemitic. But the Company, if it is supported officially and semiofficially, will everywhere provide a broad base for taxation. To this end, it will establish tax-liable branch offices everywhere. Further, it will pay double duties on the twofold transfer of goods which it accomplishes. Even in transactions where the Company is really nothing more than a real estate agency, it will temporarily appear as a purchaser, and will be set down as the momentary possessor in the register of landed property.

These are, of course, mere bookkeeping transactions. It will have to be considered and decided in each locale how far the Company can go without endangering its own existence. The Company itself will confer freely with finance ministers on the various points at issue. Ministers will recognize the friendly spirit of our enterprise and will consequently offer every concession which is demonstrably necessary for the successful conclusion of the great undertaking.

Further, direct profit will accrue to governments from the transport of passengers and goods, and where railways are state property the returns will be immediately discernible. Where they are held by private companies, the Jewish Company will receive favorable terms for transport, in the same way as does every large-scale shipper. Freight and carriage must be made as cheap as possible for our people, because every traveler will pay his own expenses. The middle classes will travel on the Cook's system, the poorer classes in emigrant trains. The Company might make a good deal by reductions on passengers and goods; but here, as elsewhere, it must adhere to its principle of not trying to raise its receipts beyond what will cover its working expenses.

In many places transport is in Jewish hands; and the transport businesses will be the first needed by the Company and the first to be liquidated by it. The original owners of these concerns will either enter the Company's service or establish themselves independently "over there." The new arrivals will certainly require their assistance, and theirs being a paying profession, which they may and indeed must exercise there to earn a living, there will be no lack of these enterprising spirits. It is unnecessary to describe all the business details of this mass movement. They must be judiciously evolved out of the original plan by many able men, who must apply their minds to achieving the best system.

SOME OF THE COMPANY'S ACTIVITIES

Many activities will be interconnected. For example: The Company will gradually introduce the manufacture of goods into the settlements which will, of course, be extremely primitive at their inception. Clothing, linens, and shoes will first of all be manufactured for our own poor emigrants, who will be provided with new suits of clothing at the various European emigration centers. They will not receive these clothes as alms, for they must not be humiliated, but in exchange for old garments. Any loss the Company sustains by this transaction will be booked as a business loss. Those who are absolutely without means will pay off their debt to the Company by working overtime at a fair rate.

Existing emigration societies will be able to give valuable assistance here, for they will do for the Company's colonists what they did before for departing Jews. The forms of such co-operation will be easily found.

Even the new clothing of the poor settlers will have the symbolic meaning, "You are now entering on a new life." The Society of Jews will see to it that long before the departure and also during the journey a spirit of solemn enthusiasm is fostered by means of prayers, popular lectures, instruction on the object of the expedition, advice on hygienic precautions in their new places of residence, and guidance in regard to their future work. For the Promised Land is the land of work. On their arrival, the emigrants will be welcomed by our chief officials with due solemnity, but without foolish exultation, for the Promised Land will not yet have been possessed. But these poor people should already see that they are at home.

The clothing industries of the Company will, of course, not produce their goods without proper organization. The Society of Jews will obtain from the local branches information about the number, requirements, and date of arrival of the settlers, and will communicate all such information in good time to the Jewish Company. In this way it will be possible to provide for them with every precaution.

PROMOTION OF INDUSTRIES

The duties of the Jewish Company and the Society of Jews cannot be kept strictly apart in this outline. These two great bodies will have to work constantly in unison, the Company depending on the moral authority and support of the Society, just as the Society cannot dispense with the material assistance of the Company. For example, the organization of the clothing industry must be directed according to a plan providing deliberately for a slow, tentative beginning, in order to avoid crises of overproduction. Wherever the Company undertakes the organization of new industries the same precaution must be exercised.

The Company must never use its superior power to exclude individual initiative. We shall work collectively only when the immense difficulties of the task demand common action; we shall, wherever possible, scrupulously respect the rights of the individual. Private property, as the economic basis of independence, must be freely developed and respected among us. Our first unskilled laborers will at once be raised to the status of proprietors.

The spirit of enterprise must, indeed, be encouraged in every possible way. The establishment of industries will be promoted by a judicious system of duties, by the supply of cheap raw material, and by the creation of a bureau to collect and publish industrial statistics.

But this spirit of enterprise must be encouraged with prudence, and planless speculation must be avoided. Every new industry must be advertised for a long period before establishment, so that those who might hit on the idea of starting a similar business six months later may be spared failure and impoverishment. Whenever a new industrial establishment is to be founded, the Company should be informed, so that all those interested may obtain full information from it on prevailing conditions.

Industrialists will be able to apply to centralized labor agencies, which will receive a commission only large enough to ensure their continuance. The industrialists might, for example, telegraph for five hundred unskilled laborers for three days, three weeks, or three months. The labor agency would then collect these five hundred unskilled laborers from every possible source, and dispatch them at once to carry out the particular agricultural or industrial project. Parties of workmen will thus be systematically drafted from place to place like a body of troops. Thus the crude form of migratory labor will be refined into a well-organized mass operation. The office will not, of course, supply wage slaves, but men who work only a seven-hour day; and, in spite of the changes of locality, they will preserve their organization, work out their term of service, and receive commissions, promotions, and pensions. Some establishments may, of course, be able to obtain their workmen from other sources, if they wish, but they will not find it easy to do so. The Society will be able to prevent the introduction of non-Jewish wage slaves by boycotting obstinate employers, by charges on transport, and by various other methods. The seven-hour workers will therefore have to be taken, and we shall bring our people gradually, and with no appreciable coercion, to adopt the standard of a seven-hour day.

SETTLEMENT OF SKILLED LABORERS

It is clear that what can be done for unskilled workers can be even more easily done for skilled laborers. These will work under similar regulations in the factories, and the central labor agency will provide them when required.

Independent craftsmen and small employers must be carefully taught, so that we may rapidly introduce advanced techniques; they must learn, even if no longer very young men, to master scientific technology, and to use water power and electricity. These men, too, must be sought out and provided by the Society's agency. The local branch will, for example, apply to the central office: "We want so many carpenters, locksmiths, glaziers, etc." The central office will publish this demand, and the right men will apply there for work. These would then travel with their families to the place where they are wanted and establish their residence there, without the trials of uncontrolled competition. A permanent and comfortable home would thus be provided for them.

METHOD OF RAISING CAPITAL

The capital required for establishing the Company was previously put at what seemed an absurdly high figure. The actual amount needed will be determined by financiers and will in any case be a very considerable sum. There are three ways of raising this sum, all of which the Society will take under consideration. This Society, the great "Gestor" of the Jews, will be formed by our best and most upright men, who must not derive any material advantage from their membership. Although the Society cannot at the outset possess any but moral authority, this authority will suffice to establish the credit of the Jewish Company in the nation's eyes. The Jewish Company will be unable to succeed in its enterprise unless it has received the Society's sanction; it will thus not be formed of any chance collection of financiers. For the Society will weigh, select, and decide, and will not give its approval till it is sure that there is a sound basis for believing that plans will be conscientiously carried out. It will not permit experiments with insufficient means, for such an undertaking must succeed at the first attempt. Any initial failure would compromise the whole idea for many decades to come, or might even make its realization permanently impossible.

The three methods of raising capital are: (1) through big banks; (2) through small and private banks; (3) through public subscription.

The easiest, fastest, and most certain method would be for the great banks to found the Company. The present great financial groups could raise the necessary funds in a short time by merely consulting together. The great advantage of this method would be that it would be unnecessary to pay in the entire billion (to keep to the original figure) all at once. A further advantage would be that the credit of these powerful financiers would also be available to the enterprise. Vast latent political forces lie in our financial power, that power which our enemies assert to be so effective. It might be so, but actually it is not. Poor Jews feel only the hatred which this financial power provokes; its use in alleviating their lot as a body they have not yet felt. The credit of our great Jewish financiers would have to be placed at the service of the National Idea. But should these gentlemen, quite satisfied with their lot, feel disinclined to do anything for their fellow Jews, who are unjustly held responsible for the large possessions of certain individuals, then the realization of this plan will draw a clear line of distinction between them and the rest of Jewry.

The great financiers, moreover, will certainly not be asked to raise an amount so enormous out of pure philanthropic motives; that would be expecting too much. Rather may the promoters and stockholders of the Jewish Company look forward to considerable profit, and they will be able to calculate beforehand what their chances of success are likely to be. For the Society of Jews will be in possession of all documents and materials bearing on the prospects of the Jewish Company. The Society will in particular have investigated the precise magnitude of the new Jewish movement, so as to provide the Company promoters with thoroughly reliable information on the degree of participation they may expect. The Society will also supply the Jewish Company with comprehensive modern Jewish statistics, thus doing the work of what is called in France a *"société d'études,"* which undertakes all preliminary research required for the financing of a great undertaking. Even so, the enterprise may not receive the valuable assistance of our moneyed magnates. These might, perhaps, even try to oppose the Jewish movement by their private connections and agents. Such opposition, as all other, we shall meet with relentless firmness.

Supposing that these magnates are content simply to turn this scheme down with a smile. Is it, therefore, done for?

No.

For then the money will be raised in another way—by an appeal to moderately rich Jews. The smaller Jewish banks would have to be united in the name of the National Idea against the big banks, forming a second and formidable financial force. But unfortunately, this would require a great deal of financing at first—for the billion would have to be subscribed in full before starting work; and, as this sum could only be raised very slowly, all sorts of banking operations would have to be undertaken and loans made during the first few years. It might even occur that, in the course of all these transactions, their original object would be forgotten; the moderately rich Jews would have created a new and large business, and Jewish emigration would be forgotten.

The notion of raising money in this way is by no means impracticable. The organization of a Christian financial combination to oppose the big banks has already been tried; that one could also oppose them with Jewish money has not been thought of until now.

But these financial conflicts would bring about all sorts of crises; the countries in which they occurred would suffer, and antisemitism would run rampant.

This method is therefore not to be recommended. I have merely suggested it, because it comes up in the course of the logical development of the idea.

Nor do I know whether smaller private banks would be willing to adopt it.

In any case, even the refusal of moderately rich Jews would not put an end to the scheme. On the contrary, it is only now that we can consider it in full earnest.

The Society of Jews, whose members are not businessmen, might try to found the Company through popular subscription.

The Company's capital might be raised, without the aid of a banking syndicate, by means of direct subscription on the part of the public. Not only poor Jews, but also Christians who wanted to get rid of them, would subscribe a small amount to this fund. A new and peculiar form of the plebiscite would thus be established, whereby each man voting for this solution of the Jewish Question would express his opinion by subscribing for a certain sum conditionally. The condition would constitute his security. The full funds subscribed would only be paid in if their sum total reached the required amount, otherwise the initial payments would be returned.

But if the whole of the required sum is raised by popular subscription, then each little amount would be secured by the great numbers of other small amounts.

All of this would, of course, need the express and firm assistance of interested governments.

CHAPTER IV. LOCAL-GROUPS

THE TRANSPLANTATION

Previous chapters have explained only how the emigration scheme is to be carried out without creating any economic disturbance. But so great a movement cannot take place without stirring up deep and powerful emotions. Old customs, old memories attach us to our homes. We have cradles, we have graves, and we know what ancestral graves have meant to the Jews. Our cradles we shall carry with us—for therein slumbers our future, rosy and smiling. The graves so dear to us we must abandon—and I think these will be the most difficult for this grasping people of ours to leave behind. But so it must be.

Economic distress, political pressure, and social obloquy have already driven us from our homes and from our graves. We Jews are even now constantly shifting from place to place, a strong current carrying us westward over the sea to the United

States, where they don't want us, either. And where will we be welcome, so long as we haven't a homeland of our own?

But we shall give a home to our people. And we shall give it, not by uprooting them forcibly from the soil that sustains them, but rather by transplanting them carefully, roots and all, in better ground. Just as we wish to create new political and economic conditions, so shall we keep sacred all of the past that is dear to our people's hearts.

This theme can only be briefly touched upon. It is the part of my plan most likely to be considered fanciful. Yet even this is possible and real, however vague and aimless it may now appear. Organization will make of it something rational.

EMIGRATION IN GROUPS

Our people will emigrate in groups of families and friends. But no man will be forced to join the group going out from his former place of residence. Each will be able to journey in any manner he chooses as soon as he has settled his affairs. Each man will pay his own way, by rail and ship, hence he will travel by whatever class suits him. Our trains and ships may well have only one class, to avoid humiliating the poor over the long journey. Though we are not taking people on a pleasure trip, we do not intend to dampen their spirits en route.

None will travel in conditions of hardship, but whoever so wishes may travel in comfortable elegance. Even under the most favorable circumstances, the movement may not draw in certain classes of Jews for several years to come; the intervening period can, therefore, be employed in selecting the best modes of organizing the journeys. Those who are well off can travel in parties if they wish. Everyone will have his own circle of friends and connections with him. We know, after all, that, with the exception of the richest, Jews have very little to do with Christians. In some countries, apart from dependents, borrowers, and flunkeys, a Jew may have no Christian acquaintances at all. The Ghetto subsists, though its walls are broken down.

The middle classes will make elaborate and careful preparations for departure. A group of travelers will be formed in each locality, large towns being divided into districts with a group in each district, who will communicate by means of representatives elected for the purpose. This division into districts need not be strictly adhered to; it is merely intended as a convenience for the poorer Jews to alleviate discomfort and prevent any attack of homesickness during their journey outwards. Everybody is free to travel either alone or attached to any local group he prefers. The conditions of travel—regulated according to classes—will apply to all alike. Any sufficiently numerous traveling party can charter a special train and special boat from the company.

The Company's housing agency will provide quarters for the poorest on their arrival. Later on, when more prosperous emigrants follow, their easily calculable lodging needs on first landing will have been supplied by hotels built by private enterprise. Some of these more prosperous colonists will, indeed, have built their houses before becoming permanent settlers, so that they will merely move from an old home into a new one.

It is not necessary to spell out their tasks for our intellectuals. Every man who rallies behind the National Idea will know what he has to do in his own circle to propagate it and to initiate action. We shall seek above all the co-operation of our religious leaders.

OUR SPIRITUAL LEADERS

Every group will have its Rabbi, traveling with his congregation. All groupings will be voluntary. The Local-Groups will each form around a Rabbi, and each Rabbi will have his own group. For it is the Rabbis who will be the first to understand us, the first enthusiasts of the cause, and from their pulpits they will inspire the others. They will not need to call special meetings or conferences for the purpose; their appeal will fit naturally into the synagogue service. And properly so. For we inherit our historic identity as a people only through the faith of our fathers, having long since absorbed into our very marrow the languages of many different nations.

The Rabbis will regularly receive the bulletins of the Society

and the Company, which they will promulgate and explain
to their congregations. And Israel will pray for us, for itself.

LOCAL-GROUP REPRESENTATIVES

The Local-Groups will appoint small committees of representatives under the chairmanship of the Rabbis. The committees will discuss and decide all practical issues in accordance
with local conditions.

Philanthropic institutions will be independently transferred
by their local groups, each institution remaining "over there"
the property of the same people for whom it was originally
founded. I think the buildings should not be sold, however,
but turned over for the assistance of indigent Christians in
the departed towns. The Local-Groups will be compensated
with free building sites and reconstruction facilities in the new
country.

This transfer of philanthropic institutions will give another
of those opportunities, which occur at different points of my
scheme, for an experiment in the service of humanity. Our
present disorganized system of private philanthropy does little
good in proportion to its expenditures. But these institutions
can and must become part of a system in which they will
supplement one another. In a new society these organizations
can be set up in harmony with modern conceptions, and may
be based on all previous socio-political experiments. This matter
is of great importance to us, since we have so many paupers.
The weaker characters among us, disheartened by an oppressive environment and spoilt by the soft-hearted charity of our
own rich, easily let themselves sink to beggary.

The Society, with the co-operation of the local groups, will
give the utmost attention to educating the people in this respect.
Many energies which now wither uselessly away will flourish
in our fertile soil. Whoever shows a genuine desire to work
will be suitably employed. Beggars will not be tolerated. Whoever refuses to do anything as a free man deserves the work-
house.

On the other hand, we shall not relegate the aged to an almshouse. An almshouse is one of the cruelest charities that our

stupid benevolence has ever invented. It is an institution where old people die out of pure shame and mortification, where they are as good as buried. But we would leave even those of the lowest grade of intelligence the happy sense of being of some use in the world. We will provide light tasks for those who are incapable of physical labor; for we must take into account the enervated poor of an already enfeebled generation. But future generations shall be brought up differently: in freedom, for freedom's sake.

We will seek to bestow the moral blessing of labor on men of all ages and of all qualities. Thus will our people find its strength again in the land of the seven-hour day.

PLANS OF THE TOWNS

The Local-Groups will delegate their authorized representatives to select sites for towns. In the distribution of land every precaution will be taken to effect a careful transfer with due consideration for acquired rights.

The Local-Groups will have plans of the towns, so that our people may know beforehand where they are to go, in which towns and in which houses they are to live. Comprehensive drafts of the building plans previously referred to will be distributed among the Local-Groups.

Whereas strict centralization will be the principle of our administration, the Local-Groups will enjoy full autonomy. In this way the transfer will be accomplished with the minimum of friction.

I do not imagine all this to be easier than it actually is; on the other hand, people must not imagine it to be more difficult than it is in reality.

THE DEPARTURE OF THE MIDDLE CLASSES

The middle classes will be drawn willy-nilly into the outward current, for their sons will be officials of the Society or Company employees "over there." Lawyers, doctors, technicians of every description, young business people—in fact, all Jews who are in search of opportunity, who are now fleeing oppression in their native lands to earn a living in foreign lands—

will assemble on a soil so full of fair promise. Others will have
married their daughters to such ambitious men. Then one
young man will send for his wife or fiancée to come out to
him, another for his parents, brothers, and sisters. Members
of a new civilization marry young. This will promote general
morality and ensure sturdiness in the new generation; and
thus we shall have no delicate offspring of late marriages, children of fathers who had already spent their energies in the
struggle of life.

Every middle-class emigrant will draw more of his kind
after him.

To the boldest, naturally, will go the best of the new world.

But here we seem clearly to have come to the chief difficulty
in the plan.

Even if we succeed in initiating a serious world-wide discussion of the Jewish Question—

Even if this debate leads to the unequivocal conclusion that
the Jewish State is a world necessity—

Even if we acquire sovereignty over some territory through
the support of the Powers—

How shall we cause the masses of Jews to move from their
present homes to this new country without coercion?

For must not their emigration, under any conditions, be
voluntary?

THE BEHAVIOR OF MASSES

Great exertion will hardly be necessary to stimulate the
migration. The antisemites provide adequate impetus. They
need only go on as they are, and the desire of Jews to emigrate
will arise where it did not previously exist and will wax
stronger where it is already present. Where Jews now remain
in antisemitic countries, they do so chiefly because even those
among them who are ignorant of history know that continual
change of residence over the centuries has brought us no lasting good. Any land which were to welcome the Jews today,
offering them even lesser advantages than the Jewish State,
would immediately attract a great influx of Jews. The poorest,
who have nothing to lose, would find their way there against

all obstacles. But I maintain, and every man may ask himself if it is not so, that because of the pressure weighing upon us there is a desire to emigrate even among our prosperous classes of society. But even the poorest alone would suffice to found a State; these are the best men for taking a country into possession, for all great ventures must have an element of desperation in them.

But when our "desperadoes" raise the value of the land by their labor, they make it increasingly attractive as a place of settlement for people with greater means.

Higher and yet higher strata will become interested in moving. The expedition of the first and poorest settlers will be conducted by Company and Society jointly, with the co-operation, also, of existing emigration and Zionist societies.

How may a multitude not subject to command be directed to a particular spot? There are certain Jewish benefactors on a grand scale who would alleviate Jewish suffering through Zionist experiments. The problem presented itself to them, too, and they thought to solve it by giving the emigrants money or means of employment. Thus, the philanthropic solution was to say: "I will pay these people to go there." Such a procedure is utterly wrong, and all the money in the world will not bring it to fulfillment.

The Company, on the other hand, will say: "We shall not pay them, we shall let them pay us. We shall merely offer them inducements to go."

A fanciful illustration will make my meaning more explicit: One of those philanthropists (whom we shall call "The Baron") and I both wish to assemble a crowd of people on the plain of Longchamps near Paris on a hot Sunday afternoon. The Baron, by promising them ten francs each, will, for 200,000 francs, bring out 20,000 perspiring and miserable people, who will curse him for having put them to so much trouble. On the other hand, I would offer the same 200,000 francs as a prize for the swiftest race horse—and I would put up barriers to keep the people off Longchamps: they would have to pay to go in: one franc, five francs, twenty francs.

The upshot would be that I would get a half-million people out there; the President of the Republic would drive up *"à la Daumont,"* and the crowds would enjoy themselves. Most of them will think it a pleasure trip in the open in spite of the heat and dust; and I should have turned my 200,000 francs into about a million from admission and gaming receipts. I can get the same people out there again whenever I please, but the Baron will not—not for the world.

Let me give a more serious illustration of the law of mass behavior in an economic situation. Let someone have it proclaimed through the streets of a town: "Whoever is willing to stand all day long, through the bitter cold of winter or the burning heat of summer, in an iron hall exposed on all sides, and there to address every passer-by and offer him fancy wares, or fish, or fruit, will receive two florins, or four francs, or anything you please."

How many people would go to the hall? How many days would they hold out if hunger drove them there? And if they held out, what energy would they display in trying to persuade passers-by to buy fish, fruit, and fancy wares?

We shall set about it in a different way. In places where trade is active (and these places we shall the more easily discover, since we ourselves direct trade whithersoever we wish), in these places we shall build large halls and call them markets. The halls might easily be worse built and more unwholesome than those mentioned before, and yet people would stream toward them. But we shall apply our best efforts, and we shall build them as well and as attractively as possible. And the people, to whom we had promised nothing, because we cannot promise anything without deceiving them, these excellent, keen businessmen will cheerfully create a most active commercial intercourse. They will harangue the buyers unweariedly; they will stand on their feet and scarcely think of fatigue. They will hurry off at dawn, so as to be first on the spot; they will form unions, cartels, anything to continue in their occupation undisturbed. And if they find at the end of the day that all their hard work has produced only one florin, fifty kreuzer, or three francs, or something similar, they will yet look forward hopefully to the next day, which may, perhaps, bring them better luck.

We have given them hope.

Would any one ask whence the demand comes which creates the market? Is it really necessary to tell them again?

I pointed out that by means of the system of *"Assistance par le Travail,"* the return could be increased fifteenfold. One million would produce fifteen millions; and one billion, fifteen billions.

This may be the case on a small scale; is it so on a large one? Capital surely yields a return diminishing in inverse ratio to its own growth. It is true, inactive and inert capital yields diminishing returns, but active capital brings in a handsomely increasing return. Indeed, this is the crux.

Am I stating facts? I call on the richest Jews to attest to it. Why do they carry on so many different industries? Why do they send men to work underground and bring up coal amid terrible dangers for meager pay? I cannot imagine this to be pleasant, even for the owners of the mines. For I do not believe, nor do I pretend, that capitalists are heartless. My desire is not to agitate, but to reconcile differences.

Is it necessary to illustrate the behavior of masses, and the means for attracting them to a desired spot, by considering religious pilgrimages?

I do not wish to offend anyone's religious sensibilities by words which might be misinterpreted.

I merely cite in passing what the pilgrimage to Mecca means in the Mohammedan world, Lourdes to the Catholics, and many other spots whence men return home comforted by their faith, or the sacred rock of Trèves. Thus we, too, shall create a center for the deep religious needs of our people. Our clergymen will be the first to understand us and go along with us.

We shall let every man find salvation "over there" after his own inclination. And among them, we shall think first and foremost of that immortal band, our cherished freethinkers, who are continually conquering new regions for humanity.

No more force will be applied against anyone than is necessary for the preservation of the State and public order; and the force necessary will not be arbitrarily defined by whatever persons happen to be in authority at any time; it will be established in constitutional laws.

Now if it be inferred from my illustrations that the multitude can be attracted only temporarily, to centers of faith, of business, or of amusement, the rebuttal is simple. Whereas one of these objects by itself would certainly only attract the masses, all these centers of attraction combined are suited permanently to hold and satisfy them. For all these centers together form that great, long-sought entity for which our people has never ceased to yearn, for which it has kept itself alive, for which it has been kept alive by external pressure: A homeland! When the movement is underway we shall draw some along with us, let others follow, others again will be swept into the stream, and the last will be forced out in our wake.

These, the laggards, will be the worst off, both in the old country and the new.

But the vanguard, who go with faith, enthusiasm, and courage, will have the best positions.

OUR HUMAN MATERIAL

There are more misconceptions abroad concerning Jews than concerning any other people. And we have become so depressed and discouraged by our age-old suffering that we ourselves parrot and believe these errors. One of them is that Jews have an immoderate love of trade. Now it is well known that wherever we are permitted to take part in the rising of classes we hastily remove ourselves from business. By far the great majority of Jewish businessmen send their sons to study the humanities. Hence the so-called "Judaization" of all intellectual professions. But even in the lower economic strata, our love of trade is not so great as is commonly held. In European countries there are large masses of Jews who are not traders, and who are not afraid of hard work either. The Society of Jews will be in a position to prepare scientifically accurate statistics of our manpower. The new tasks and prospects that await our people in the new country will satisfy our present handicraftsmen and will transform many present small traders into manual workers.

A peddler who travels about the country with a heavy pack on his back is not as contented as his persecutors imagine. The seven-hour day will transform all of his kind into workmen. They are good, misunderstood people, who now suffer perhaps more grievously than any. The Society of Jews will, moreover, concern itself from the outset with their training as artisans. The profit motive will be encouraged in a wholesome manner. Jews are thrifty, resourceful, and adaptable. Such people are qualified for any means of earning a living, and merely making small trading unremunerative will be enough to cause those now occupied as peddlers to give up this trade altogether. This could be brought about, for example, by encouraging large department stores, carrying all commodities. These general stores are already crushing small trading in large cities; in a new civilization they will quite preclude its existence. The establishment of these stores has the further advantage of making the country immediately habitable for people accustomed to a higher standard of living.

HABITS

Is a reference, even a passing one, to the minor habits and comforts of the common man in keeping with the serious nature of this pamphlet?

I think so. And moreover, it is very important. For these daily habits are the thousand and one fine threads which together go to make up an unbreakable cable.

Here, too, certain narrow notions must be set aside. Whoever has seen anything of the world knows that just these daily habits can easily be transplanted everywhere. The technical achievements of our day, which this scheme intends to employ fully in the service of humanity, have heretofore been principally used for the provision of such habitual needs. There are English hotels in Egypt and on the mountaintops in Switzerland, Viennese cafés in South Africa, French theater in Russia, German opera in America, and the best Bavarian beer in Paris.

When we journey out of Egypt again, we shall not leave the fleshpots behind.

Every man will find his habits provided for again in the transplanted Local-Groups, but they will be better, more beautiful, and pleasanter than before.

CHAPTER V. SOCIETY OF JEWS AND JEWISH STATE

NEGOTIORUM GESTIO

This pamphlet is not intended for lawyers. I can therefore touch only cursorily, as on so many other things, upon my theory of the legal basis of a state. I must, nevertheless, lay some stress on my new theory, which could be maintained, I believe, even in technical presentation.

According to Rousseau's now antiquated view, a state is formed by a social contract. Rousseau held: "The conditions of this contract are so precisely defined by the nature of the agreement that the slightest alteration would make them null and void. The consequence is that, even where they are not expressly stated, they are everywhere identical, and everywhere tacitly accepted and recognized . . . "

A logical and historical refutation of Rousseau's theory was never, nor is it now, difficult, however terrible and far-reaching the effects of that theory may have been. The question whether a social contract with "conditions not expressly stated, yet unalterable" existed before the framing of a constitution is of no practical interest to states under modern forms of government. The legal relationship between government and citizen is in any case clearly established now.

But prior to the framing of a constitution, and during the creation of a new state, these principles assume great practical importance. We know and see for ourselves that states still continue to be created. Colonies secede from the mother country; vassals fall away from their suzerain; newly opened territories are immediately formed into free states. It is true that the Jewish State is conceived as a peculiarly modern structure on unspecified territory. But a state is formed, not by an area of land, but rather by a number of men united under a single sovereignty.

The people is the subjective, land the objective foundation of a state, and the subjective basis is the more important of the two. One sovereignty, for example, which has no objective basis at all, is perhaps the most respected one in the world. I refer to the sovereignty of the Pope.

The theory of rationality is the one at present accepted in political science. This theory suffices to justify the creation of a state, and cannot be historically refuted in the same way as the theory of a contract. Insofar as I am concerned only with the creation of a Jewish State, I am well within the limits of the theory of rationality. But when I touch upon the legal basis of the state, I have exceeded them. The theories of a divine institution, or of superior power, or of a contract, and the patriarchal and patrimonial theories do not accord with modern views. The legal basis of a state is sought either too much within men (patriarchal theory, and theories of superior force and contract), or too far above them (objective patrimonial theory). The theory of rationality leaves this question conveniently and carefully unanswered. But a question which has seriously occupied doctors of jurisprudence in every age cannot be an absolutely idle one. As a matter of fact, a mixture of the human and the transhuman goes into the making of any state. Some legal basis is indispensable to explain the oppressive relationship in which subjects occasionally stand to rulers. I believe it is to be found in the *negotiorum gestio*, the body of citizens representing the *dominus*, and the government represents the *gestor*.

The remarkable legal insight of the Romans created a noble masterpiece in the *negotiorum gestio*. When the property of an incapacitated person is in danger, anyone may step forward to save it. One who does is the *gestor*, the director of affairs not strictly his own. He has no warrant—that is, no human warrant. His warrant derives from a higher necessity. This higher necessity may be formulated by a state in different ways, as its formulation may also differ in accordance with the varying ideas at different levels of culture. The *gestio* is intended to serve the welfare of the *dominus*—the people—of whom the *gestor* himself is one.

The *gestor* administers property of which he is joint owner. His joint proprietorship enables him to recognize the urgency that warrants his intervention, and demands his taking charge in peace or war; but in no sense can he claim to delegate valid authority to himself on the grounds of his co-ownership. Even under most favorable conditions, he can no more than presume the consent of the innumerable other co-proprietors.

A state is created by a nation's struggle for existence. In any such struggle it is impossible to obtain proper authority in due form beforehand. In fact, any preliminary attempt to obtain a regular decision from the majority would probably ruin the undertaking at the outset. For partisan division would render the people defenseless against external dangers. We cannot all be of one mind; the *gestor* therefore simply takes the leadership into his hands and marches in the van.

Action by the *gestor* of a state is sufficiently authorized if the common cause is in danger, and the *dominus* is prevented, either by want of will or by some other reason, from helping itself.

But the *gestor* becomes similar to the *dominus* by his intervention, and is bound by the agreement *quasi ex contractu*. This is the legal relationship existing before, or more correctly, created simultaneously with, the state.

The *gestor* thus becomes answerable for every form of negligence, even for the failure of business undertakings, and the neglect of such affairs as are intimately connected with them, etc. I shall not further enlarge on the *negotiorum gestio*, nor apply the concept in connection with the state, for it would take us too far from the main subject. One remark only: "Business transactions, if approved by the owner, are just as effectual as if originally carried on by his authority."

And how does all this affect our case?

The Jewish people is at present prevented by its dispersion from conducting its own political affairs. Besides, it is in a condition of more or less severe distress in various parts of the world. It needs, above all things, a *gestor*. This *gestor* cannot, of course, be a single individual. Such a one would appear either ridiculous or, since he would appear to be working for his own interests, contemptible.

The *gestor* of the Jews must be a "moral person" in every sense of the word. That is, then, the Society of Jews.

THE GESTOR OF THE JEWS

This organ of the national movement, whose nature and functions we may now consider, will actually come into being before everything else. Its formation is perfectly simple. The requisite "moral person" will arise out of the circle of energetic English Jews whom I apprised of my scheme in London.*

The Society will have scientific and political tasks; for the founding of a Jewish State, as I conceive it, presupposes the application of scientific methods. We cannot journey out of Egypt today in the simple fashion of antiquity. We shall first obtain an accurate account of our numbers and strength. The Society of Jews is the new Moses of the Jews. The undertaking of that great and ancient *gestor* of the Jews in primitive times bears much the same relation to ours that some wonderful lyrical drama of old bears to a modern opera. We play the same melody with far many more violins, flutes, harps, violoncellos, and bass viols, with lights, *décor*, choirs, magnificent costumes, and with the first singers of the day.

This pamphlet is intended to initiate a general discussion on the Jewish Question. Friend and foe will join in it, but not, I hope, in the tones of sentimental apologetic and violent abuse that has hitherto prevailed. The debate should be objective, comprehensive, sober, and politically oriented.

The Society of Jews will gather all available pronouncements of statesmen, parliaments, Jewish communities, societies, whether in speeches or writings, at meetings, in newspapers or books.

* Dr. Herzl addressed a meeting of the Maccabean Club, at which Israel Zangwill presided, on November 24, 1895, three months before publication of *The Jewish State*. Three months after its publication, the Club rejected his proposals.

Thus the Society will ascertain for the first time whether the time has really come when the Jews must and wish to go to the Promised Land. The Society will receive from every Jewish community in the world material towards a comprehensive collection of Jewish statistics.

Further tasks, such as expert investigation of the new land and its natural resources, co-ordinated planning of migration and settlement, laying the groundwork for legislation and administration, etc., must be intelligently developed in line with the objective.

In relation to the outer world, the Society will attempt, as I have already explained in the general section, to be recognized as a state-forming power. The free assent of many Jews will confer on it the requisite authority *vis-à-vis* governments.

Internally—that is to say, *vis-à-vis* the Jewish people—the Society will create the first indispensable agencies, the nuclei out of which the public institutions of the Jewish State will later evolve.

Our first object is, as I have said, sovereignty assured by international law over a portion of the globe adequate to meet our fair needs.

What is the next step?

THE OCCUPATION OF THE LAND

When peoples migrated in antiquity, they let themselves be borne, drawn, and tossed about by chance. Like locust swarms they lighted wherever their mechanical flight happened to take them. For in antiquity the globe was not known to man.

But this modern Jewish migration must proceed in accordance with scientific principles.

Only some forty years ago gold mining was carried on in an extraordinarily primitive fashion. What adventurous days those were in California! A report brought desperadoes together from every quarter of the globe; they stole pieces of land, robbed each other of gold, and finally gambled it away, as is the wont of robbers.

But today! What is gold mining like in the Transvaal today?

No more adventurous vagabonds, but sedate geologists and engineers manage the gold-mining industry. Ingenious machinery separates the ore from the surrounding rock. Little is left to chance. So must the most modern techniques be used in investigating and taking possession of the new Jewish Land.

As soon as we have secured the land, the ship of the occupation group will set sail.

Aboard ship will be representatives of the Society, the Company, and the Local-Groups.

These land occupiers will have three tasks: (1) an accurate, scientific investigation of all the natural resources of the country; (2) the organization of a tight, centralized administration; (3) the parceling of land. These tasks complement one another and will be carried out in accord with the now familiar objective.

One thing remains to be explained—namely, how the land is to be occupied by the several Local-Groups.

In America the occupation of newly opened territory is set about in truly forthright fashion. The settlers assemble on the frontier, and at the appointed time make a simultaneous and violent rush for it.

This will not be the approach in the new land of the Jews. Plots in the provinces and towns will be sold at auction, and paid for not in money, but in work. The general plan will have ascertained what streets, bridges, regulated waterways, etc., are necessary to bear the expected traffic. These will be grouped according to provinces. Within these provinces, sites for towns will be similarly sold by auction. The Local-Groups are not venturing beyond their means. The large communities will receive large sites for development. Outstanding efforts will be rewarded by the establishment of universities, technical schools, academies, research institutes, etc., and governmental organs which do not have to be concentrated in the capital will be dispersed throughout the country.

The personal interest of the buyers, and if necessary local assessments, will assure the proper execution of what has been undertaken. Just as we cannot, and indeed do not wish to, obliterate individual differences, so will the differences between the Local-Groups continue. Everything will shape itself quite naturally. All acquired rights will be protected and every new development will be given adequate scope.

Our people will be fully and clearly apprised of all these matters.

We shall not defraud or cheat others, any more than we shall cheat ourselves.

Everything will be systematically worked out in advance. In the elaboration of this plan, which I am capable only of suggesting, our keenest minds will participate. Every social-scientific and technical achievement of our age, and of the yet more advanced age which will be reached before the gradual execution of the plan is accomplished, must be put to the service of the project. Every useful invention now available and which will be available must be applied. Thus we can put into effect an unprecedented form of land occupation and state founding, with unparalleled chances of success.

CONSTITUTION

One of the great commissions which the Society will have to appoint will be the council of state jurists. This must formulate the best and most modern constitution that is possible. I believe that a good constitution should be of moderately flexible nature. In another work I have explained in detail what forms of government I hold to be the best. I consider a democratic monarchy and an aristocratic republic to be the finest forms of state. The form of a state and the principles of its government must constitute a balance of counterpoised forces. I am a staunch advocate of monarchic institutions, because they make possible a continuous policy and represent union of the interests of a historically illustrious family, born and educated to rule, with the needs of the preservation of the state. But our history has been too long interrupted for us to attempt to re-institute that. The very attempt would lay us open to ridicule.

Democracy without the salutary counterbalance of a monarch is extreme in its likes and dislikes, tends to idle parliamentary disputations, and produces that base class of men—the professional politicians. Nor are the present-day nations really fit

for democracy, and I believe they will become ever less fit
for it. For pure democracy presupposes the prevalence of a
very simple morality and our own morality becomes ever more
complex with the advance of commerce and civilization. *"Le
ressort d'une democratie est la vertu,"* said wise Montesquieu.
And where may virtue be found today, if we mean political
virtue? I have no faith in the political virtue of our people,
because we are no better than the rest of modern man and
because freedom will bring out contentiousness first. I also
consider government by referendum unsatisfactory, because
in politics there are no simple questions which can be answered merely by Yes and No. The masses are more prone
even than parliaments to be misled by fantastic ideas and
swayed by vigorous demagogy. It is impossible to formulate
wise internal or external policy in popular assembly.

Politics must work from the top down. But this is not to
say that anyone in the Jewish State will be repressed, but every
Jew will be able to rise, every one will wish to rise. Thus a
great upward surge is bound to energize our people. Every
individual will try to raise himself, thus raising the whole
body of citizens. The ascent will take a form beneficial to the
State and useful to the National Idea.

Hence I incline to an aristocratic republic. This would satisfy the ambitious spirit of our people, which has now degen-
erated into petty vanity. Many of the institutions of Venice
come to mind; but all that caused the ruin of Venice must
be avoided. We shall learn from the historical mistakes of
others, just as we shall learn from our own; for we are a
modern nation and wish to become the most modern. Our people who are receiving the new country from the Society will
gratefully accept also the new constitution it offers them.
Should any resistance arise, the Society will break it. The
Society cannot permit its work to be disturbed by obtuse or
malicious individuals.

LANGUAGE

It might be suggested that our lack of a common current
language would present difficulties, for we cannot converse

with one another in Hebrew. Who among us knows enough Hebrew to ask for a railway ticket in that language? We have no such people. But it is really a very simple matter. Every man retains his own language, the cherished homeland of his thoughts. Switzerland offers conclusive proof of the possibility of linguistic federalism. We shall remain in the new country what we now are here, nor shall we ever cease to recall with nostalgia the native lands which we were compelled to leave.

We shall give up those miserable stunted jargons, those Ghetto languages which we now employ. These were the stealthy tongues of prisoners. Our educators will give due attention to this matter. The language which proves itself to be of greatest utility for general intercourse will without compulsion establish itself as the national tongue. Our community of race is peculiar and unique. We know ourselves as bound together only by the light of our ancestral faith.

THEOCRACY

Shall we, thus, end by having a theocracy? No! Faith unites us, knowledge makes us free. We shall therefore permit not the least theocratic tendency to come to the fore on the part of our clergy. We shall know how to restrict them to their temples, just as we shall restrict our professional army to their barracks. Army and clergy shall be honored, as their noble functions require and deserve. But they have no privileged voice in the administration of the state which confers distinction upon them, else they would conjure up external and internal complications to vex us.

Every man will be as free and unrestricted in his belief or his unbelief as he is in his cultural ties. And should it happen that men of other creeds and other nationalities come to live among us, we shall accord them honorable protection and equality before the law. We have learned toleration in Europe. This is by no means said sarcastically. The antisemitism of today can only in a very few places be taken for the old religious intolerance. It is, for the most part, a movement among civilized nations whereby they try to exorcise a ghost from out of their own past.

LAW

When the State Idea begins to approach realization, the Society of Jews will appoint a council of jurists to lay the groundwork of its laws. During the transition period these must act on the principle that every immigrant Jew is to be judged according to the laws of the country which he has left. Thereafter legal uniformity is to be sought. The laws must be modern, making use of the best precedents available. This might become a model code, embodying all the just social demands of the present day.

ARMY

The Jewish State is conceived as a neutral country. It will require only a professional army, equipped, by all means, with every requisite of modern warfare, to preserve order internally and externally.

THE FLAG

We have no flag. We need one. Who would lead many men must raise a symbol above their heads.

I visualize a white flag, with seven golden stars. The white field symbolizes our pure new life; the stars are the seven golden hours of our work day. For the Jews shall march into the new land bearing the badge of labor.

RECIPROCITY AND EXTRADITION TREATIES

The new Jewish State must be in due form, with a decent regard for our future honorable position in the world.

Therefore all obligations in the old countries must be scrupulously fulfilled. The Society of Jews and the Jewish Company will grant cheap passage and all settlement benefits to those only who present an official certification from the local authorities: "Affairs left in good order."

Every just private claim originating in the abandoned countries will be heard more readily in the Jewish State than anywhere else. We shall not wait for reciprocity, we shall act purely for the sake of our own honor. We shall thus perhaps find, later on, that law courts will be more willing to hear our claims than now seems to be the case in some places.

It is self-evident, from the foregoing remarks, that we shall surrender Jewish criminals more readily than any other state, till the time comes when we can enforce our penal code on the same principles that all other civilized nations do. There will, therefore, be a period of transition during which we shall receive Jewish criminals only after they have paid all penalties. But having made amends, they will be accepted without any restrictions whatever, so that a new life may begin.

Thus emigration may become for many Jews a crisis with a happy outcome. Bad external circumstances, which ruin many a character, will be removed, and this change may mean salvation to many who are lost.

Here I should like briefly to relate a story I came across in an account of the gold mines of the Witwatersrand. Once a man came to the Rand, settled there, tried his hand at various things, though not at gold mining, till he founded an ice factory, which did well. He soon won universal esteem by his respectability, but after some years he was suddenly arrested. He had committed some defalcations as a banker in Frankfurt, had fled from there, and began a new life under an assumed name. But when he was taken away as prisoner, the most respected people in the place appeared at the station, bade him a cordial farewell and *au revoir*—for he was certain to return.

How much this story reveals!

A new life can regenerate even criminals. And we have relatively few criminals. There is an interesting statistical study on this point worth reading, *The Criminality of Jews in Germany*, by Dr. P. Nathan of Berlin, who was commissioned by the Society for Defense against Antisemitism to make a collection of statistics based on official reports. Of course, this pamphlet, which teems with figures, has been prompted, like many another "defense," by the error that antisemitism can be refuted by reason. We are probably disliked as much for our merits as for our faults.

BENEFITS OF THE EMIGRATION OF THE JEWS

Governments, either voluntarily or under pressure from the antisemites, will give some attention to the present plan, and they may perhaps even receive it, here and there, with a sympathy which they will also accord to the Society of Jews.

For the emigration I have in mind can create no economic upheavals. Such crises as are bound to arise anywhere in the wake of Jew-baiting would rather be prevented by the realization of this plan. A great period of prosperity would set in in those countries which are now antisemitic. For, as I have repeatedly said, there will be an internal migration of Christian citizens into the positions slowly and systematically evacuated by the Jews. If we are not merely suffered, but actually assisted, to do this, the movement will have a generally salutary effect. It is also a narrow view, which should be abandoned, to suppose that the departure of large numbers of Jews may lead to the impoverishment of their countries. It is different from a flight resulting from persecution, for then property is indeed destroyed, as it is ruined in the confusion of war. Quite different is the peaceable, voluntary departure of colonists, everything being done with due consideration for acquired rights, and in absolute accordance with law, openly and by light of day, in full view of the authorities and under the scrutiny of public opinion. The emigration of Christian proletarians to different parts of the world would be brought to a standstill by the Jewish movement.

The states would have a further benefit in the enormous increase of their export trade; for since the emigrant Jews "over there" would for a long time to come be dependent on European products, they would necessarily have to import them. Under the control of Local-Groups an equitable exchange would take place and the customary needs would have to be filled for a long time yet by the accustomed sources.

One of the greatest benefits may well prove to be the consequent easing of the social question. Social dissatisfaction would be allayed during the twenty or more years which the emigration of the Jews would occupy, in any case throughout the whole transition period.

The shape which the social question may ultimately take depends entirely on the development of our technical resources.

Steam power concentrated men around machines in factories where they were in oversupply and where they made one another miserable. Our present enormous, injudicious, and unsystematic rate of production is the cause of continual severe crises which ruin both employers and employees. Steam crowded men together; electricity will probably scatter them again, and may perhaps bring about a more prosperous condition of the labor market. In any case our technical inventors, who are the true benefactors of humanity, will continue their labors throughout the period of the emigration of the Jews, and they will discover things as marvelous as those we have already seen, or indeed more wonderful even than these.

The word "impossible" has ceased to exist in the vocabulary of technical science. If a man who lived in the last century were to return to earth, he would find the life of today full of incomprehensible magic. Wherever we moderns appear with our inventions, we transform the desert into a garden. To build a city takes in our time as many years as it formerly required centuries; America offers endless examples of this. Distance has ceased to be an obstacle. The spirit of our age has gathered fabulous treasures into its storehouse. Every day this wealth increases. A hundred thousand heads are occupied with speculations and research at every point of the globe, and what anyone discovers belongs the next moment to the whole world.

We will use and carry on experiments on every frontier of science in the Jewish Land; just as we shall institute the seven-hour day as an experiment for the benefit of humanity, so shall we proceed in everything else in the same humanitarian spirit, and build the new land as a land of experiment and a model state.

After the departure of the Jews, the enterprises which they have created will remain. Even Jewish enterprise will still be active wherever it is truly welcome. Jewish capitalists will continue to invest their liquid funds in those places where they are familiar of old with local conditions. Because of persecution, Jewish funds are frequently sent abroad to be invested in the remotest of foreign ventures, but in that time it will return, thanks to the amicable solution of the problem, and contribute to the further prosperity of the lands the Jews have left.

CHAPTER VI. CONCLUSION

How much remains to be elaborated, how many defects, how many harmful superficialities, and how many useless repetitions in this pamphlet which I have so long considered and so frequently revised!

But a fair-minded reader, who has sufficient understanding to grasp the spirit of my words, will not be repelled by these defects. He will rather be roused thereby to enlist his intelligence and energy in a project which is not one man's alone, and improve it.

Have I not explained obvious things and overlooked important objections?

I have tried to meet some objections; but I know that there are many more, high-minded and base.

It is one of the high-minded objections that the Jews are not the only people in the world who are in a state of distress. But I should think that we might well begin by removing a little of this misery, be it only our own for the time being.

It might further be said that we ought not to create new distinctions between people; we ought not to raise fresh barriers, we should rather make the old disappear. I say that those who think in this way are amiable visionaries; and the Homeland Idea will go on flourishing long after the dust of their bones will have been scattered without trace by the winds. Universal brotherhood is not even a beautiful dream. Conflict is essential to man's highest efforts.

Well, then? The Jews, in their own State, will likely have no more enemies, and in their prosperity they will decline and dwindle, so that the Jewish people will soon disappear altogether? I imagine that the Jews will always have sufficient enemies, just as every other nation. But once settled in their own land, they can never again be scattered all over the world. The Diaspora cannot be revived, unless all of civilization collapses. Only a simpleton could fear this. The civilized world of today has sufficient power to defend itself.

The base objections are innumerable, just as there are indeed more base men than noble in this world. I have tried to refute some of the narrow-minded notions. Whoever would rally behind the white flag with the seven stars must assist in this campaign of enlightenment. It may be that it is against many a malicious, narrow-minded, short-sighted Jew that the battle will first have to be joined.

Will it not be said that I am providing weapons for the antisemites? How so? Because I admit the truth? Because I do not maintain that there are none but excellent men among us?

Will it not be said that I am suggesting a way in which we can be injured? This I categorically deny. My proposal can be carried out only with the free consent of a majority of Jews. Action may be taken against individuals, even against groups of the most powerful Jews, but never and by no means by governments against all Jews. The equal rights of the Jew before the law once granted cannot be rescinded, for the first attempt would immediately drive all Jews, rich and poor alike, into the ranks of revolutionary parties. The very beginning of official discrimination against the Jews has invariably brought about economic crises. Very little, therefore, can effectually be done against us that will not redound to the detriment of the perpetrator. Meantime hatred grows apace. The rich do not feel it much. But our poor! Let us ask our poor, who have been more severely proletarized since the last resurgence of antisemitism than ever before.

Will some of our well-to-do say that the pressure is not yet severe enough to justify emigration, and that even the forcible expulsions that have occurred show how unwilling our people are to depart? True, because they do not know whither! Because they only pass from one trouble on to the next. But we are showing them the way to the Promised Land. And the splendid force of enthusiasm must fight against the terrible force of habit.

Persecutions are no longer as vicious as they were in the Middle Ages? True, but our sensitivity has increased, so that we feel no diminution in our suffering. Prolonged persecution has strained our nerves.

Will people say, again, that the venture is hopeless, because even if we obtain the land with sovereignty over it, the poor only will go along? It is precisely they whom we need at first! Only desperate men make good conquerors.

Will some one say, If it were feasible it would have been done long ago?

It has never yet been possible. Now it is possible. A hundred, even fifty years ago it would have been sheer fantasy. Today it is reality. The rich, who enjoy a comprehensive acquaintance with all technical advances, know full well how much can be done for money. And this is how it will go: precisely the poor and simple, who have no idea what power man already exercises over the forces of Nature, will have the staunchest faith in the new message. For these have never lost their hope of the Promised Land.

Here you have it, Jews! Not fiction, nor yet fraud! Every man may convince himself of it, for every man will carry over with him a portion of the Promised Land—one in his head, another in his arms, another in his acquired possessions.

Now, all this may appear to be a drawn-out affair. Even in the most favorable circumstances, many years might elapse before the founding of the state is under way. In the meantime, Jews in a thousand different places will suffer insult, mortification, abuse, drubbings, depredation, and death. But no; once we begin to execute the plan, antisemitism will cease at once and everywhere. For it is the conclusion of peace. When the Jewish Company has been formed, the news will be carried in a single day to the utmost ends of the globe by the lightning speed of our telegraph wires.

And immediate relief will ensue. The intellectuals whom we produce so superabundantly in our middle classes will find an immediate outlet in our organizations, as our first technicians, officers, professors, officials, lawyers, physicians. And so it will continue, swiftly but smoothly.

Prayers will be offered up in the temples for the success of the project. And in the churches as well! It is the relief from an old burden, under which all have suffered.

But first the minds must be enlightened. The idea must make its way into the uttermost miserable holes where our people dwell. They will awaken from barren brooding. For into all our lives will come a new meaning. Every man need think only of himself, and the movement will become an overwhelming one.

And what glory awaits the selfless fighters for the cause!

Therefore I believe that a wondrous breed of Jews will spring up from the earth. The Maccabees will rise again.

Let me repeat once more my opening words: The Jews who will it shall achieve their State.

We shall live at last as free men on our own soil, and in our own homes peacefully die.

The world will be liberated by our freedom, enriched by our wealth, magnified by our greatness.

And whatever we attempt there for our own benefit, will redound mightily and beneficially to the good of all mankind.

PROTEST RABBIS

THE latest development in the Jewish movement is the Protest Rabbis. Max Nordau has already branded this type with a word that will remain. These are the people who, themselves sitting in a safe boat, use their oars to batter the heads of those drowning men who seek to clamber up over the sides of their boat. If there is, in addition, an appointment as "spiritual leader" to one of the larger congregations, then the Protest Rabbi is all set. Five such Protest Rabbis have issued the following declaration in the *Berliner Tageblatt* and elsewhere:

"The Executive Committee of the Association of Rabbis in Germany: Dr. Maybaum (Berlin), Dr. Horovitz (Frankfurt), Dr. Guttmann (Breslau), Dr. Auerbach (Halberstadt), Dr. Werner (Munich) make the following announcement: 'Through the call for a Zionist Congress and through the publication of its agenda, such mistaken notions have been spread about the whole subject of Judaism and about the objectives of its adherents that the undersigned Executive Committee of the Association of Rabbis in Germany regards it as proper to make the following explanation:

1. The efforts of so-called Zionists to found a Jewish national state in Palestine contradict the Messianic promises of Judaism as contained in the Holy Writ and in later religious sources.

2. Judaism obligates its adherents to serve with all devotion the Fatherland to which they belong, and to further its national interests with all their heart and with all their strength.

3. However, those noble aims directed toward the coloniza-

"Protestrabbiner," in *Gesammelte Zionistische Werke*, Vol. 1 (Berlin, Jüdischer Verlag, 1934), pages 169–174.

tion of Palestine by Jewish peasants and farmers are not in contradiction to these obligations, because they have no relation whatsoever to the founding of a national state.

Religion and patriotism both thus lay upon us the duty of asking all who are concerned with the welfare of Judaism to stay away from the above-mentioned Zionistic endeavors and most particularly from the Congress which is still being planned, despite all the warnings against it.' "

This is a remarkable document. The first impression that we get from it is that it will not exactly raise the esteem in which the Jews are held. The entire declaration is, as every Jew can see at first glance, directed toward the outside. It is one of those contemptible and despicable solemn declarations that whine for the favor of the enemy.

Luckily not all Rabbis are like this. We could mention names, such as those of Mohilever in Bialystok, Zadok Kahn in Paris, Rülf in Memel, Gaster in London, and many many more, with only the highest esteem. And we do not do this in any spirit of partisanship. Zionism is not a matter of parties. One can come to Zionism from any party, just as Zionism includes all parties that make up the life of the people. Zionism is the Jewish people on the march. And that is why the behavior of the Protest Rabbis is appalling.

Whoever wishes to turn away from the Jewish nation from which he stems and go over to some other people, let him do so. We Zionists will not stop him. But he then becomes a stranger for us. His new affairs are no concern of ours, but neither are ours any concern of his. It is not for him to mix into what we have to say, and if he is wise, he will not even try, for if he continues to be concerned about internal Jewish affairs, it can only make him an object of suspicion among the Teutons, the Gallics, the Anglo-Saxons. If he wants to get colleagues for his assimilationist solution of the Jewish question, the best way to do that is by showing how well he is being received, how fully he is being accepted, how comfortably off he finds himself.

But, to belong to Judaism, one might almost say to practice one's Judaism professionally, and at the same time to fight it, that is something against which all sense of decency must rise up in protest. . . .

Zionism, as we see ever more clearly, will become a beneficent crisis of Jewry. The opposing viewpoints which ensue must of necessity lead to a clearing up of rotten conditions, and finally to a purification of the national character. It is all for the best. It is for the best, too, that some rabbis should take such a position against their own people. And were it merely that a new characterization has been won for these gentlemen— that, too, is already of some value. A Mohilever, a Rülf, noble, admirable men, who in their loyal hearts suffered along with their poor co-religionists, who stand in the very heart of their people, there where they are being most cruelly persecuted— these would not bear a name any different at all from that of some first-class wedding or funeral speaker. Now we have the distinguishing mark. So that they may no longer be confused with the good Rabbis, we will call those synagogue employees who protest against the deliverance of their people, the "Protest Rabbis."

(July 16, 1897)

FIRST CONGRESS ADDRESS

DELIVERED AT BASLE, AUGUST 29, 1897

FELLOW DELEGATES: As one of those who called this Congress into being I have been granted the privilege of welcoming you. This I shall do briefly, for if we wish to serve the cause we should economize the valuable moments of the Congress. There is much to be accomplished within the space of three days. We want to lay the foundations of the edifice which is one day to house the Jewish people. The task is so great that we may treat of it in none but the simplest terms. So far as we can now foresee, a summary of the present status of the Jewish question will be submitted within the coming three days. The tremendous bulk of material on hand is being classified by the chairmen of our committees.

We shall hear reports of the Jewish situation in the various countries. You all know, even if only in a vague way, that with few exceptions the situation is not cheering. Were it otherwise we should probably not have convened. The unity of our destiny has suffered a long interruption, although the scattered fragments of the Jewish people have everywhere endured similar vicissitudes. It is only in our days that the marvels of communication have brought about mutual understanding and union between isolated groups. And in these times, so progressive in most respects, we know ourselves to be surrounded by the old, old hatred. Antisemitism—you know it, alas, too well!— is the up-to-date designation of the movement. The first impression which it made upon the Jews of today was one of astonishment, which gave way to pain and resentment. Perhaps our enemies are quite unaware how deeply they wounded the sensibilities of just those of us who were possibly not the primary objects of their attack. That very part of Jewry which is modern and cultured, which has outgrown the Ghetto and lost the habit of petty trading, was pierced to the heart. We can assert it calmly, without laying ourselves open to the suspicion of wanting to appeal to the sentimental pity of our opponents. We have faced the situation squarely.

Since time immemorial the world has been misinformed about us. The sentiment of solidarity with which we have been reproached so frequently and so acrimoniously was in process of disintegration at the very time we were being attacked by antisemitism. And antisemitism served to strengthen it anew. We returned home, as it were. For Zionism is a return to the Jewish fold even before it becomes a return to the Jewish land. We, the children who have returned, find much to redress under the ancestral roof, for some of our brothers have sunk deep into misery. We are made welcome in the ancient house, for it is universally known that we are not actuated by an arrogant desire to undermine that which should be revered. This will be clearly demonstrated by the Zionist platform.

Zionism has already brought about something remarkable, heretofore regarded as impossible: a close union between the ultramodern and the ultraconservative elements of Jewry. The fact that this has come to pass without undignified concessions on the part of either side, without intellectual sacrifices, is further proof, if such proof is necessary, of the national entity of the Jews. A union of this kind is possible only on a national basis.

Doubtless there will be discussions on the subject of an organization the need for which is recognized by all. Organization is an evidence of the reasonableness of a movement. But there is one point which should be clearly and energetically emphasized in order to advance the solution of the Jewish question. We Zionists desire not an international league but international discussion. Needless to say this distinction is of the first importance in our eyes. It is this distinction which justifies the convening of our Congress. There will be no question of intrigues, secret interventions, and devious methods in our ranks, but only of unhampered utterances under the constant and complete check of public opinion. One of the first results of our movement, even now to be perceived in its larger outlines, will be the transformation of the Jewish question into a question of Zion.

A popular movement of such vast dimensions will necessarily be attacked from many sides. Therefore the Congress will concern itself with the spiritual means to be employed for reviving and fostering the national consciousness of the Jews. Here, too, we must struggle against misconceptions. We have not the least intention of yielding a jot of the culture we have acquired. On the contrary, we are aiming toward a broader culture, such as an increase of knowledge brings with it. As a matter of fact, the Jews have always been more active mentally than physically.

It was because the practical forerunners of Zionism realized this that they inaugurated agricultural work for the Jews. We shall never be able, nor shall we desire, to speak of these attempts at colonization in Palestine and in Argentina otherwise than with genuine gratitude. But they spoke the first, not the last word of the Zionist movement. For the Zionist movement must be greater in scope if it is to be at all. A people can be helped only by its own efforts, and if it cannot help itself it is beyond succor. But we Zionists want to rouse the people to self-help. No premature, unwholesome hopes should be awakened in this direction. This is another reason why public procedure, as it is planned by our Congress, is so essential.

Those who give the matter careful consideration must surely admit that Zionism cannot gain its ends otherwise than through an unequivocal understanding with the political units involved. It is generally known that the difficulties of obtaining colonization rights were not created by Zionism in its present form. One wonders what motives actuate the narrators of these fables. The confidence of the government with which we want to negotiate regarding the settlement of Jewish masses on a large scale can be gained by plain language and upright dealing. The advantages which an entire people is able to offer in return for benefits received are so considerable that the negotiations are vested with sufficient importance a priori. It would be an idle beginning to engage in lengthy discussions today regarding the legal form which the agreement will finally assume. But one thing is to be adhered to inviolably: the agreement must be based on rights, and not on toleration. Indeed we have had enough experience of toleration and of "protection" which could be withdrawn at any time.

Consequently the only reasonable course of action which our movement can pursue is to work for publicly legalized guarantees. The results of colonization as it has been carried on hitherto were quite satisfactory within its limitations. It confirmed the much disputed fitness of the Jews for agricultural work. It established this proof for all time, as the legal phrase has it. But colonization in its present form is not, and cannot be, the solution of the Jewish question. And we must admit unreservedly that it has failed to evoke much sympathy. Why? Because the Jews know how to calculate; in fact, it has been asserted that they calculate too well. Thus, if we assume that there are nine million Jews in the world, and that it would be possible to colonize ten thousand Jews in Palestine every year, the Jewish question would require nine hundred years for its solution. This would seem impracticable.

On the other hand, you know that to count on ten thousand settlers a year under existing circumstances is nothing short of fantastic. The Turkish government would doubtless unearth the old immigration restrictions immediately, and to that we would have little objection. For if anyone thinks that the Jews can steal into the land of their fathers, he is deceiving either himself or others. Nowhere is the coming of Jews so promptly noted as in the historic home of the race, for the very reason that it is the historic home. And it would by no means be to our interest to go there prematurely. The immigration of Jews signifies an unhoped-for accession of strength for the land which is now so poor; in fact, for the whole Ottoman Empire. Besides, His Majesty the Sultan has had excellent experiences with his Jewish subjects, and he has been an indulgent monarch to them in turn. Thus, existing conditions point to a successful outcome, provided the whole matter is intelligently and felicitiously treated. The financial help which the Jews can give to Turkey is by no means inconsiderable and would serve to obviate many an internal ill from which the country is now suffering. If the Near East question is partially solved together with the Jewish question, it will surely be of advantage to all civilized peoples. The advent of Jews would bring about an improvement in the situation of the Christians in the Orient.

But it is not solely from this aspect that Zionism may count upon the sympathy of the nations. You know that in some lands the Jewish problem has come to mean calamity for the government. If it sides with the Jews, it is confronted by the ire of the masses; if it sides against the Jews, it may call considerable economic consequences down upon its head because of the peculiar influence of the Jews upon the business affairs of the world. Examples of the latter may be found in Russia. But if the government maintains a neutral attitude, the Jews find themselves unprotected by the established regime and rush into the arms of the revolutionaries. Zionism, or self-help for the Jews, points to a way out of these numerous and extraordinary difficulties. Zionism is simply a peacemaker. And it suffers the usual fate of peacemakers, in being forced to fight more than anyone else. But should the accusation that we are not patriotic figure among the more or less sincere arguments directed against our movement, this equivocal objection carries its own refutation with it. Nowhere can there be a question of an exodus of all the Jews. Those who are able or who wish to be assimilated will remain behind and be absorbed. When once a satisfactory agreement is concluded with the various political units involved and a systematic Jewish migration begins, it will last only so long in each country as that country desires to be rid of its Jews. How will the current be stopped? Simply by the gradual decrease and the final cessation of antisemitism. Thus it is that we understand and anticipate the solution of the Jewish problem.

All this has been said time and again by my friends and by myself. We shall spare no pains to repeat it again and again until we are understood. On this solemn occasion, when Jews have come together from so many lands at the age-old summons of nationality, let our profession of faith be solemnly repeated.

Should we not be stirred by a premonition of great events when we remember that at this moment the hopes of thousands upon thousands of our people depend upon our assemblage? In the coming hour the news of our deliberations and decisions will fly to distant lands, over the seven seas. Therefore enlightenment and comfort should go forth from this Congress. Let everyone find out what Zionism really is, Zionism, which was rumored to be a sort of millennial marvel—that it is a moral, lawful, humanitarian movement, directed toward the long-yearned-for goal of our people. It was possible and permissible to ignore the spoken or written utterances of individuals within our ranks. Not so with the actions of the Congress. Thus the Congress, which is henceforth to be ruler of its discussions, must govern as a wise ruler.

Finally, the Congress will provide for its own continuance, so that we do not disperse once more ineffectual and ephemeral. Through this Congress we are creating an agency for the Jewish people such as it has not possessed heretofore, an agency of which it has stood in urgent need. Our cause is too great to be left to the ambition or the whim of individuals. It must be elevated to the realm of the impersonal if it is to succeed. And our Congress shall live forever, not only until the redemption from age-long suffering is effected, but afterwards as well. Today we are here in the hospitable limits of this free city—where shall we be next year?

But wherever we shall be, and however distant the accomplishment of our task, let our Congress be earnest and high-minded, a source of welfare to the unhappy, of defiance to none, of honor to all Jewry. Let it be worthy of our past, the renown of which, though remote, is eternal!

MESSAGE TO THE AMERICAN ZIONIST CONFERENCE IN FEBRUARY 1898

Mr. president! For the first time, American Zionists are gathering for a conference. It is happening at a moment when Europe is looking with more intense interest than usual toward the young giant state on the other side of the ocean. When we here, each evening, read what has taken place over there in the morning, then we have no doubts as to the victory of the star-spangled banner of the Union, that flies so high.* And when we at the same time observe the historical continuity, then we, particularly we Jews, are in the grip of strange emotions. The new world, which stands forth so powerfully today, was still lying undiscovered when Spain cruelly drove our forefathers from its borders. Today that once great power is close to its downfall. But that is the least of the wonders. There have always been wars and triumphs by land and sea, and the rise and fall of states. Much more remarkable are the conditions under which all this is proceeding in our own time. On iron rails men and goods speed across continents, great steamships hasten over the oceans of the world, in a single hour we receive news reports of events in places which, in our fathers' time, would have been inconceivably great distances. But one thing only is still as it was when the Turks conquered Byzantium, when Columbus set sail in his *caravalle*, when men

* This was the time of the Spanish-American War.

"Botschaft an die amerikanische Zionisten-konferenz, 1898," in *Gesammelte Zionistische Werke*, Vol. 1 (Berlin, Jüdischer Verlag, 1934), pages 274 ff.

rumbled over the highway in stagecoaches—and that single thing is the plight of the people scattered over the face of the globe—the people to which we belong. Yes, after a short breathing space for us modern "emancipated" Jews, bad times have come again. Under a new slogan, the old hatred has raised its ugly head once more, not only in the backward countries of Asia and Asia Minor, but also in those that are called civilized. A dream, an illusion it was for us to believe that antisemitism would disappear. It grew; it is growing. It conquers territories for itself which had seemed forever lost to it, such as France, the France of Dreyfus. Yes, according to reports that are hard to believe, it is even supposed to have made its appearance in free America. You, gentlemen, will know yourselves what of all this is true. It would seem that that unhappy Jewish proletarian who sets foot in the New World brings over with him a little antisemitism in the wretched rags of his beggar's garb. Is there to be no end of wretchedness and no escape from misery?

Then—an idea sprang up in the minds of Jews. You already know it, this idea—for that it is which unites you today. You know that to cure the age-old *misère* the most modern means are called for, a solution *up to date*. We know that we are in possession of all the remedies and aids of the present, and we are still supposed to be as incapable of helping ourselves as were our fathers in the ghetto? No! We *can* help ourselves and we *will* help ourselves. We are experienced in science, skilled in communications, able to work, enterprising, toughened. What we need is nothing but some sure soil on which we can do our work unmolested. And you know, too, what that soil is called, you know what name is given to that movement. Zionism! Eighteen hundred years of misery and hope are contained in that word.

There are depraved Jews who scoff at it; narrow-minded ones who fight it. But our movement, at first kept secret, then laughed at, then fought against, has within itself the whole strength of a people that simply cannot be destroyed. The spirit of peoplehood had only to be shaken into life. The people's will had to be given a voice. Just a year ago all that seemed impossible. Now it has come to pass. In August, 1897, at the

Congress in Basle, the program of Zionism was set forth in
final form:

"A publicly and legally assured Homeland for those Jews
who cannot or do not want to be assimilated in their present
places of abode!"

But the so-called "practical" men, the superclever ones, the
men who know it all, will scoff: You call that a program?
Mere words; nothing but fine speeches! Is this thing capable
of being achieved?

Nothing can be achieved if hands are laid idly in the lap.
Everything can be achieved if there is a firm will, and one
goes to work. We must proceed systematically and unswerv-
ingly. Everywhere able helpers in our cause are becoming
activated—Christians, too, not only Jews. Now is not the proper
time to set forth in detail everything that has been done since
the Congress in Basle to enlighten the governments involved
and public opinion with regard to our wholly loyal and humanitarian efforts. Let me rather speak to you here about a
subject in which you collectively and individually can contribute to the realization of the idea. I take it for granted that
you will be happy to do so.

The first Congress gave us the assignment, among other
things, of creating an effective financial arm for the movement.
That will be the Jewish Colonial Bank. The leaders of the
Zionist movement naturally have nothing further to do with
the bank, except to see that it is founded and maintained by
honest and trustworthy men. The principles underlying the
bank which is to be set up are already known in America. Its
seat will be in London. The capital stock is to be two million
pounds sterling, in shares at one pound sterling. Immediately
following the first announcement, notices of subscriptions began to pour in from all parts of the world. From this there
arose the idea of making the capital stock larger from the very
beginning. For the bigger it is, the more powerfully will the
bank be able to enter into financial transactions, and the quicker
will it serve to reach its final goal. From a distinguished
leader of finance, who consented to join it, there came the
plan for setting up the bank with a capital of five million

pounds. Now we must know approximately in what measure we can count on the participation in the subscriptions of the already organized Zionists. For the present, a payment of the amounts pledged is *not required*. The organizational leaders merely have to check on the reliability of the subscribers and to vouch for them. Here I recommend to your conference that you discuss this question fully, and that you start at once the campaign for the Jewish Colonial Bank, and inform the Congress Bureau in Basle of the results. . . .

The Jewish masses, with the help of this Colonial Bank, will be able to stand on their own feet. That is what we are striving for. We go cautiously but determinedly forward. What we want is justice. What we are demanding for the Jewish people is only what they deserve.

And, gaining adherents, this demand hurries over the length and breadth of all the lands wherever Jews live and sigh. Everywhere the word of freedom makes hearts that are not hardened beat faster. Everywhere friends spring up for the Jewish people when it shows itself capable of having an ideal. For the very worst that they were able to say against us was that we had no national ideal. Our Jewish opponents say that the antisemites are disposed in friendly fashion to Zionism. The anti-Zionists just do not understand that that is an advance sign of the peace that we are bringing to this hate-poisoned affair of mankind. A Jewish colonization movement to the land of our fathers represents amelioration for the lands that have grown sick with antisemitism; it also increases prosperity and order in the East. No matter how minor the former attempts at colonization in Palestine may have been, yet they did show that the soil is still good. Every soil is good onto which a laboring man steps. And there, of course, is the land where, in the golden days of history, milk and honey flowed. So it will be again, when the sorely tried Jews return home once more to the unforgettable land of their fathers.

With Zion's greetings,
Sincerely yours,
TH. HERZL

SECOND CONGRESS ADDRESS

DELIVERED AT BASLE, AUGUST 28, 1898

. . . THE new Jewish movement came before the world as a strange apparition, incomprehensible to many. Some considered it a ghost of former times. Was not the Jewish people dead and forgotten? But we had felt dimly, half-consciously as it were, that this was not true. Death is the end of all suffering—whence came it that we suffered? In us the words of the thinker were paraphrased: "I suffer, therefore I am!" And gradually, as wrong succeeded wrong, this realization assumed more definite form, until the national consciousness stood before us in its entirety, not as yet the common property of all, but equipped with a mighty capacity to spread abroad. And in truth it conquered, vanquishing heads and hearts, winning old and young, and the first Congress of the Zionists was a manifestation of our reanimated national consciousness. . . .

Our words must have rung true, for the Congress called forth widespread sympathy even from those who were formerly indifferent or antagonistic to the Jews. Every genuine nationality which does not hide behind a strange mask has a fundamental right to respect and toleration on the part of other nations, provided it does not menace their existence. Even though our times are clouded by antisemitism, we must not forget that they were preceded by more magnanimous days, when all the civilized nations bestowed equal rights upon us. Their intentions were good, but the results were inadequate. Who was to blame—we or the others? Perhaps both, or rather conditions of long standing which were not to be eradicated by laws and ordinances. The laws were kindlier than the usages. We witnessed the reaction, the tremendous welling-up of re-

317

gret on the part of those nations which had so recently shown us indulgence. From the emancipation which cannot be rescinded and the antisemitism the existence of which cannot be denied, we have drawn new and important conclusions. It could not have been the historic import of our emancipation that we cease to be Jews, for we were repulsed whenever we wanted to intermingle with the others. The historic import of our emancipation was rather that we provide a home for our liberated nationality. This we could not have done before. We can do it now if we desire it with all our might. . . .

We are ready to bring about the constructive period of Jewry. We have everything in abundance—people, materials, plans. We need nothing more than—a site!

Of course, the site which is suited to use is of a peculiar nature. No spot on earth has been so coveted as this, and many nations desired it so intensely that the ardor of their longing dried it up. We, however, believe that this desolate corner of the Orient has, like us, not only a past but also a future. On that soil, where so little grows at present, there grew ideas for all mankind. And for that very reason nobody can deny that there is a deathless relation between our people and that land. If there is such a thing as a legitimate claim to a portion of the earth's surface, all peoples who believe in the Bible must recognize the rights of the Jews. As a matter of fact, they may do so without envy or anxiety, for the Jews are not, and will nevermore become, a political power. . . .

As we were steadfast in the darkest days so let us be thankful and modest if better days should come. And how shall we conjure up those better days, which still lie beyond our field of vision? Will they bring us no more than the possession of land, increased consideration, untroubled rest? No! Those of us who are today prepared to hazard our lives for the cause would regret having raised a finger, if we were able to organize only a new social system and not a more righteous one. . . .

THIRD CONGRESS ADDRESS

DELIVERED AT BASLE, AUGUST 15, 1899

. . . THERE is another thing: we are not here to occupy ourselves with the internal affairs of the individual countries of
which we happen to be citizens. Any such attempt would only
serve to produce a false impression of our Congress. We are
here for the sole purpose of taking counsel on the situation of
our people and of working out, under the supervision of public
opinion, a solution which shall be lawful as well as humane.
That we have no other end in view has been demonstrated by
all our previous actions. Thus we ourselves draw incontestable
boundaries about our activities. We want to occupy ourselves
with the welfare of the Jewish people. That is our right. It is
also our duty. . . .

Here then is a people striving for existence, for honor, and
for liberty. It seeks to abandon a suffocating atmosphere and
to go forth into the sunshine. Under present conditions the
Jews have three roads before them: one is apathetic submission
to insult and poverty; another is revolt, outspoken hostility to
an unjust social system. Ours is the third road. We want to
mount to a higher grade of civilization, to spread well-being
abroad, to build new highways for the intercourse of peoples,
and to forge an opening for the coming of social justice. And
just as our beloved poet transformed his sorrows into songs,
so upon the loom of our sufferings we shall weave progress
for mankind whom we serve.

ZIONISM

. . . It was surely a daring thing to do, when my friends and I in 1897 called together the first Congress. We ran a terrible risk, one which might frighten off an otherwise courageous man—namely, the risk of becoming a laughing stock. Since the Sanhedrin which Napoleon I convened in Paris in 1806, also only under peculiar circumstances, such an attempt had not been made. In the ninety years since, the fitness of the Jews for a national assembly has diminished considerably. It may be assumed that the Jewish nation, despite the ineffable persecutions, or perhaps just because of them, survived to the end of the eighteenth century dispersed but unbroken. At this time the Jewish people, which had survived the destruction of its state for so long, experienced two convulsions, one internal and the other external. Moses Mendelssohn dealt the internal blow; the French Revolution the external one. The noble Prussian philosopher, Lessing's friend, wanted to see Judaism survive merely as a religious denomination, and the great revolution granted human rights even to the poor Jews. The emancipation of the Jews was gradually copied by one civilized state after another. The emancipation loosened the soil in which Mendelssohn's thought-seed flowered splendidly. And what neither murder, nor plundering, nor being driven from country to country, burning at the stake, and proscription had been able to accomplish during the frightful centuries—came to pass under the sunny rays of love: the Jewish sense of peoplehood was lost. What is a nation? A historical grouping of people of rec-

"Zionismus," in *Gesammelte Zionistische Werke*, Vol. 1 (Berlin, Jüdischer Verlag, 1934), pages 371–386.

ognizable homogeneity, which is held together by a common foe. When the Jews, as Mendelssohn wished, came together only for religious services and for the rest adjusted themselves to the people among which they happened to be living, then they were no more related to each other than are perhaps the various peoples of the respective Christian rites. The history of the group was to be put to an end, its homogeneity was to become unrecognizable, and through the emancipation, the group was rid of the external enemy. The enemy, however, is the iron hoop that holds a nation together. It sounds like a tautology, like the most banal truism to remark: nations will last as long as they are hostile to each other. But that is the simple truth. The road to universal humanity is still a long one, even though it is not without hope of attainment. We too want to march along it, but in a different way than the magnanimous Mendelssohn did it. We do not want to give up our own nationality; on the contrary, we want to cherish it, and that, not by any means aggressively, but only defensively. Moreover, we want to cultivate a friendly feeling toward other peoples and also to help lessen the antagonisms that exist between them. For such a task the Jewish people is perhaps peculiarly fitted, because its members were for so long scattered among the various peoples.

That is the idealistic basis for our Zionism. Of course, we did not come upon it out of idealism, pure and simple. The truth as to how we got to this is unfortunately less praiseworthy, but we are perfectly ready to admit it. We were led to it by the new enemy which attacked us just when we were in the process of complete dissolution: by antisemitism. I am still aware what an impression it made upon me when I, in the year 1882, as a twenty-year old, read Dühring's book on the Jewish question, a book which is as full of hate as it is brilliant. I think that prior to that I really no longer knew that I was a Jew. Dühring's book had an effect on me as if I had received a blow on the head. And that same thing probably happened to many a Western Jew who had already completely forgotten his peoplehood. The antisemites reawakened it in him. Of course, from such stimulation to a conscious decision such as is expressed in the present-day Zionist movement, there is still a long way to go. I, for my part, required twelve or thirteen years, and I beg for forgiveness when I report this. Perhaps I may be permitted to do it for two reasons: first, because we always best study whatever is human in our own selves, and secondly, because there is a bit of historical actuality about it.

For what made me into a Zionist was the Dreyfus case. Not the present one in Rennes, but the original one in Paris, which I witnessed in 1894. At that time I was living in Paris as a newspaper correspondent and attended the proceedings of the military court until they were declared secret. I can still see the defendant coming into the hall in his dark artillery uniform trimmed with braid. I still hear him give his credentials: "Alfred Dreyfus, Captain of artillery," in his affected nasal voice. And also the howls of the mob in the street in front of the École Militaire, where he was degraded, still rings unforgettably in my ears: "Death! Death to the Jews!" Death to all Jews, because this one was a traitor? But was he really a traitor? At that time I had a private conversation with one of the military attachés who has been much talked of recently. The Colonel did not know much more about the whole affair than had appeared in the papers; yet he believed in the guilt of Dreyfus, because to him it appeared impossible that seven officers should have been able to declare a comrade guilty without the most convincing proof. I, on the other hand, believed in his innocence, because I did not consider a Jewish officer capable of being a traitor to his country. Not that I regarded the Jews in general as better than other human beings. But under the particular circumstances in the case of Captain Dreyfus, who personally did not even make a favorable impression on me, the whole thing appeared unlikely to me. A Jew who, as an officer on the General Staff, has a career of honor lying open before him, is incapable of committing such a crime, I said to the Colonel. In a lower stratum of society, I would deny such a possibility among Jews as little as among Christians. In Alfred Dreyfus' case, however, it was psychologically impossible. A wealthy man, who had chosen this career only through ambition, simply could not have committed the most dishonorable of all crimes. The Jews, as a result of their long having to do without civic honor, often have a pathological urge for honors, and in this regard a Jewish army officer is a Jew raised to the highest degree. My line of reasoning at that time was probably that of all of our coreligionists since the beginning of the affair. Just because for all of us the psychological impossibility was so clear from the very beginning, the Jews had foreshadowings on all sides as to the innocence of Dreyfus, even before the memorable campaign to establish the truth began.

From this attitude of the Jews, unfavorable conclusions were drawn as to our solidarity in all, even the worst things. I certainly hold no brief against the national solidarity of the Jews, yet in this case, there was something else in the picture. The Jews were just simply the first who guessed at the miscarriage of justice, because to them the crime seemed impossible and because they had had countless victims of false accusations to mourn for in the course of the centuries. Now, however, they were supposed to guard against entertaining a sentimental or melodramatic view of the Dreyfus case. This is more than an abstract occurrence; it is connected to a quivering, tortured human being. One might well say that the fate of the poor Captain is only an illustration that serves the coarser perception of a movement of the spirit that is taking place in the land of the French. For the philosophical observer, for a long time, it has no longer been a matter of the guilt or innocence of a Jewish artillery officer. The question of a miscarriage of justice merits the sympathy of all, but we must have no other attitude toward it than if it concerned the suffering members of any other people. As long as men administer justice, there can and there will be miscarriages of justice and the just men of all faiths and of all nations will find common ground in the wish to rectify the error.

But the Dreyfus case contains more than a miscarriage of justice: it contains the wish of the vast majority in France to damn one Jew and through him all Jews. "Death to the Jews!" the crowd yelled when they ripped the Captain's stripes from his uniform. And since that time "Down with the Jews" has become a battle cry. Where? In France! In republican, modern, civilized France, one hundred years after the Declaration of the Rights of Man. The Dreyfus case can be compared historically only to the revocation of the Edict of Nantes. That, too, took place after a long time. More than ninety years had passed since Henry IV had issued his Edict when Louis XIV retracted freedom from the Huguenots. It is true that the State is no longer the "I" of a Sun King; the State coincides with the will of the people, but yet the result is similar. The people, at least a very large part of it, no longer wants human rights for the Jews. The edict of the great Revolution is revoked.

And here we are at the matter that concerns us, here we are at the lesson in history that any unprejudiced observer must draw from the Dreyfus case. Up to that time most of us had believed that the solution of the Jewish question was to be expected from the gradual progress of mankind toward tolerance. But if an otherwise progressive, surely highly civilized people could come to such a pass, what was there to be expected from other peoples, who even today are not at the height at which the French have already been for a hundred years.

For the Jews there is no other help and salvation than the return to their own nation and their establishment on their own ground and soil. I wrote that in my book *The Jewish State* in 1895, under the shattering impressions of the first Dreyfus trial. When I reached these conclusions I was still a stranger to my own people. I know but little of the conditions of our poverty-stricken masses, and nothing at all of the new movements in Judaism. It was only through my writing that I got into these circles, that I learned of the men who long or shortly before me had written similar things. Who knows whether I would have dared to issue my book if the more significant works of the German Hess and the Russian Pinsker had been known to me? When I dared do it, I regarded myself as a lone wolf uttering an old and completely forgotten appeal.

Meanwhile, Zionism had already made its appearance. It existed in thought, word, writing, and deed. What is Zionism? The attempt to create a legally assured Homeland for the Jewish people in Palestine (Basle Program of 1897). The wish for a return to the historical fatherland had actually, since the destruction of our realm, slumbered in the deepest layers of our national soul. The outcry full of longing, "Next year in Jerusalem!" one generation had handed down to the next, and only in the last decades of our national decline had, among many rabbis, the watery interpretation become customary that the Jerusalem of this remark really should read London, Berlin, or Chicago. When one explains away Jewish traditions in this wise, then verily there remains little more of Judaism than the annual salaries that these gentlemen draw. But as opposed to such convenient and dishonest commentators, during the past twenty years, under the new pressure of antisemitism, a more sturdy race arose. The ideas of Hess, the manly suggestions of Pinsker, Rülf, Birnbaum, and others contributed a great deal to the education of our youth in East Europe, the latest Jew-baiting in Russia and Romania brought home to individual rich philanthropists the idea that something would have to be done for the frightened-off swarms of their unfortunate co-religionists who were wandering from country to country. Baron Hirsch tried to settle the homeless in Argentina, Baron Edmond Rothschild undertook the same thing in Palestine. Besides, in the various cities Colonization Associations were formed; they are called by a fine collective name, *Hovevei Tsion*, the Lovers of Zion. In England their leader was Colonel Goldsmid. But these individual groups, working independently of each other and without a common plan, could not reach the goal, although they did indeed offer proof that was extremely important for our exclusive activity—namely, that Jews are well fitted for agricultural work. The Jew wants to fertilize the earth with the blood and sweat of his toil—but only one single soil—that of Palestine. Baron Hirsch had left this idealistic aspect out of his calculations, that is why his experiment in Argentina miscarried, and, as has already been mentioned, his colonists elected delegates to the Zionist Congress. On the other hand, the experiments in Palestine were successful. There you will find Jewish farmers in thriving colonies. Unfortunately only a few, and the Lovers of Zion are unable to settle more of them, because the land belongs to the Turkish government, which became suspicious after the very strong influx of Jews and finally, in the year 1891, closed its borders to Jewish immigration.

After my friends and I had assured ourselves of this situation, we determined to become active in two directions. First of all, we wanted to bring together into one movement all these isolated endeavors and proclaim it to the world. Secondly, we wanted to enter into bona fide negotiations with the Turkish government, in order to achieve legal assurances for the large-scale settlement. For it is clear that nothing would have been accomplished if the colonists were left at the mercy of minor bureaucrats, and perhaps, after a short respite, after heroic labors, could again be driven away.

These considerations led us, in 1897, to call the first Zionist Congress in Basle. The success was astounding. I do not know how much fate will still permit me to see of the realization of our idea, whether I will be present when the Jewish people begins to make the land of our fathers fruitful and flourishing, to build streets, harbors, railroads, canals, water works, houses, fine cities, and the temple. But this I do know, that on that August Sunday of 1897 in Basle I experienced something tremendous, perhaps the greatest thing that the whole movement has to give. On that day, the Jewish people found itself once more. Two hundred representatives of organizations from all over the world gathered together in Basle, and they declared amidst sobbing and shouts of jubilation that there is still a Jewish people, that this people has not succumbed and does not want to succumb. That is the main thing. When once a people's consciousness and a people's will are in evidence then all that remains is to find sensible ways and means to realize them. A people is inexhaustible in strength, just as it is not limited by the time limits of an individual. Naturally, the realization ought not be unduly delayed, or else the clearest strivings grow pale and unreal as dreams. Accordingly, we did not tarry overmuch among the sentimental dreams of rediscovery but made every effort to go forward. . . .

It is in the logical order of our work that we should enlighten the governments and public opinion as to our work. That is done in many ways. The Jewish question exists more or less in every country. The United States, too, particularly New York with its suddenly swollen population of several hundred thousand proletarian Jews, is interesting itself in the matter. For the United States the Zionist solution represents the diversion of a probably unwanted immigration. In the East European mass hovels of misery, there still throng millions of Jews who otherwise will cross the Atlantic, out of their hunger depress the wages existing over there, and with the courage of desperation generally thrust themselves into the economic struggle. Of course they can protect themselves a little, not altogether, against debarkation difficulties and the like. But it will be more praiseworthy and more American if the freest people on earth were to support the striving for freedom of the Jewish people and, instead of making more difficult the road to America, were to help make easier the road to Zion. The voice of the United States is heard in Europe and in the Orient. . . .

When I was preparing my first publication on this subject and informed some of my friends of my plan, they were frightened lest I thereby make myself forever impossible in the eyes of all sensible men. Since I would not let myself be dissuaded, they advised me at least to offer my idea in the noncommittal and entertaining form of a novel, with love stories, the fates of individual human beings, and a depicting of future conditions in the land of the Jews. After all, that was more in keeping with my current role of dramatist and feuilletonist. I did realize that this would be a good propaganda means for the idea and would spare me the danger of making myself thoroughly ridiculous. But then no action would have resulted from it. People would have spoken of it in the drawing rooms and railroad coaches, and some would perhaps have wept secretly into the book. And what would have been accomplished thereby? Still another fairy tale in the thousand and one nights of suffering. No, it was to be day and deed. We had to arouse the Jewish people instead of lulling it. And, indeed, it has let itself be aroused, it is stretching its limbs, it is getting into action, which we name Zionism, after its goal. And now, I believe, now the hour has come to tell the Jewish people the story of the future. It will be a romance and will take place twenty years from now. I shall show the society, the institutions which we can create—not perchance with aids that are yet to be discovered or invented, but with those which our present-day culture already has at its command. We have arrived at the end of the nineteenth century after the birth of Christ. Mankind already possesses many tools for happiness, but they are not yet utilized correctly. It remains to be shown how much justice, goodness, and beauty can be brought down to earth, if it is sincerely desired.

What unexpected times these are in which we live! Communication between people has become free and easy. Distances have been virtually eliminated. The War Powers are beginning to consult together with regard to everlasting peace. Ever more and more matters are brought up in international meetings. There are no longer any limits to science and art. The great poets and philosophers create their works for the entire world. Public opinion is no longer limited to one place, one city, one country. A misfortune that happens here can, within the next few hours, be known at the antipodes, and will arouse sympathy there. An invention which benefits mankind is loudly proclaimed by a hundred thousand heralds. The signal needs only to be given of an injustice that is committed anywhere, and in all parts of the world it calls forth storms of indignation. What strange times these are! In the not too distant past, all this would have been declared impossible, and he who wished for it would have been regarded as a mad dreamer. And behold, the mystical becomes the natural, as if the times that had been prophesied wanted to fulfill themselves. Thus it comes about that modern men, standing firmly in their own epoch, regard that matter as natural, necessary, and capable of being performed for which in countless houses of God, for centuries, prayers upon prayers have risen up to Heaven: The return of the Jews!

(1899)

FOURTH CONGRESS ADDRESS

. . . ENGLAND, mighty England, free England, with its world-embracing outlook, will understand us and our aspirations. With England as a starting point we may be sure that the Zionist idea will soar further and higher than ever before. . . .

Our activities and the progress we have made can be summed up in a single sentence: We are organizing Jewry for its coming destiny. . . .

Our progress is laborious, yes, and full of affliction. But it will prove our courage and our faithfulness. Let those who crave immediate results withdraw from our ranks. And if the final victory takes its time in coming to us we shall at least be able to point to a moral gain growing out of the material need of our people. We shall have shown that Jewry is still capable of an idealism which defies danger, endures privation, and possesses the infinite patience through which great ends are achieved.

FIFTH CONGRESS ADDRESS

DELIVERED AT BASLE, DECEMBER 26, 1901

. . . THE question of what we shall do with the settlers causes us no embarrassment. We want to attach them to the earth, to make them permanent dwellers on the land. They shall live near the soil and by the soil, not keep an anxious eye upon the fluctuations of prices as impotent tradesmen do. Their concern with barter shall be limited to the disposition of the products which they raise in excess of their needs. Each settlement shall administer its own affairs as an agricultural productive association, in accordance with the principles which experience and science have taught us. We must hold to these principles if by the grace of God we obtain the publicly legalized guarantees mentioned in our platform. Thus the foundation can be laid for the permanent peace which the Jewish people long for so intensely.

What building is to rise upon the broad and steadfast basis of an industrious agricultural population? What sort of modern and habitable edifice? That will depend upon the people itself when once we shall have secured for it the molding of its own destiny. There is room in Palestine for all the forces of Jewry, for the untaught as well as for the highly cultured. No longer will it be necessary to exclude Jewish children from institutions of learning as is done in some places at the present time. And perhaps it is not altogether to the discredit of the Jews that they consider the cultural restrictions imposed upon them as the greatest of present-day afflictions. We shall not even touch upon other forms of oppression, lest our Congress become another Wailing Wall. We must not complain, but we must work, all the more because those who have hitherto represented Jewish interests have shown themselves incapable of accomplishing anything whatsover. To give alms is not to help. Alms are merely the tie which binds the lazy rich to the lazy poor. But these two categories do not represent the whole of the Jewish people. . . .

Fellow Delegates, we whom you have commissioned to execute your wishes have completed our first task. We were, so to speak, the mechanics who were to install an electric plant. We built the machinery which could transform energy into current, we laid the wires, frequently in places which previously seemed inaccessible, and thus our modest task is accomplished. Survey it today!

The main feature of our plant was this Congress, a body representative of those who are dispersed all over the world, a Jewish forum which has gained in respect from year to year, thanks to the earnestness and the honorable intentions of the men whose words were heard here. Even now watchwords go forth from here to the entire Diaspora. In all the lands of Europe, in North and South America, in North and South Africa, as far as Siberia, India, and Australia, we find Zionist societies endorsing the Basle platform. This year, for the first time, there is a simultaneous demonstration everywhere, the World Zionist Day, in which many hundreds of thousands of Jews are participating.

Through our societies an unexpected vitality has surged through Jewry. There are innumerable cases of individual effort which, taken collectively, represent a mighty power. The spiritual and moral benefits of Zionism are already considerable; even our opponents cannot deny it. A Pleiad of poets, artists, and scholars have been roused and inspired by our idea. Strangely enough they are not only Jews, as we have seen. That proves that we are proclaiming and striving for something that is common to all mankind. And already rays of light have penetrated to many a dark corner in which the poor of our people dwell. Toynbee Halls, popular cultural centers, are flourishing in a number of places. In the school and in the home an ideal is present before the eyes of the young. The students in the universities are animated by a new spirit. Workmen and tradesmen meet together for intellectual discussions. Moreover, physical development is cultivated in athletic clubs, sociability in glee clubs. Mutual-aid associations are springing up. And all this under the banner of Zionism! But we can do no more than to establish the institutions—the nation itself must support and nourish them.

This is true, above all, of the financial medium of our movement. The Jewish Colonial Trust in London is now ready for business. Our opponents spoke much ill of it in advance. But there were neither founders' profits, shares, nor advantages of any kind for the board of directors, and the administration has no aim but to assure the common property against danger.

Furthermore, we must see to it that this possession of ours is guarded with the greatest conscientiousness, economically and overcautiously rather than overdaringly. The Congress exercises supervision over the Trust through bodies elected by it; that is what constitutes the value of this arrangement. An account of the administration must be given publicly. The means which are to be devoted to our national aim cannot be utilized for other purposes through the caprice or the mistakes of individuals. This financial institution must be directed according to the rules laid down by the Congress and with the care of a good, scrupulous *paterfamilias*. And now that it is in existence we can proceed to the execution of the plan which our late friend, Professor Schapira, of the University of Heidelberg, presented to the First Congress: the creation of a National Fund. The money will be deposited in the Jewish Colonial Trust in London. In the course of our deliberations you will be informed of the new proposal and enabled to come to a decision with regard to it. The people shall be not only the founder of this fund, but its permanent administrator as well. This will prevent an arbitrary disposition which might conflict with the founder's purposes.

Thus in a certain sense we can say that we have completed our first task. To a great extent the institutions are merely indicated and admit of improvement, but in any case they are extant. The Jewish people can build them up, strengthen them, and utilize them if it so wishes. We took all manner of pains to give our achievement an impersonal character. That alone makes for permanence. Not one of us is indispensable any longer. Neither the death nor the defection of any one of us would impede the progress of our work.

How soon the machinery which we have prepared will begin to operate we cannot determine. It does not depend upon us here. We were able to establish the plant, but we cannot supply the energy. The energy must be supplied by the whole Jewish people—if it so wills.

SIXTH CONGRESS ADDRESS

DELIVERED AT BASLE, AUGUST 23, 1903

FELLOW DELEGATES: We are assembling for the sixth Zionist Congress in the good city of Basle, which has earned our gratitude on former occasions. Again we come together in mingled hope and anxiety.

In truth, the situation of the Jews throughout the whole world is no more favorable at present than it was in the years of the earlier Congresses. The statement we issued from this forum in former years regarding the situation of our people holds good at the present moment. Here and there a change has doubtless taken place, but not a change for the better. Many of us thought things could grow no worse, but they did grow worse. Misery has swept over Jewry like a tidal wave. Those who lived in the depths have been submerged. If the inhabitants of higher, more protected spots deny the truth of this shocking fact they are not doing credit either to their insight or to their hearts. Of course, merely to admit that the Jews are in a pitiable plight does not do much good. At best it leads to philanthropic endeavors, which, however praiseworthy they may be in individual cases, are to be censured from a higher, more comprehensive point of view, because notwithstanding their oftproved futility they salve the consciences of those who share the responsibility. It is easy to say: "Well, well, we do what we can!" There are some people who pat themselves on the back, if after having read in the morning paper of a brutal Jewish massacre they send a paltry contribution to the newspaper for acknowledgment. But even those who tax themselves in proportion to their fortunes cannot fulfill their duty with money alone. Money does not restore life to the dead, health

335

to the maimed, parents to the orphaned. And how can alms relieve the fear of those who, although they themselves have not been the victims of assault, continue to live in the selfsame circumstances? Their turn may come at any moment.

As a matter of fact we Zionists have recourse to these arguments against our will. It is distasteful to us to turn disasters to political ends and to search for propaganda material in the anguish of the unfortunate. But we must state from this platform how great was our pain and our wrath when we learned of the hideous occurrences of Kishinev, and how overwhelming our grief to think that Jews must live under such conditions. Poor, careworn existences that met their end in martyrdom! We shall cherish their memory and provide for their survivors, and then lose no time in useless demonstrations, but devote our living care to the living.

The bloody days of the Bessarabian city must not cause us to forget that there are yet other Kishinevs, not alone in Russia. Kishinev exists wherever Jews undergo bodily or spiritual tortures, wherever their self-respect is wounded and their possessions are damaged because they are Jews. Let us save those who can still be saved!

It is high time. Whoever does not blind himself to visible signs must perceive that the situation has undergone an ominous change for the worse. We Zionists have predicted this change for years—and now that it has come we are none the less sorrowful. . . .

Meanwhile things are progressing continuously. In England, hitherto the last refuge unconditionally open to us, a royal commission was appointed to investigate alien immigration—"alien," to avoid the use of the word "Jewish." The recommendations of the report do not admit of a single doubt as to what kind of immigration the commission had in mind. It is evident how hard a struggle free and magnanimous England has waged within itself, how difficult it finds the enactment of a drastic measure against unfortunate creatures, and for what reason it has instituted a special protracted investigation before deciding to act. For there are age-old principles, glorious as banners, which will not emerge untarnished if England no longer affords a sanctuary to innocent unfortunates. And the same may be said of America, which became a great country for the very reason that it was a sanctuary. . . .

Since we assembled here for the fifth time I have again had the honor of being summoned to Constantinople on two occasions by His Majesty the Sultan. On both these occasions, however, in February and in August, 1902, the pourparlers remained without effect. Of course, I could not venture upon a course of action which would not have been compatible with our Basle Platform, and a colonization plan calling for scattered, unrelated communities in different parts of the Turkish Empire could not have satisfied our national aspirations. The only thing to be gathered from all these troublesome negotiations was that His Majesty the Sultan continues to be kindly disposed to the Jewish people. This fact is undoubtedly cheering and valuable, but it offers us no practical advantages. Given the kindly sentiments of the ruler and the indisputable benefits to be gained by the Turkish Empire it would appear that the obstacle in our path is to be sought in the attitude of the great powers which are interested in the Near East, especially Russia. That we need not look for resistance on the part of Germany we know from the German Emperor. In 1898 when, together with the Zionist delegation, I had the honor of being accorded a reception in Jerusalem, His Majesty assured us of his sympathetic attitude toward the movement. The word of an Emperor must not be twisted or subtilized. Nor was there any reason to apprehend opposition on the part of England, as we can see from events which I shall now relate to you.

After the ill-success of the last negotiations with Constantinople, and as a result of the steadily increasing misery prevailing among the Jews, we found ourselves forced to take another course of action. Therefore, last October I entered into communication with several members of the British Cabinet and made them the proposition that they grant our people a concession on the Sinai Peninsula for colonization purposes. Not only the secretaries, to whom I desire to express my warmest thanks on this occasion, but the higher officials of the British Government who are concerned with matters of this kind received me with the heartiest good will and met me more than half way. I was informed that as the territory in question was under Egyptian dominion it would be necessary to enter into direct negotiations with the Egyptian Government. However, the English Government generously offered to give me its recommendation, and expressed the hope to its representative in Egypt, Lord Cromer, that the project be taken into favorable consideration by him as well as by the Counsellors of His Highness the Khedive. As a preliminary measure the British Government gave us permission to send a commission composed of experts to the tract of land in question with a view to examining its fitness for colonization purposes and its possibilities. In order to obtain the consent of the Egyptian authorities to the sending of the commission and their co-operation in our project, our representative, Mr. Greenberg, set out for Egypt at the end of October equipped with letters of recommendation from the English Government.

Lord Cromer and the Egyptian Secretary for Foreign Affairs received him with great affability and, after giving the matter due consideration, consented to the sending of the commission. In addition to this they agreed to allow a representative of the Egyptian Survey Department to accompany the commission. Thereupon the commission was organized with the following personnel: Messrs. Kessler, Marmorek, Goldsmid, Stephens, Professor Laurent, Dr. Soskin, Dr. Hillel Joffe, and Mr. Humphreys, the representative of the Egyptian Government.

The commission arrived in Egypt toward the end of January and set out for the Sinai Peninsula in the beginning of February. In the meantime our representative, Mr. Greenberg, left England and went to Egypt once more to submit to Lord Cromer and the Egyptian Government plans for a charter covering a tract of land in the Sinai Peninsula. After protracted negotiations our agent received a note from the Egyptian Government wherein it declared itself to be in accord with the basic provisions of the projected charter—namely, Jewish autonomy for the tract of land in question and municipal rights for the whole of the ceded territory, under condition that the report of the commission be favorable, and that it convince the government of the feasibility of colonizing the Peninsula.

In the beginning of March the members of the commission returned to Egypt, and in order to meet them I traveled there myself. I laid various propositions before Lord Cromer and the Egyptian Government, but as I was compelled to go back to Europe I entrusted the further negotiations to a member of the commission.

Protracted discussions followed, which, I am sorry to say, resulted in a statement by the Egyptian Government to the effect that it could proceed no further in the matter, as expert opinion held that it would be impossible to supply the Pelusian plain with a sufficient amount of water, and that consequently it would be impossible to colonize El-Arish or any other part of the Peninsula.

When the officials of the British Government with whom I had previously been in touch learned of the expert opinion which had been expressed to the Egyptian Government and of the decision which had been necessary in consequence, they immediately made me the proposition of ceding another tract of land for Jewish colonization purposes.

This territory has not the historic, traditional, and Zionist significance of the Sinai Peninsula; but I do not doubt that the Congress, acting as the representative of the Jewish people as a whole, will consider this new offer with the warmest gratitude. The proposition relates to an autonomous Jewish settlement in East Africa, with a Jewish administration, Jewish local government, and a Jewish official at its head, under the suzerainty, I need not add, of Great Britain. When this proposition was made I did not feel myself justified, considering the plight of Jewry and the immediate necessity of ameliorating this plight, in taking any steps other than obtaining permission to submit the proposition to the Congress. However, in order that the matter might be of sufficiently definite interest to all of us it was necessary to formulate the proposition in such a way that it would take into consideration the national aspirations so dear to us all. Consequently our representative had a number of conferences with the members of the British Cabinet and with the chiefs of departments, in which the matter was thoroughly gone into. These conferences were of a satisfactory nature. . . .

Zion it is not and can never be. It is merely an expedient for colonization purposes, but, be it well understood, an expedient founded upon a national and political basis. We shall not and cannot give the Jewish masses the marching signal on the strength of this arrangement. It is and must remain an emergency measure destined to allay the perplexity prevailing in philanthropic undertakings at the present time and to prevent our losing touch with the scattered fragments of our people.

This was the situation up to a few days ago, when it developed in such a way as to promise results of the utmost importance. Events which are universally known made it necessary for me to undertake a journey to Russia in the interests of the Jewish people. I had the welcome opportunity of coming in touch with the Russian Government, and I may say that I met with a fair understanding of our Zionist aspirations and heard expressions of a benevolent desire to be of real assistance to us. As a matter of fact I admit that on this occasion I was not only a Zionist— you will not blame me, I know. I spoke not only in behalf of the Zionists but for all the Jews in Russia. I took pains to recommend a number of improvements in their sad situation and received the assurance that these alleviatory measures would be taken into consideration in the immediate future. But more important were the assurances I received concerning the Zionist movement. I am in a position to state that the Russian Government will not impede the progress of the Zionist movement, provided it retains the quiet and lawful character which has hitherto distinguished it. Moreover, the Russian Government is ready to co-operate with the Zionists in an emigration undertaking on condition that the expenses it incurs are covered.

Finally, and this is the most important fact of all, the Russian Government is willing to use its influence with His Majesty the Sultan in furthering our efforts to obtain Palestine. The importance of this statement, which I am empowered to make to the Zionist Congress, is surely evident to you all. A promise of this nature from the Russian Government signifies a diplomatic asset the value of which cannot be overestimated. Not only is a tremendous obstacle removed, but suddenly powerful aid is at hand. Its effects are yet to be seen; but we may continue to strive for Eretz Israel with renewed courage and with brighter prospects than ever before.

Of course, some people will perceive none but the gloomy aspects of these developments. The help of the Powers, they will say, signifies nothing good. Either they want to be rid of us or they want to deny us admission. So be it! If it portends injustice toward our people we shall reply to it in the future. In our future, in our country! And our answer shall consist in the advancement of human civilization.

CONCLUDING SPEECH

AT THE SIXTH ZIONIST CONGRESS, BASLE,
AUGUST 1903

... The sixth Zionist Congress has been remarkable in many ways. Our experiences have been both encouraging and depressing. One of the most encouraging experiences was the welcome offered for the first time to the Congress by the Jewish community of Basle. It has been a difficult, but also a very important Congress, not only owing to the number who took part in it, but also to the nature of our deliberations. It has been proved that the Zionists are to be relied upon. We have seen the truth of the saying, *"On ne s'appuie que sur ce qui resiste."* We can lean only on what is capable of resisting.

On the occasion of a very difficult decision by vote, for which we are all willing to take the responsibility, we saw that a considerable part of the Congress members, some perhaps very reluctantly, thought it necessary to express their confidence in their leaders, because they felt and understood that the leaders were in a difficult position. But this is not intended as a reproach to the other members; they have only shown what was their point of view. I must admit that we cannot always go the straightest road. The straightest road is overhead, as the crow flies. We cannot travel by it as long as we cannot walk on the clouds. If we could go the straightest road to our goal we should need no leaders, for we all know where Zion is. I do not think we ought to allow the mass of our people to become more miserable still in order to make strong Zionists of them. I believe that by strengthening them we shall strengthen Zionism. But because many misunderstandings have arisen among

Published in *The Maccabaean*, organ of the Federation of American Zionists, Vol. V, No. 4, October, 1903, pages 258–259.

us, I must repeat before we part what I said at the opening of the Congress, "Zion it is not and can never be."

If you read those words again, which have been forgotten in the meantime, you will perhaps admit that they might easily have found a place in a speech made by one of our supposed opponents. And if any of you think the words I have quoted a mere phrase, then there is also the following statement, "We shall not and cannot give the Jewish masses the marching signal on the strength of this arrangement." I think we may safely say, after all that has occurred, that we have not for a single second, or with a single thought, departed from the Basle program. When in one of those difficult moments, of which we have had many, I thought that all hope must be abandoned for our lifetime, I was about to propose an expedient to you, and also to say a word of consolation which at the same time constituted a pledge on my part. "If I forget thee, O Jerusalem, may my right hand wither." But I have found that the words of consolation I intended to say were not needed. . . .

This Basle program, which I helped to draw up, remains unaltered. I have done my utmost to create this Congress, which shows in miniature and in rudimentary form many beginnings of future and better organization. We have begun many reforms which will not be made elsewhere for a long time to come. We have freedom of opinion, and we respect all religious and political convictions on a national basis; the equal rights of women, fellowship of the weak, and many other things are a part of our program. This Congress is our first institution, and I trust that it may ever remain the best, greatest, and most honorable of our institutions, which we will transplant into the fair land of our fathers, the land which we need not explore to love. . . .

IMPRESSIONS OF THE FIRST CONGRESS

Vienna, September 3, 1897

IF I were to sum up the [Basle] Congress in a few words—words I shall be most careful not to speak in public—I would say: in Basle I founded the Jewish State.

If I said that aloud today, I would be met by universal laughter. Perhaps in five years, certainly in fifty, everyone will see it. The State is already founded, in essence, in the will of the people to the State; yes, even in the will of one individual, if he is powerful enough (the *l'État c'est moi* of Louis XIV). The territory is only the concrete manifestation; and even where it possesses a territory, the State is always something abstract. The Church State, too, exists without a territory, or else the Pope would not be sovereign.

In Basle I created this thing which is abstract and which is therefore invisible to the great majority of people. . . .

A BLESSING ON THE JOURNEY

THE publishers of this paper have set for themselves a task that is at once fine and great, joyous and difficult: they wish to imbue our youth, our hope in the secondary schools, with the Zionist ideal.

There is no more splendid work to be done in the preparation of the Jewish people for its coming destiny. The students of today are to become journeymen and master craftsmen, and are to relieve us, who are actively at work today, in the work of Zionism.

One time I called Zionism an ideal that had no end. And I truly believe that Zionism will not stop being an ideal even after the attainment of our land of Palestine. For in Zionism, as I understand it, there is contained not only the striving for a legally assured homeland for our poor people, but also the striving for moral and spiritual perfection. . . .

"Reisesegen," from the Viennese monthly magazine for Jewish youth, *Our Hope* (first issue, March, 1904), in *Gesammelte Zionistische Werke,* Vol. 1 (Berlin, Jüdischer Verlag, 1934), page 497.